Ubiquity and Autonomy

Editors
Kory Bieg, Danelle Briscoe, Clay Odom

Copy Editing
Gabi Sarhos

Graphic Identity
Bruno Canales, Kory Bieg, Danelle Briscoe, Clay Odom

Layout + Design
Crystal Torres, Kory Bieg, Danelle Briscoe, Clay Odom

Printer
IngramSpark

Conference hosted by The University of Texas at Austin School of Architecture, Austin, Texas

ISBN 978-0-578-57872-9

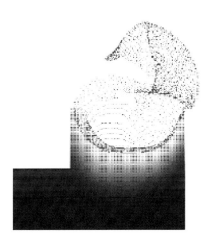
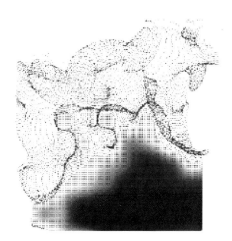
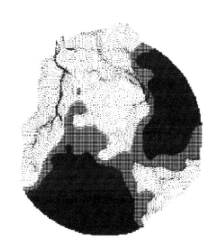

PROJECTS CATALOG

Projects Catalog of the 39th Annual Conference of the
Association for Computer Aided Design in Architecture

THE UNIVERSITY OF TEXAS AT AUSTIN
SCHOOL OF ARCHITECTURE
Austin, Texas

CONTENTS

INTRODUCTION

08 **Kathy Velikov**
Reframing Future(s)

10 **Kory Bieg, Danelle Briscoe, Clay Odom**
Ubiquity and Autonomy

KEYNOTES and AWARDS

16 **Thom Mayne**
ACADIA 2019 Lifetime Achievement Award
Keynote

20 **Harlen Miller**
Keynote

24 **Dominique Jakob**
Keynote

28 **Dana Cupkova**
ACADIA Teaching Award of Excellence

32 **Roland Snooks**
ACADIA Digital Practice Award of Excellence

36 **Jose Sanchez**
ACADIA Innovative Research Award of Excellence

40 **Chris I. Yessios**
ACADIA Society Award for Leadership

44 **Catie Newell**
Taubman College MS Digital and Material Technologies
ACADIA Innovative Academic Program Award of
Excellence

PEER-REVIEWED PROJECTS

50 **Brandon Clifford, Jo Lobdell, Tyler Swingle,
Davide Zampini**
Walking Assembly Craneless Tilt-Up Construction

56 **Brandon Clifford, Jo Lobdell, Tyler Swingle,
Davide Zampini**
Janus A Self Erecting Colossus

62 **Ester Hong Fen Lo, Leon Yi-Liang Ko**
Precise Imprecision: Flexible Construction with
Robotics

68 **Jinhui He, Xiaojie Cao, Tsz Yan Ng, Wes McGee**
Precarious Stand

74 **Shan Chun Wen, Maryam Aljomairi, Misri Patel**
Kneucrete CNC Knits for Programmable Hybrid
Formworks

80 **Joseph Choma**
Paper Folding to Foldable Composites

86 **Roger Hubeli, Julie Larsen**
Origami Concrete Robotic Folding Fabrication

92 **Shelby Elizabeth Doyle, Erin Linsey Hunt**
Melting Augmenting Concrete Columns with Water
Soluble Formwork

98 **Ronald Rael, Virginia San Fratello**
MUD Frontiers/Zoquetes Frontizeros

104 **Christian J. Lange, Donn Holohan**
Ceramic Information Pavilion

110 **Jeffrey F. Day**
FLOCK\\Proof of Concept

116 **Blair Satterfield, Alexander Preiss, Derek Mavis,
Graham Entwistle**
Zippered Wood: Small Material Moves Can Bend Large
Systems

122 **Christoph Klemmt, Rajat Sodhi**
Plaisiophy

128 **Igor Pantic, Christoph Klemmt, Andrei Gheorghe**
Styx

134 **Christoph Klemmt, Igor Pantic**
Bryx

140 **Joel Lamere, Cynthia Gunadi**
Lost House

146 **Manuel Jimenez Garcia**
NECTARY - Modular Assembly System

152 **Faysal Tabbarah**
Where Do The Twigs Go?

162 **Anat Uziely, Chun Nien Ou Yang**
Spatial Felted Structure

168 **Lee-Su Huang, Gregory Thomas Spaw, Jakob Marsico**
Resonant Stacks

174 **Nancy Diniz, Frank Melendez**
Expanded Perceptions Blending Physical and Virtual
Environments through Mobile Sensed Data

178 **Behnaz Farahi**
Iridescence: Bio-Inspired Emotive Matter

184 **Jason Kelly Johnson, Nataly Gattegno**
Lightweave

188 **R. Scott Mitchell, Diana Yan, Alex Weisfeld**
The Arroyo Bridge: Collaborative Robotics for Large
Scale Construction

194 **Adam Marcus, Matt Hutchinson**
Component/Assembly: Prototyping Domestic Space

200 **Niccolo Casas, Gabriel Esquivel, Garrett Farmer,
Nicholas Houser, Oswaldo Veliz**
Hypersecting Objects

206 **Daniele Profeta**
Arctic LiDAR Logistic Landscapes of the Arctic

212 **Uwe Rieger, Yinan Liu**
LightTank A Cross Reality Sculpture

218 **Nicolas Azel, Marantha Dawkins**
Wilding Agents

ACADIA CREDITS

224 Conference Chairs
225 Closing Panel
226 Session Chairs
230 Peer Review Committee
234 ACADIA 2019 Sponsors

Introduction
Reframing Future(s)

Kathy Velikov

President, Association for Computer Aided Design in Architecture
Associate Professor, University of Michigan Taubman College of
Architecture and Urban Planning
Founding Partner, rvtr

The ACADIA Conference and its Proceedings and Project Catalog publications present an annual moment when the design community takes the pulse of computational design across research, academia, and practice. With a full paper double blind peer review process and an acceptance rate of under 30% for technical papers, ACADIA is one of the most selective conferences in the field. Beyond this, ACADIA also strives to lead in discourse around the present and future state of computational design and its surrounding culture(s). Each annual conference takes on a specific theme around which the membership is invited to engage in conversation, and inevitably, at each conference new discussions and debates come to the fore.

Last year, in 2018, we held the annual conference, Re/calibration: on imprecision and infidelity, in Mexico for the first time in ACADIA's 38-year history. This was significant for not only opening up ACADIA to a broader international community, but also for the charge put forward by the conference chairs to rethink computational design relative to broader discourses of craft, labor, and social impact. The article by Viola Ago in The Architect's Newspaper makes an insightful summary of the significance of conference location and the conversations that it aimed to provoke: "The cultural implications of holding the conference in Mexico City were best explained by keynote speaker and professor at the Universidad Iberoamericana CDMX and principal at Estudio MMX, Diego Ricalde's analysis punnily titled PPP (Prejudice, Paradox, Pragmatism). Ricalde speculated that Mexico's architectural culture is at a moment where the unproductive division of old world single-vision, analog thinking, and new world "digital hysteria" needs to come to an end. Ricalde's call for action can be read as a parallel to this year's ACADIA theme "Recalibration: On Imprecision and Infidelity". The theme encouraged participants to rethink a machine-driven infatuation with nano-centric precision, and recover other avenues of thinking and making."[1]

The 2019 conference, Ubiquity and Autonomy, promises a no less provocative conversation around the pervasiveness of connected digital platforms and algorithmic processes on the one hand—when it actually takes considerable effort to not engage computational technologies in almost every aspect of design than to do so—and the seeming retrenchment of architectural factions into disciplinary autonomy focused on aesthetics, representation, and theory on the other. We look forward to seeing how this conversation will evolve in the discussion sessions and presentations. Another topic anticipated to be part of the discussions this year will surely be the speed with which relatively recent technologies such as AR/VR/MR, generative design, and machine learning are being rapidly adopted within the industry and profession, as well as in extra-disciplinary fields, and perhaps faster than the advancements in fabrication and advanced manufacturing. This year's conference is remarkable in the presence of professional firms who are leading in both computational design and leading edge constructed projects worldwide, and this is particularly evidenced in the selections for Keynotes and Workshops that have been curated by the Conference Chairs. If one of ACADIA's goals is to bridge gaps between academia and practice, Ubiquity and Autonomy is certainly poised to make steps toward that aim.

On behalf of the ACADIA membership and the Board, I would like to thank the 2019 Conference Chairs, Kory Bieg, Danelle Briscoe, and Clay Odom for the incredible work they have done to conceive of, plan, and execute the Annual Conference and the associated Peer Review Process and Publications, as well as Benjamin Rice for his work on the Workshop organization. I would also like to extend many thanks to Dean Michelle Addington hosting ACADIA at the The UT Austin School of Architecture, and to the staff and students who have worked behind the scenes to make the conference and workshops a success.

This year was also significant for ACADIA, as we went a long way in increasing the organization's inclusiveness, professionalism, and transparency. Over the past year, the ACADIA Board has developed and adopted two important policies that affirm our core beliefs as an organization: the Publication Ethics Guidelines and the ACADIA Code of Conduct. The Publication Ethics provides our guidelines for standards and best practices in peer review publication for authors, reviewers, and technical chairs. This will help ensure that ACADIA maintains the highest standards in academic publication, and reinforces the organization's commitment to transparency and integrity throughout the process. The Code of Conduct is a set of expectations for behavior that we expect at all ACADIA sponsored activities, including conferences, workshops, Board meetings, and social media interactions. One way to increase the diversity and inclusiveness of an organization or society is to establish expectations for inclusive and welcoming behavior and interactions, and the Code of Conduct will help us to ensure that all ACADIA activities and events are safe, professional, and inclusive spaces, and encourages respectful dialogue among ACADIA participants and members. I would particularly like to acknowledge the members of the ACADIA Scientific Committee who did significant work in developing these documents: Andrew John Wit, Lauren Vasey, Christoph Klemmt, Phillip Anzalone, Tsz Yan Ng, and Skylar Tibbits.

I would also like to acknowledge and thank the dedicated members of the ACADIA Board and Officers, who volunteer countless hours to helping the organization and the annual conference to run smoothly. In particular the leadership and contributions of Vice President Jason Kelly Johnson, Treasurer Mike Christensen, Communications Officer Adam Marcus, and Development Officer Alvin Huang have been invaluable. I would also like to extend my gratitude to ACADIA's sponsors, who not only provide financial support, helping to ensure that the annual conference is a high quality event, but are also active members of the ACADIA community and its activities. In particular, the continued scholarship sponsorship by Autodesk, now in its fourth year, has enabled us to provide travel scholarships for accepted students to travel to present at the conference, and to support the work of emerging researchers. In 2018 ACADIA additionally supported 24 students from Mexico City with reduced local rates so that they were able to afford to attend the conference. This year we are working with our sponsors and local institutions to continue this relationship and exchange. Each year we struggle to maintain affordable conference ticket rates, especially for students and recent graduates, against the very real costs of hosting such an event. The annual conference would not be possible without incredible amounts of volunteer time from the Conference Chairs and the Board, significant in-kind support from the host institution, and the financial support of our sponsors. One of our goals for the coming year will be to make content from ACADIA's conferences more accessible to the public through our website. I look forward to the ways that ACADIA and its members will continue to lead as the computational design field matures and transforms in the future.

Notes:

[1] Viola Ago, "Acadia 2018 focused on imprecision in digital design," *The Architects Newspaper*, January 28 2019 [https://archpaper.com/2019/01/acadia-2018-focused-on-imprecision-in-digital-design/]

Ubiquity and Autonomy

Introduction to the Paper and Project Proceedings of the 39th annual
ACADIA Conference

Kory Bieg

Associate Professor, The University of Texas at Austin

Danelle Briscoe

Associate Professor, The University of Texas at Austin

Clay Odom

Associate Professor, The University of Texas at Austin

The telegraph was one of the first technological breakthroughs to turn physical objects into digital bits. This transformation necessitated the construction of a large-scale, infrastructural network of wires to relay this new form of information. The implications were so profound that critics warned of an advancing technology "annihilating time and space."[1] Through its aggressive nature, the digital was for the first time altering the very constants by which we had for centuries understood and defined the analog world. That was almost 200 years ago. The late 1950s again saw a boom in development spurred by the race to reach the moon. In fact, the first digital interface, the DSKY, was developed specifically for the Apollo Program by Charles Draper and his team from MIT. Digital interfaces then found their way into use by everyday people around the world. A few years later, Gordon Moore made a bold prediction that has since dominated much of the speculation regarding computation. Moore stated that the number of transistors on a microchip would double every two years—this exponential doubling of computer speed came to be known as Moore's Law. After years of Moore's prediction proving true there is growing consensus that, barring breakthroughs in quantum computing, such growth will end within the decade. Despite a leveling of computational speed, access to that speed has become ubiquitous, giving way to a different form of computational economy that is digital by its very nature (block Chain, Big Data, AR/VR, AI, etc.). Powerful computers now impact almost every aspect of our lives, and as Keller Easterling notes, "non-human, inanimate objects possess agency and activity"[2] in a way that is unprecedented. We find ourselves at a moment where there is no longer a divide between analog and digital processes; the digital world is as ubiquitous and inescapable as the material, and has, in many ways, replaced it.

The counterpart of ubiquity is autonomy. As technology continues to proliferate and embed itself into the world, becoming increasingly ubiquitous and available to the masses, new forms of autonomy are emerging. In 1990, the World Wide Web was launched. For the past 30 years, we have been engrossed in a shared network culture and absorbed in a universe of information. In some ways, the web has liberated us. We are no longer dependent on large corporate conglomerates. The market has been dispersed, and we have much more freedom to choose with whom we do business. As Alec Ross, the Senior Advisor for Innovation in the State Department under President Obama, noted, "With coded markets available to even the smallest vendors, a trend has arisen that pushes economic transactions away from physical stores or hotels and toward individual people, as they connect either locally or online."[3] Instead of reinforcing the smooth and unobstructed projection of existing modes of operation, ubiquitous access to the web has allowed for new niche communities to emerge, communities that are in some ways highly specialized and capable of achieving discrete, sole source transactions in a way that would be impossible for any large company. Such diffusion and proliferation is, in itself, a form of ubiquity. As we have seen time and time again, when individuals gain access to technology or companies innovate small markets from within, they eventually either redefine existing industries or form new ones.

In many ways, the state of ubiquity and the spark of autonomy chart the rise and fall of companies, industries, and technology. The history of American Online (AOL) for example, is one that began with growth. AOL started as a small online host for multi-player games, and eventually acquired Netscape as its online internet platform. Its ubiquity invited competition and soon rivals fought for their share of market space. The AOL merger with Time Warner was the largest in history at the time until AOL split with Time Warner, in an attempt to regain its prior status as an independent industry giant. Instead, AOL gradually declined in the wake of other companies that had grown autonomously and claimed their own foothold in a rapidly changing marketplace.

In architecture, we are seeing a similar transition from the ubiquitous use of tools and techniques to more autonomous modes of production. Since the 1990s, the 'digital' in architecture has spread through academia and the profession. The digital has become completely ubiquitous; one would be hard-pressed to find an office or school not using computers or emerging technologies. Now that total acceptance of and access to technology has arrived, it is time to question these tools anew and look for other ways to innovate from within. In his essay, Software Monocultures, Mark Foster Gage warns against uniformity of any kind. Gage advises us to heed the lesson learned from the great Potato Famine—a devastating event attributed to reliance on the uniformity of potato genetics, allowing a single disease to wipe out entire crops.[4] Our dependence on single software platforms for the design of buildings has produced a similar "monoculture" laden with the same dangers and pitfalls that befell those who relied on a single breed potato. Gage is not alone. The discourse of architecture has been drifting toward theories and practices of a more autonomous nature, whereby practices leverage access to digital tools and techniques to develop approaches which often favor articulation and separation.

In the paper and project proceedings from this year's ACADIA Conference, we see a resistance to the familiar use of ubiquitous technologies and a search for autonomy within the expanding reach of our discipline. This extension has multiplied the range of topics that are within these pages and re-energized familiar terrain. The ubiquitous technologies of CNC fabrication, 3d printing, and even robotic manufacture have matured over the past decade, but we have also seen an increase in the fear that automation will soon replace skilled labor. Some of the work in this book directly responds to that fear, searching for new ways in which to use technology to promote design and fabrication while continuing to engage the unique capacity of humans to create. We are starting to search for alternative ways to incorporate digital technologies into architecture—not to displace the analog with digital, but to deliver autonomy back in the hands of individuals. As Ross notes, "robots can be a boon, freeing up humans

to do more productive things—but only as long as humans create the systems to adapt their workforces, economies, and societies to the inevitable disruption."[5] The overlap of previously disconnected technologies is partly responsible for this exciting development.

This year, we saw an increase in areas of research using Augmented Reality (AR) and Virtual Reality (VR) in relation to Robotics, and these explorations introduce new questions about our place in a digitally constructed world. Both AR and VR displace the individual into a completely accessible and ubiquitous other; a point made by some of the more theoretical papers. In many ways, our avatars are not extensions of our self, but objects that exist outside the subject through which to engage other objects that may be virtual, material, or just as likely, digital and physical hybrids. In this realm, alternative forms of autonomy must emerge in order for progress to continue. As Elon Musk has noted, "Over time I think we will probably see a closer merger of biological intelligence and digital intelligence..."[6] As the agency of our bodies is replaced by more efficient machines, we should understand how our creative thoughts and actions might not only survive, but thrive in this new domain. While Artificial Intelligence (AI) can think faster and sift through information more accurately, it processes information differently. AI does not replace our minds, but, as we have seen with the advance of human-robot collaborations, it is an opportunity for expanding human intelligence and creativity. AI fosters autonomy and as Bruce Sterling famously stated, "Autonomy is independence."[7]

So what is next? If the last decade was about the advance of architectural technology into unified and specialized areas of research, the next decade might bring about the expansion of that same research into new fields, new territories, and other disciplines. If the papers from this year's conference are bellwethers for the next phase in computational design, we will see an even greater increase in overlapping technologies and a further fracturing of the mainstream use of well-worn digital tools. As Adam Greenfield notes in his book Radical Technologies, "The truly transformative circumstances will arise not from any one technology standing alone, but from multiple technical capabilities woven together in combination."[8] This mutual exchange, this coupling between ubiquity and autonomy, will fuel innovation and continue to progress.

Ubiquity not only promotes autonomy; it is the reason for it. After all, the vast infrastructure of telephone lines is mostly unnecessary now that cell phones have become the favored form of universal access to a communication regime that began with the telegraph. The new localized (cellular) and distributed access of mobile phones has, in a strange way, facilitated an autonomy that goes well beyond what a hard wired phone network could ever achieve. The cyclical revolution between ubiquity and autonomy will continue and opportunities to advance the field will remain. Ubiquitous access to technology could and sometimes does point to irrelevance or even loss of entire sectors. However, such access also heralds new potential for developing the disciplinary expertise and autonomy required to maximize ubiquity's impact. ACADIA represents a collective of researchers at the forefront of our discipline's investment in digital technology and computational design and it will be exciting to see how this community answers this call and propels the next revolution of autonomous innovation in response to and in spite of society's universal adoption of technology.

NOTES:
[1] James Gleick, The Information: A History, A Theory, A Flood, (New York: Pantheon Books, 2011), 148.

[2] Keller Easterling, "An Internet of Things," E-Flux Journal #31 (Jan 2012). http://www.e-flux.com/journal/an-internet-of-things/14

[3] Alec Ross, The Industries of the Future, (New York: Simon & Schuster, Inc., 2016), 93.

[4] Mark Foster Gage, "Software Monocultures," in Composites, Surfaces and Software: High Performance Architecture, eds. Mark Foster Gage and Greg Lynn, (New Haven: Yale School of Architecture, 2010), 108.

[5] Ross, 37.

[6] Rima Sabina Aouf, "Humans need to become cyborgs to survive, says Elon Musk," Dezeen, last modified February 15 2017, https://www.dezeen.com/2017/02/15/elon-musk-humans-become-cyborgs-survive-artificial-intelligence-technology-news/?li_source=base&li_medium=rhs_block_1

[7] Adam Greenfield, Radical Technologies, (London: Verso, 2017), 275.

[8] Greenfield, 273.

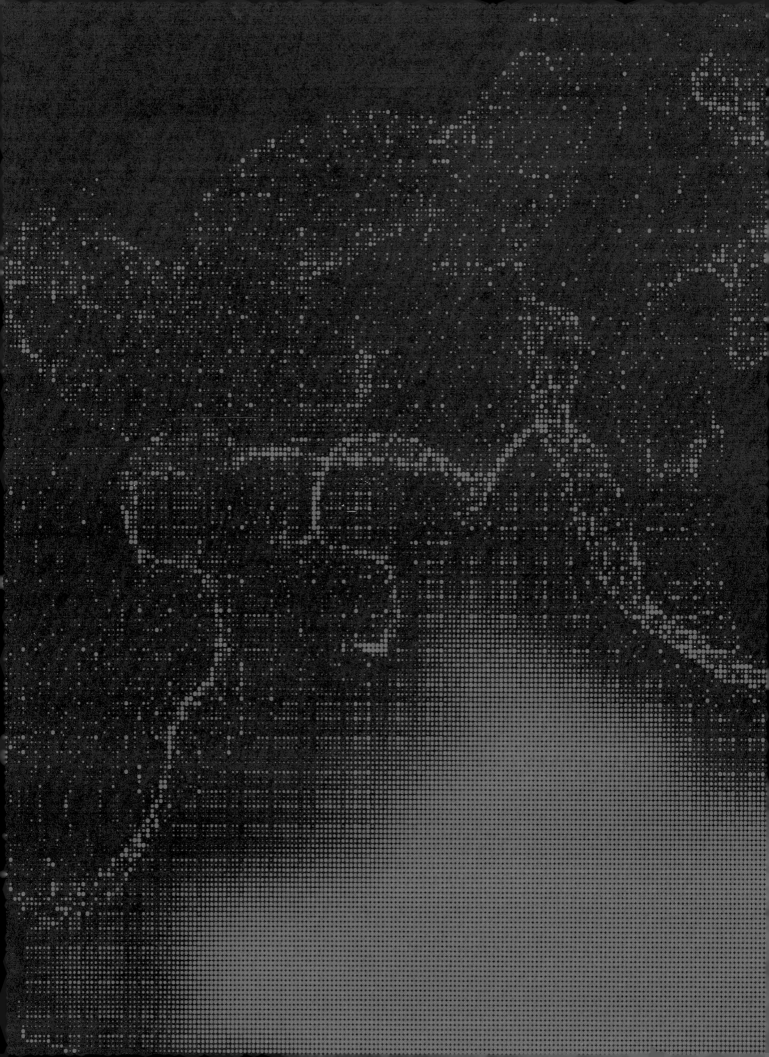

KEYNOTES + AWARDS

Thom Mayne

ACADIA 2019 Lifetime Achievement Award
KEYNOTE
Founding Principal, **Morphosis**

Thom Mayne founded Morphosis in 1972 as a collective practice of architecture, urbanism and design, rooted in rigorous research and innovation. Working globally across a broad range of project types and scales, Morphosis is recognized for its innovative and sustainable designs for cultural, civic and academic institutions, including the Bloomberg Center at Cornell Tech, the Perot Museum of Nature and Science, and 41 Cooper Square, the academic building for The Cooper Union. As Founding Principal of Morphosis, Mayne provides overall vision and project leadership to the firm.

Throughout his career, Mayne has remained active in the academic world. In 1972, he helped to establish the Southern California Institute of Architecture (SCI-Arc). Since then, he has held teaching positions at Columbia, Yale (the Eliel Saarinen Chair in 1991), the Harvard Graduate School of Design (Eliot Noyes Chair in 1998), the Berlage Institute in the Netherlands, the Bartlett School of Architecture in London, and many other institutions around the world. He was a tenured Professor at the University of California Los Angeles Architecture and Urban Design (UCLA A.UD) from 1993 – 2019. There has always been a symbiotic relationship between Mayne's teaching and practice, evidenced in his concurrent position as Executive Director of the Now Institute, Morphosis' research arm that collaborates with academic institutions to create design-based solutions for the pressing issues of the day, from mobility, urban revitalization, and sustainability, to public policy, planning, and community outreach. Fueled by the power of design-based thinking at all levels of education, Mr. Mayne founded the Thom Mayne Young Architects program in 2015 to provide elementary school children at underperforming schools with an introduction to architecture that hones their problem-solving skills across all areas of their education.

Mayne's distinguished honors include the Pritzker Prize (2005) and the AIA Gold Medal (2013). He served on the President's Committee on the Arts and Humanities under President Obama. With Morphosis, Thom Mayne has been the recipient of 29 Progressive Architecture Awards, over 120 American Institute of Architecture Awards and numerous other design recognitions. The firm has been the subject of various group and solo exhibitions throughout the world, including a large solo exhibition at the Centre Pompidou in Paris in 2006. Morphosis buildings and projects have been published extensively; the firm has been the subject of 33 monographs.

1 Perot Museum of Nature and Science (Photo © Jasmine Park)

2 Perot Museum of Nature and Science (Photo © Jasmine Park)

4 Kolon One and Only Tower (Photo © Jasmine Park)

3 Kolon One and Only Tower (Photo © Jasmine Park)

5 Kolon One and Only Tower (Photo © Jasmine Park)

MORPHOSIS FIRM PROFILE

Morphosis is a global architecture and design firm, creating compelling work that is intelligent, pragmatic, and powerful. For more than 40 years, Morphosis has practiced at the intersection of architecture, urbanism, and design, working across a broad range of project types and scales, including civic, academic, cultural, commercial, residential, and mixed-use; urban master plans; and original publications, objects, and art. Committed to the practice of architecture as a collaborative enterprise, founder and Pritzker Prize-winning architect Thom Mayne works in tandem with Partners Arne Emerson, Ung-Joo Scott Lee, Brandon Welling, and Eui-Sung Yi, and a team of more than 60 architects and designers in Los Angeles, New York, Shanghai and Seoul. At the root of all Morphosis projects is a focus on rigorous research and innovation, prioritizing performance-driven design that is

environmentally, socially, and economically sustainable. Through its research arm, The Now Institute, the firm collaborates with academic institutions to create design-based solutions for the pressing issues of the day, from mobility, urban revitalization, and sustainability to public policy, planning, and community outreach.

Morphosis has received 29 Progressive Architecture awards, over 120 American Institute of Architects (AIA) awards, and numerous other honors. Morphosis buildings and projects have been published extensively; the firm has been the subject of 33 monographs. With Morphosis, Thom Mayne has been the recipient of the highest recognitions in architecture, including the Pritzker Prize (2005) and the AIA Gold Medal (2013).

6 Bill and Melinda Gates Hall (Photo © Matthew Carbone)

7 Emerson College Los Angeles (Photo © Jasmine Park)

8 Emerson College Los Angeles (Photo © Jasmine Park)

Harlen Miller

KEYNOTE

Harlen Miller is a Senior Associate and practicing Design Architect at UNStudio's Amsterdam office. He joined UNS in 2012 after moving from Los Angeles, where his background was cultivated in architecture, film, narrative arts, and high-concept futurist thinking. The ability to analytically problem-solve through digital tooling has allowed him the unique opportunity to design bizarre and speculative typologies ranging from 300m towers, fashion, islands, Ferris wheels, boats, cars, jewelry, furniture, body modification and screen writing.

Harlen is the Lead Coordinator of UNStudio's Computational Knowledge Platform which develops digital strategies and customized tools for rationalizing complex geometry and building systems through computational, parametric and BIM modeling workflows. The Computational Knowledge Platform operates as both an internal / external sub-consultancy for project teams and industry manufacturers while simultaneously value engineering projects in accordance to cost constraints, expedited delivery timelines, and fabrication efficiency.

Harlen received his Master of Architecture from UCLA where he attended classes at the School of Theater, Film, and Television sparking his fascination with the narrative arts. This experience helped shape many of the projects he has been responsible for, such as UNStudio's proposal for the 'Chicago Museum of Film and Cinematography' which houses 100 years of Hollywood's most treasured cinematic memorabilia. The ability to translate story-telling through architecture with the help of Hollywood conceptual film designers and branding strategists has also lead to his involvement on large scale urban masterplans and islands that are currently under construction in Dubai (Porto Island), Bengaluru (Karle Town Centre) and Seoul (Masterplan Eunma Housing Development).

Currently, Harlen is leading the design of the 'wasl Tower', a benchmark 308 meter super-high-rise structure located in the heart of Dubai's City Center, next to the Burj Khalifa. Set for completion in the winter of 2020, the 'wasl Tower' will have one of the world's tallest ceramic façades, setting a regional standard for the use of indigenous materials and sustainability. Its responsiveness and ability to acclimatize to local temperatures through passive shading and cooling techniques articulated throughout the façade, set this building apart in the harsh desert climate. Its complex geometric silhouette offers a variable 360 degree viewing angle which required a unique digital workflow in order to achieve an accurate design translation into construction, team efficiency, and improved coordination with sub-consultants.

In 2015 UNStudio was asked to partner with United Nude, an innovative Dutch shoe design studio, to produce a line of 3D printed stiletto high-heels (RE-Inventing Shoes) beside designers, Ross Lovegrove, Zaha Hadid, Fernando Romero, and Michael Young. Harlen's

1   Nippon Moon Observation Wheel: Osaka, Japan

2   Nippon Moon Observation Wheel: Osaka, Japan

3   UNX2 3D Printed Shoe 2, United Nude, W Hotel (Photo @ Dasha
    Martynova)

4   UNX2 3D Printed Shoe 3, United Nude, W Hotel (Photo @ Dasha
    Martynova)

research and digital dissection of the human foot led to
a functioning prototype (UNX2) that was exhibited at the
London and New York 'Fashion Week' as well as the W Hotel
Amsterdam. This approach to digitally re-interpreting
products has led to collaborations with Mercedes, Audi,
and new proposals for classical typologies such as the
Osaka 'GOW Nippon Moon' Ferris wheel in Japan.

His role at UNS, within the building industry, and
neighboring creative fields, has allowed for the examination
of technology and its subsequent impact on all related
design professions with a focus on the physiological effects
associated with its adoption. Harlen's digital research
runs parallel to his involvement with Human Resource
management, recruitment, and the training of 'next-
generation designers' entering the workforce which he
frequently writes and lectures on.

5   al Wasl Tower: Dubai, UAE

6   Digital Rationalization Process, al Wasl Tower: Dubai, UAE

7   Construction Process, al Wasl Tower: Dubai, UAE

Dominique Jakob

KEYNOTE

Since its first projects, Jakob + MacFarlane architects has been oriented as an experimental laboratory in architecture focused on environmental transition and digital culture. The agency's interest is in programmatic and urban social innovations where the passion for construction and innovation is manifested in projects such as the Orange Cube in Lyon and the Frac Centre in Orléans among a few examples. The agency is involved in research on links between the technicality and the materiality of each project to anchor each of them in their temporal relationship and site.

Their main projects include the Restaurant Georges Pompidou Centre (2000), the reconstruction of the theater of Pont-Audemer in Normandy (2001), the library Florence Loewy Books by Artists in Paris (2001), Ricard Foundation for contemporary Art (2007) and Docks - City of Fashion and Design, 100, Herold in Paris (2008), the Orange Cube and RBC showroom in Lyon in 2010, the FRAC Centre in Orléans (2013) and Euronews global headquarters of the European information TV channel in Lyon (2014). Recent projects are a 50-meter multi-program tower of municipal and childhood equipment with social housing «Community House» in the city center of Knokke-Heist in Belgium, the school of architecture and urbanism (FA+U) of the city of Mons in Belgium, a set of cinemas in Pont-Audemer, housing and equipment buildings in La Rochelle and Montpellier, the «FRAC arthothèque du Limousin» in Limoges and the digital arts and culture center «Trinum» at Lomme-Lille. In 2019, the agency won two competitions for international calls for projects «C40-Reinventing Cities» in Saint-Denis Pleyel and Reykjavik.

Jakob + MacFarlane has been invited to participate in selected international competitions such as the New Contemporary Art Museum in Liège, Belgium, the International Competition for the Taipei Performing Arts Center in Taipei, Taiwan and the Mumbai Memorial Competition site in Mumbai, India. They are regularly invited to participate in conferences and juries in prestigious institutions such as the Architectural Association of London, the Centre Georges Pompidou, and the Monterey Design Conference. Their projects have been exhibited in museums around the world, including the Victoria & Albert Museum (London, 2003), SFMOMA (San Francisco, 2004), the Museum of Architecture (Moscow , 2000), the Artist Space (New York, 2003), Carnegie Melon (USA, 2001), the Mori Art Museum (Tokyo, 2004), the Centre Pompidou, the Pavillon de l'Arsenal (Paris), the Bartlett School Gallery (London, 1997), as well as international architecture festival Orleans / Archilab (1999, 2001, 2003). They were also part of the French selection for the Biennale of Architecture in Venice in 2002, and the international selection in 2004 and 2008. Publications: 'FRAC Centre - Les Turbulences' (HYX 2013) - 'Phase - The Architecture of Jakob + MacFarlane' (AADCU 2012) - 'Jakob + MacFarlane - Les Docks' (HYX 2011) - 'Hors-Serie #02 - Jakob + MacFarlane' (Archistorm 2011) - 'Jakob + MacFarlane' (NeoArchitecture 2006)

1   Euronews (Photo © Nicolas Borel)

2   Docks Cite De La Mode Et Du Design (Photo © Nicolas Borel)

4   Herold (Photo © Nicolas Borel)

3   Georges Euronews (Photo © Couturier)

5   Les Turbulences FRAC Centre (Photo © Nicolas Borel)

DOMINIQUE JAKOB is a partner of JAKOB+MACFARLANE ARCHITECTS, which she founded with BRENDAN MACFARLANE in 1998. She received a bachelor degree in Art History from the University of Paris in 1990 and grad-uated from the Architectural School of Paris-Villemin in 1991. She has taught at the Ecole Speciale of Architecture in 1999-2000 and at both Architectural School of Paris Villemin and Malaquais from 1994 to 2004. She has been a visiting teacher at Sci-Arc in Spring 2018. She is an external examiner for Bartlett-School of architecture for 2018-2022. She became a permanent member of the French Architecture Academy in 2016.

Dominique was offered the Officer Insignia award for services to Arts and Letters by the French Ministry of Culture in 2011.

6   Cube Orange (Photo © Nicolas Borel)

Dana Cupkova

ACADIA Teaching Award of Excellence

Architecture is fundamentally a part of larger planetary ecology. In my teaching I seek to engage the notion of ecological attunement beyond the environmentalist paradigm, questioning the implication of the binary logic between objects and environmental ethics. The ambition is to examine architecture(s) that inquire into energy as a primary inspiration for formation of matter. Promoting a shift away from purely data-driven rationales, the desire is to engage students in design of sensorial subjectivities as part of our collective aesthetic and ecological experience.

My work is situated within an expanded field of architecture as it relates to ecology and technology. The primary agenda that bridges my research with teaching is rooted in the definition of architecture as an environmentally contingent object. Focused on shaping materials relative to behaviors, I introduce students to computational strategies that enable them to experiment with fusing natural and constructed environments and to think of architecture as a living, self-regulating organism, attuned to its ecological awareness.

In this time of acute social and climate crises it is critical to develop new design thinking that considers the issues of ecology and perception central to design. Along with understanding the effects of material systems in both time and space, we need to reinvent processes that help us shape the built environment and the practice of architecture. Problems that were historically framed as outside of the discipline and relegated to art, biology or engineering optimization have the potential to become seamlessly integrated into design workflows. At the same time, the idea of experimentation and creativity should be reframed not as purely a subjective mode of expression, but as an imaginative exploration informed by new knowledge, collected at the fringes of our field. This framework is foundational to my belief that an expanded definition of the discipline has to emerge, a definition deeply impacted by the interdisciplinary thinking and ethical imperative linked to an socio-ecological framework.

Computational processes profoundly impact our understanding of the world, and precipitate new forms of human awareness, empathy and interactions with the built environment. In my teaching I actively engage emergent technologies, material prototyping, and testing. The goal is to expand the range of design techniques that link modes of inquiry to design logics, and design logics to ways of making at multiple scales. With this approach I hope to encourage students to explore new perceptions and material sensibilities; to design towards adaptive responses to specific contexts, thus recognizing architecture as a material and environmental practice deeply embedded within local cultural urban landscapes.

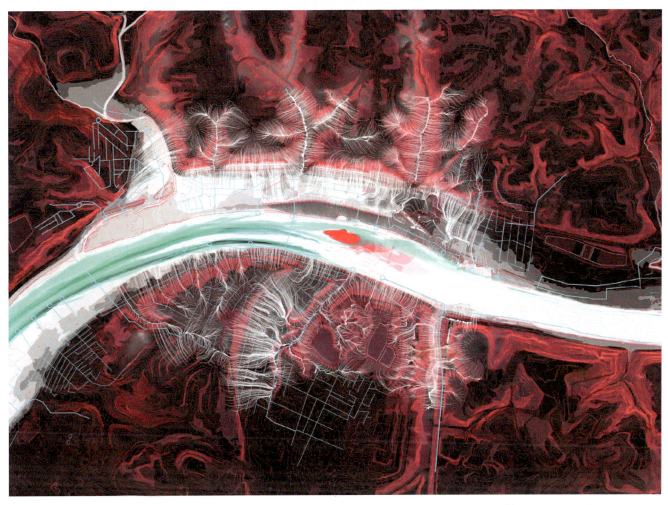

1   Studio Course at Carnegie Mellon School of Architecture (SoA CMU): Environment, Form, Feedback (Student: Ryu Kondrup, Third Year Undergraduate, 2018)

2   Studio Course at Cornell University: Fuzzy Logics (Student: Greg Gyulai, Second Year Graduate, 2011)

3　Workshop at University of Calgary (Students: Chris Berg, Josh Schellenberg, 2018)

4　**Seminar Course** at SoA CMU: Shaping Environments (Student: Ben Snell, 2016)

The use of drawing and simulation is critical. The drawing itself always straddles empirical and metric-based input, yet I feel a kind of visceral ambivalence towards this tension between the determinacy of the data and the ineffability of the sublime. The concept of drawing that the students are charged with is centered on visualizing connections between perceptive form and its contingency on invisible forces. By mapping behavioral processes, through now common computational means, technology can become an integral force that enables more intuitive communication with the environment.

I think of teaching as a continuous exploration rather than a communication of the known. Our cultural bias, especially in academia, approaches the construction of knowledge through disciplinary focus. However, the natural world is cohesive beyond these narrow lenses that we created for ourselves to understand it. I am attracted to ambiguities in our perceptions. Descriptions of effects can be reductive through singular disciplinary focus, as phenomena are processes that are based both in physics and aesthetics simultaneously. Visualizing the non-visual leads to seeing the world differently. New descriptions create shifts in meaning of that can be simultaneously constructed as both scientific and cultural. This is critical, as much as it is deeply ecological in nature. Ecological boundaries are fuzzy and non-distinct. They belong to multiple territories. Large scale processes and formation are symptomatic of these conflicts.

I believe that we have an imperative within academia to question, to provoke and uproot an idea that specific technologies or tools offer objective solutions. In the classroom, I like to negotiate my pedagogy between usefulness and creative play, ultimately questioning how information can affect design thinking, to probe new sensibilities and interpretations of our future collective realities.

5   **Seminar** Course: at SoA CMU Shaping Environments (Students: Aman Tiwari, Aprameya Mysore, Contingent Landscapes: Projection mapping detail, 2016)

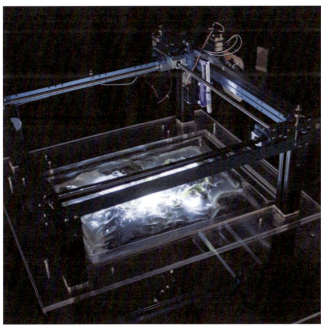

6   Detail from above: Robotic slime printing machine

7   Detail from above: Close-up of slime network simulating urban connectivity

Roland Snooks

ACADIA Digital Practice Award of Excellence

The work of Studio Roland Snooks attempts to define a behavioral approach to architectural design—one in which architecture emerges from the behavior of complex systems and their interaction with design intention. This is an approach that has been developed over the past seventeen years of practice through Kokkugia, Studio Roland Snooks, and research undertaken at RMIT University.

Emergent processes of formation create intensive, heterogeneous, intricate, complex phenomena. These processes have come to define our contemporary understanding of the nature of becoming, which stands in contrast to established notions of design and intention. The experimental design research of the studio speculates on this relationship between emergent processes of formation and architectural design intention, and explores the strange and specific qualities of the architecture that is drawn out of this interaction.

The work of the studio operates within a larger architectural and cultural concern for complex systems and their role in algorithmic design processes. The original contribution of this work to the larger milieu is the articulation of a design process in which architectural intention is embedded within emergent processes. This is a reconceptualization of design intention as behaviors that interact in a self-organizing process of formation – Behavioral Formation. Intention, in this process, is recast as discrete, micro-scale architectural decisions, relationships, or procedures that are encoded as behaviors within multi-agent algorithms. The local interaction of these agents self-organizes architectural design intention at the macro-level. This methodological approach, began in 2002, and developed through the work of the studio, has played a pioneering role in establishing a multi-agent algorithmic approach to architectural design. More importantly, Behavioral Formation enables a departure from the contemporary adoption of indexical algorithms: defining, instead, an approach that embeds and intertwines the architect's design intention within emergent processes.

Behavioral Formation develops, and exploits, an intricate intertwining of intention and emergence. The design intention of the architect is both encoded within algorithmic systems of emergence and operates externally to the algorithm in a feedback loop conditioned by explicit decisions and the evaluation of emergent outcomes. This approach is an important shift from the dominant contemporary architectural use of algorithms where design intention is limited solely to iterative evaluation. The implications of working through these highly iterative, non-linear, computational design processes are manifest as a compression of hierarchies, a blurring of geometric types, and the uncoupling of geometric elements from architectural roles.

Behavioral Formation posits a primarily morphogenetic design methodology. The primary form of intention operates at the micro-scale of algorithmic behavior and is conditioned by

1   Floe (2018)

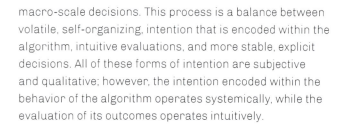

2   Hawthorn Public Art (2016)

6   NGV Pavilion (2016)

6   Nine Elms - Retroactive Form Study (2018, Centre Pompidou)

macro-scale decisions. This process is a balance between volatile, self-organizing, intention that is encoded within the algorithm, intuitive evaluations, and more stable, explicit decisions. All of these forms of intention are subjective and qualitative; however, the intention encoded within the behavior of the algorithm operates systemically, while the evaluation of its outcomes operates intuitively.

This algorithmic approach draws on a subset of complexity theory known as 'swarm intelligence', which can be defined as the local interaction of autonomous agents from which collective behavior emerges. The translation of this logic into architectural design involves encoding architectural design behaviors that range from specific tectonic decisions to more abstract behaviors designed to produce emergence at a larger scale. This approach to design enables an integration of intention with the volatility of emergence. This is not a process of creating emergent form that can later be applied to, or crafted into, architecture. It

6   Painterly Form 1 (2015)

4 SensiLab (2017)

5 SensiLab, robotic fabrication (2017)

is a methodology of creating a specific and intentional architecture that is designed through, not after, emergence. The tendencies and limitations of the agent-based algorithms developed through the work of the studio have been exploited, exaggerated, and developed into a highly personal formal language. This language of hairy, fibrous, blurred, and geological articulations is not an indexical outcome of agent-based processes, but the interaction of individual subjectivity and the generative capacity of these algorithms. As this research has evolved, the concern has shifted from the development of a broadly applicable behavioral design process to the specificity of the projects and their strange qualities. These qualities are developed through the interaction of behavioral processes and somewhat idiosyncratic intention. This body of work aims to establish both a behavioral approach to architectural design and to tease out the strange specificity of its architecture through the interaction of self-organization and subjective intention. Ultimately, the ambition of this architectural design work is not processual; instead, it is concerned with the specific qualities, characteristics, and affects of the architecture created through this approach that exceed—but are integrally dependent upon—their generative processes.

Jose Sanchez

ACADIA Innovative Research Award of Excellence

Jose Sanchez is an assistant professor at the University of Southern California where he develops research to design physical and digital architectural systems that enable cooperation between users. To do so, he uses the medium of video games, so that design becomes a form of play for a vast global community. His designs are intensively participatory, allowing and encouraging players to share knowledge and collaborate in the production of design patterns as a form of shared value. His research builds upon earlier work on participation but innovates by using video games to educate, produce architectural literacy, and crowdsource design solutions, enabling crowds to generate large repositories of architectural knowledge for the public domain.

His research on participatory systems can be divided into two strands: physical and digital. Both are systems in the sense that I define a set of parts that work together to produce buildings or architectural fields. The physical systems he designs allow him to create building components that both interact with each other and incorporate forms of design intelligence such as logics of aggregation. Digital systems, on the other hand, allow him to establish a dialogue with the general public. For his digital projects he uses video games as social platforms in which players interact with preestablished architectural rules. The information presented to the players provides feedback regarding architectural and ecological performance, which subsequently allows them to operate as designers, making informed decisions.

Jose has conducted design research by developing architectural building systems, designing video game interfaces, and through academic publications. Each design he has put forward over the past years advances some aspect of a larger architectural agenda—namely, how can digital culture contribute to the production of an architectural commons, defined as publicly accessible repositories of architectural knowledge that can facilitate access to affordable construction and ecological urban patterns. The building systems he has developed address this agenda by providing preengineered solutions that can generate patterns and be manipulated and combined by the general public. The video game interfaces he has designed address this agenda by providing a digital simulation of physical systems, allowing for manipulation and the process of social recombination to occur at a much larger scale. In this sense, his projects put forward a design proposition that encourages the coordination of building parts using digital platforms with the purpose of affording decentralized production.

One of his design contributions is the video game Block'hood. Block'hood is a neighborhood simulation video game that tracks ecological interdependences between urban units. The game engages nonexpert audiences into thinking architecturally and ecologically, generating architectural literacy regarding environmental challenges. The game was initially released in 2016 as an early access title and was then continuously updated using

1 Block'hood, video game. Vertical Neighborhood simulation.

2   Block'hood, video game. Screenshot of gameplay

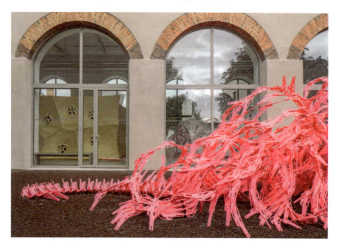

3   Bloom installation at Frac Centre, Orleans France.(Collaboration with
     Alisa Andrasek)

4   Folly.age prototype (Developed with the support of Diego Pinochet and
     Felipe Veliz.)

player feedback until its official release in 2017. Since its
completion, Block'hood has been translated into eleven
languages, and has engaged over a hundred thousand
players in more than fifteen countries and has garnered 1.7
million views on YouTube.

The nexus between architecture and games that was
brought to fruition with Block'hood grew out of an earlier
project, Bloom, which was an interactive installation
developed for the London 2012 Olympic Games. Designed
in collaboration with Alisa Andrasek. Bloom theorized
questions of production and manufacturing by making an
economic and social statement. Economically, the serial
repetition of one identical unit allows the project to be
affordable, proposing that the task of customization and
architectural differentiation be conducted through the
process of recombination rather than by manufacturing
different components. In turn, Bloom was able to respond
to its context and take on different forms in each iteration.

Socially, the project posits that there is no optimal form,
but rather that design value is spontaneously generated
through the participation and consensus of users.

Hi latest research project is a new video game name
Common'hood. Common'hood continues the research
initiated in Block'hood but has a significantly more
ambitious scope. The game is no longer a diagram of how
the city operates, but rather a one-to-one representation of
materials, tools, human labor, and automation. The project
intends to be both a 3-D modeling tool and a social network
for architecture, one that is designed to address the ethical
concerns of user exploitation and data surveillance by
focusing on encouraging players to share, trade, and remix
architectural designs. The game communicates that each
design intent is associated with a series of dependencies
that are mediated by the scarcity of materials, technology,
capital, and knowledge, issues that are not ordinarily
considered in the design process.

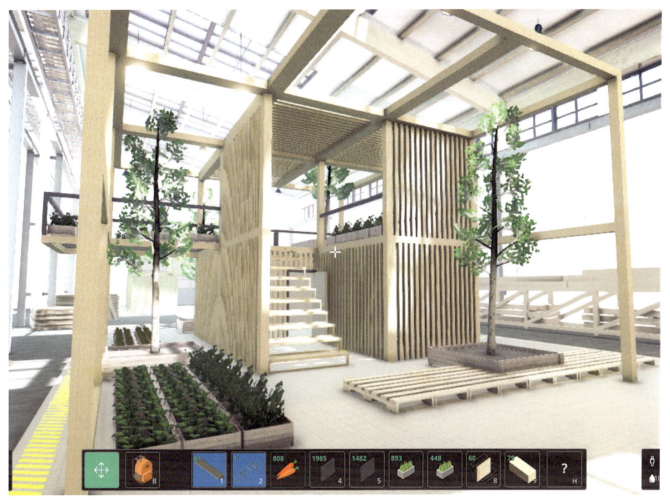

5 Common'hood video game. Screenshot of designs created by players.

6 Common'hood video game. Screenshot of online sharing system.

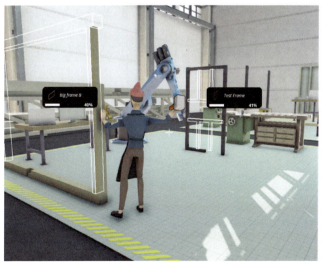

7 Common'hood video game. Screenshot of workers and robots developing architecture.

Chris I. Yessios

ACADIA Society Award for Leadership

ARCHEOLOGY OF SELF

My title conforms to that of Greg Lynn's exhibition at the Canadian Centre for Architecture, *The Archeology of the Digital*, which I have to note included only 4 projects while a lot more was happening at the time. A more complete documentation of the times would be *Pioneers of CAD in Architecture*.

In January 1968, after my studies in Architecture, I came to the USA to study City Planning, which I did for about a year. During that year I took courses in cybernetics and computers and fell in love with the new technologies. Then I met Chuck Eastman who was starting a new Graduate Program at Carnegie-Mellon University (C-MU) dealing with the use of computers in Architecture. In January 1969 I became his first doctoral student.

C-MU was an exiting place at the time, Herbert Simon (Nobel Prize) and Allen Newell (Turing Prize) were heavily involved in Artificial Intelligence (AI) research and promising that a computer program will be beating Chess Masters within three years. Chuck's group's initial projects involved problem solving protocol analysis aimed at understanding how designers work. Next, we were actually writing programs that generated spatial configurations. We were applying mostly exhaustive searches but soon we also started developing heuristic techniques. Interestingly, we were representing spaces as alphanumeric matrices as line drawings were still at their infancy and essentially non-existent. This is exactly what led me to my subsequent interests in graphic representations and modeling, first in 2D and then in 3D. Also, influenced by Chomsky's work, I became interested in linguistic structures I called *space languages* that could represent spatial configurations. My approach was quite different from George Stiny's at UCLA whose *shape grammars* were based on production rules. I was above all interested in implementing space languages, which I did with FOSPLAN and SIPLAN. The later was actually my doctorate thesis project at C-MU. Another research project that I undertook at C-MU were the Boolean operations. The solution we did with Chuck Eastman was in 2D and it was defined as an automaton. I later did a 3D version at Ohio State.

I graduated from C-MU in 1973 and took a job at The Ohio State University (OSU). As we acquired our first Tektronix terminals, we offered both beginning and more advanced computer courses, which became increasingly popular over time. Fast forward, in 1978, I became the Director of a newly established Special Graduate Program in Computer Aided Architectural Design (CAAD) and a number of research projects were funded that supported graduate students and provided new equipment. Most notable was a project that IBM sponsored for some 3 years and provided, in addition to financial support, our own dedicated mainframe and a number of state of the art refresh graphic terminals. The aim of this project was to get the students to design with computers in their design classes. However, before this could happen a prototypical modeling application called Archimodos had

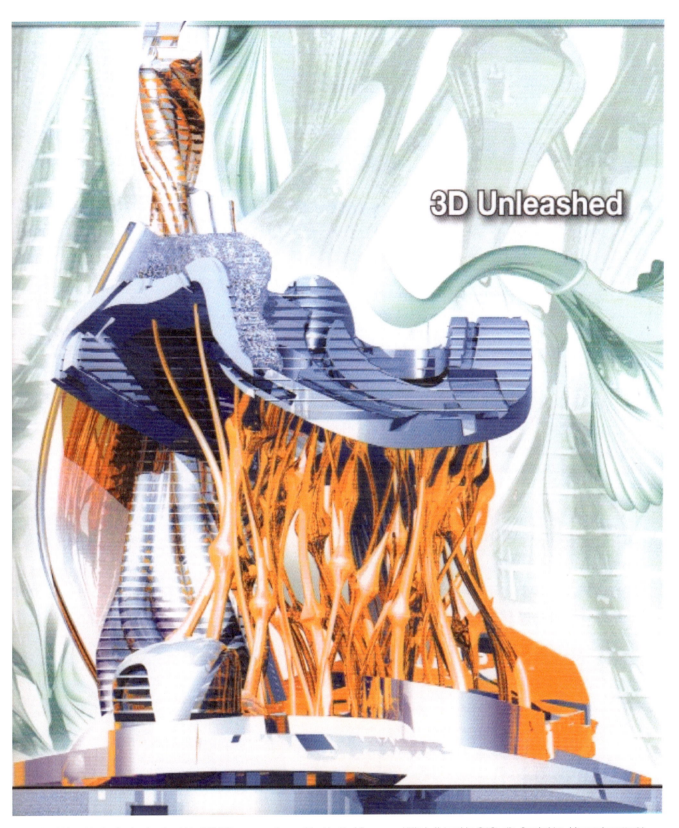

3D Unleashed

1   Peristal City (Winning Design for the eVolo 2006 Skyscraper Competition) by Neri Oxman and Mitchell Joachim OJ Studio, Cambridge, Massachusetts: "A cluster of soft elevators comprise a space for a new tall building type. Our intentions combined fluidic muscle technology with the elevator to mimic a peristaltic circulatory effect." (in•form•Z, June 2005)

2   Change or Visualizing Knowledge by Michael Meier, vasp datatecture, GmbH, Zurich, Switzerland: "Our ambition was to create an object that you almost could not craft." (in•form•Z, June 2005)

to be developed. Archimodos was actually used in a number of classes, including one that Peter Eisenman taught as a visiting Professor. For a description of that class see *A Fractal Studio* in Acadia 1985. Another research project that is worth mentioning was *CKAAD-Expert: A Computer and Knowledge Aided Architectural Design Expert System*, sponsored by the National Science Foundation (NSF). Parts of these projects were done as thesis work by our students and, over the years, I took special pride in seeing many of them presenting papers at Acadia. A few came back at a later time as keynote speakers (Marcus Novak) or to receive awards (Kostas Terzidis).

The arrival of personal computers made our mainframe obsolete and especially when the Apple Macintosh arrived it offered the interactivity we had dreamed of for some time. The problem once again was that there was no serious software running on the personal computers. Thus we were faced with the task of developing new software for the Macs, the hardware of our choice. To do that we needed funds, which we soon found out, were not available for doing work that had been done before. This is when a graduate student of mine, David Kropp, and myself decided to finance it ourselves and do it privately. About a year and a half later (February 14, 1991) version I of form.Z arrived..

What is form.Z all about? The generation of forms that go far beyond what human designers can produce with manual means. It is the reinforcement of our imagination and creativity. In the nearly 30 years of its existence there are myriad of examples, but space here allows me to only display a couple. Form.Z is a lot more than a "style of smooth and curving lines and surfaces..." as Mario Carpo observes in *The Second Digital Turn*. According to him "tools for thinking" have already arrived. I admit I do not see them. As an old timer, I can't help it recalling the *Architecture*

3　Transformed House, a set for The Cat in the Hat by Victor Martinez, Santa Monica, California: "The challenge of this film was to create a visual language that alluded to the whimsical, surreal world that Dr. Seuss has created in his stories and artwork, without literally copying the art." (in•form•Z, June 2005)

Machine and all the early promises for smart automated design. None of this has happened in spite of the impressive progress that other areas of AI have made. Obviously, there is a lot more work to be done.

REFERENCES

Greg Lynn (Ed.): Archeology of the Digital, Canadian Centre for Architecture, Sternberg Press, 2013

Mario Carpo: The Second Digital Turn, Design beyond Intelligence, The MIT Press, 2017

Nicholas Negreponte, The Architecture Machine, The MIT Press, 1970

N. Chomsky, Syntactic Structures, Mouton and Company, The Hague, 1957

Alfred Kemper (Ed.): Pioneers of CAD in Architecture, Hurland/Swenson Publishers, 1985

Chris Yessios, FOSPLAN: A Formal Space Planning Language, in Environmental Design Research and Practice, W. Mitchel (Ed.), Los Angeles, California, 1972 and Charles Eastman, An Efficient Algorithm for Finding the Union, Intersection and Difference of Spatial Domains, Institute of Physical Planning, Carnegie-Mellon University, Pittsburgh, Pennsylvania, 1972

Site Planning with SIPLAN, in the Design Activity DMG/DRS International Conference, London, United Kingdom, 1973

TEKTON: A System for Computer Aided Architectural Design, in Proceedings of CAD 82 Conference, Brighton, United Kingdom, 1982

A Fractal Studio, in ACADIA 87 Proceedings, University of North Carolina, Raleigh, North Carolina, 1987

CKAAD-Expert: A Computer and Knowledge Aided Architectural Design Expert, in NSF Design Theory and Methodology Workshop, Rensselaer Polytechnic Institute, Troy, New York, 1988

Catie Newell

ACADIA Innovative Academic Program Award of Excellence
Taubman College: MS Digital and Material Technologies

THE DEXTERITY OF MAKING

The process of making is our greatest design opportunity.

Architecture and construction are a complex entangling of materials, systems, and production logics. New technologies and ways of making are constantly stepping over one another, advancing at uneven rates, and negotiating or disrupting industries' established standards and methods. Building our lived environments in the boom of computationally-driven design and fabrication technologies is an effort that requires constant experimentation and the ability to recognize both opportunity and error. It requires us to observe material behavior, follow the flow of machine logics, create new tools for new tasks, and understand the wisdom in collaboration. The University of Michigan's Taubman College Master of Science in Architectural Research, Digital and Material Technologies concentration contributes to our evolving discipline through our unending pursuit of making, both digitally and physically, placing the power and weight of new forms of architectural fabrication at the center of our educational program.

The MSDMT concentration is an intensive 10-month post-professional degree program that concentrates on the fundamental question of how architects make. The program is committed to attuning its students to the relationships between material realities and computational advances, mentoring them to understand the logics of fabrication resources, and teaching them to recognize synergies between what they build and its impact in the larger material or digital environment. The core value of the program is an attentive alignment between the architect and the materials, instruments, and processes necessary to create any system or component. It thrives on experimenting with how the future will be built, correlating the possibilities of now with the expectation of new materials, methods, and machines.

This is not something that any one mind or machine can handle. It requires collaboration between researchers, makers, and our institutions. Our program originally grew out of the intensity of faculty research: in light of the research programs then under way, Taubman College invested in fabrication equipment that other disciplines had already adopted, allowing the faculty to expand their material practice in making large-scale built objects. Placing the machines within an architectural education program established a base of knowledge in digital computation and fabrication that was spread across a group of faculty. Concurrently, the college's Research Through Making grant program was established to support faculty projects that took risks on new methods and material systems. With these shared resources in place, the MS in Digital Technologies was formed in 2010, focusing on design computation and fabrication. The Material Systems concentration, invested in material systems and environmental inputs and outputs, formed shortly afterwards, in 2011. Students witnessed and shared in new collaborations that were happening between

1   End effector application (Taubman College © 2018).

2   Full scale mock-up (Catie Newell, 2017).

3   Progress review (Taubman College © 2018).

faculty members across both concentrations as we continued to expand our new knowledge and practice in the lab. Our programs, entangled in shared pursuits across the concentrations and the advancements capable with the clear merger, then came together as the single concentration Digital and Material Technologies.

Keeping to this ethic of close collaboration and coordination around shared fabrication resources, our students' course of study is structured around (1) gaining practical mastery of the tools of their work, and (2) using that mastery in the service of a collaborative capstone project, working in teams with other students, faculty members, and industry partners. The students begin with intensive tutorials and hands-on use of our machine resources, learning each machine's type of making, and understanding how to modify it with tool heads, jigs, and the use of multiple machines in coordination. As they gain technical expertise, they are also asked to question how and why this expertise should be deployed in making, challenging the common practices of

the built world and questioning their role in it. As instruction continues, students are trained within comingling themes of robotics, materials, computation, and systems, allowing them to find some of their own affinities or innate working logics. Courses shift and change based on the faculty involved in any given year, but these courses also intersect and inflect one another, either through faculty direction or through the fluid development of projects within the same cohort. The final capstone offers a major project, often linked to an industry partner. This project grounds all of us in the realities of making.

This research curriculum, coordinated closely with ongoing faculty research, is a testing ground for operating in an age of constantly-changing digital technologies and material productions. It seeks new processes of making, ever aware of unforeseeable changes, and builds the skills necessary to find and make new ways of creating space. It is within this making that we as a field can learn from the world as we change with it.

4   Assembly through hololens (Matias del Campo, 2018).

5   Material systems discussion (Taubman College © 2018)

6   CNC Knitting test, (Sean Ahlquist, 2017).

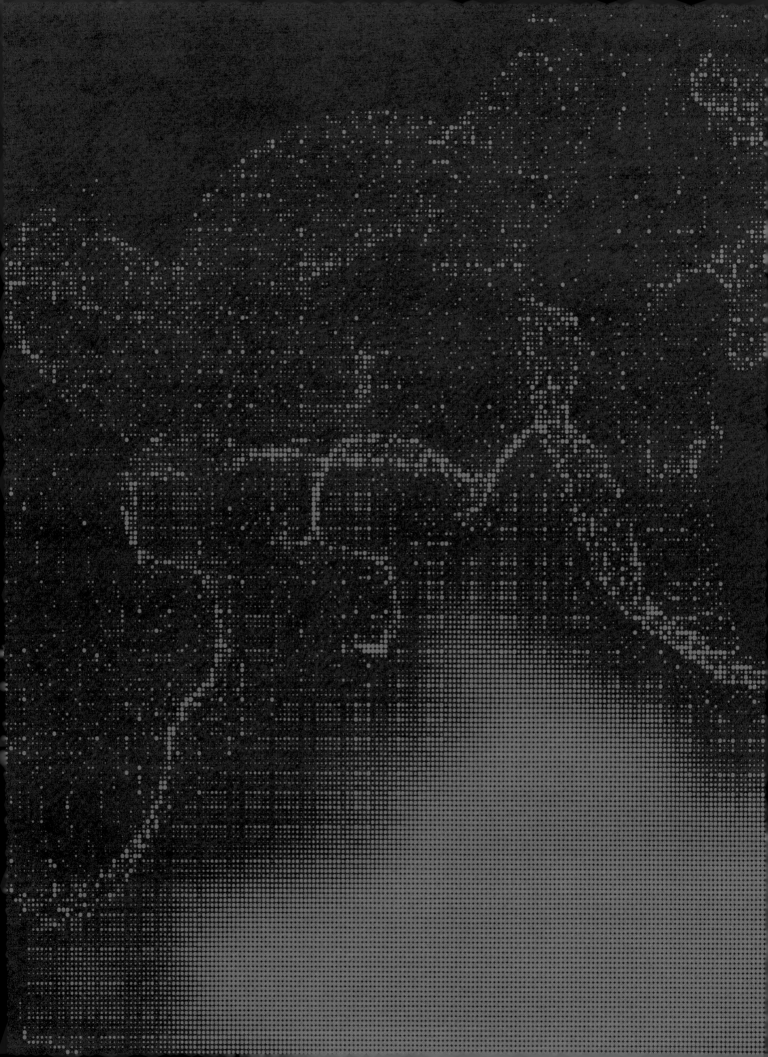

PROJECTS

Walking Assembly
Craneless Tilt-Up Construction

Brandon Clifford
MIT/Matter Design

Jo Lobdell
Matter Design

Tyler Swingle
Matter Design

Davide Zampini
CEMEX Global R&D

1   *Walking Assembly* prototype elements

The mysterious knowledge surrounding the transportation and placement of megaliths used by ancient societies eludes contemporary building practices. The construction of massive elements in architecture, particularly tilt-up construction, is largely dominated by reliance on external structures and mechanisms such as cranes and tilting tables (Brown 2014). This reliance has irreducible implications on costs and access to the potentials of massive construction.

Since its invention, concrete is the most used manufactured material in the world with "three tonnes of concrete (...) used annually per person" (Brito 2013). Inherent to concrete is mass, and much of the work surrounding intelligent futures for concrete has focused on reducing mass and deploying the material where needed. These examples include work by Abd Elrehim (2019), Jewett (2018), and Liew (2017). As beneficial as these efforts are, mass is not the only parameter, and it can even be advantageous to have when improving the thermodynamic performance as shown in the Hsu House (Cupkova and Azel 2015). The challenge of today is identical to moments of the past when ancient civilizations such as the Romans or Egyptians erected incredibly massive megalithic assemblies without the energy consumption of mechanical cranes (Diebner 1991). While much is still uncertain about the ancient Egyptian and Roman methods, archaeologists have proven that the colossal statues of the Moai Rapanui were carved using a highly calibrated relationship between the curvature of the form and the center of mass (COM) of the object, enabling the Moai to march forward when tugged side to side (Hunt 2012).

PRODUCTION NOTES

Designer:	Matter Design
Industry:	CEMEX Global R&D
Size:	6.3m x 3m
Mass:	5,970kg
Material:	Concrete
Date:	2019

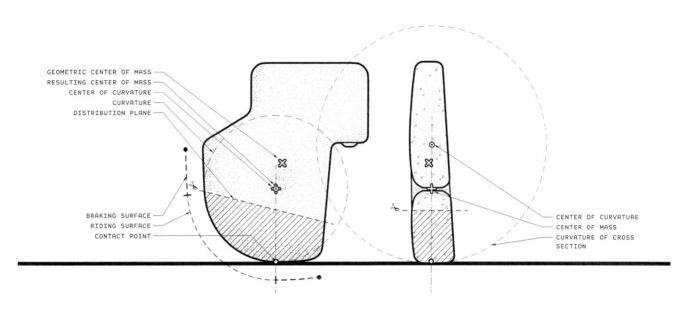

GEOMETRIC CENTER OF MASS
RESULTING CENTER OF MASS
CENTER OF CURVATURE
CURVATURE
DISTRIBUTION PLANE

BRAKING SURFACE
RIDING SURFACE
CONTACT POINT

CENTER OF CURVATURE
CENTER OF MASS
CURVATURE OF CROSS
SECTION

2   Key of the various geometries that compose an element

Walking Assembly taps into the potentials of innovative concrete technologies and ancient methods of transportation and assembly of megalithic architecture to inform contemporary practice by embedding intelligence into building elements to assemble without the aid of external lifting. The project employs recursive solver computation to locate two densities of concrete in the design process to ensure the safe and stable movement of the massive elements. The computation surrounds two key geometries—the form of the element and the COM. The forms of the elements are constrained by the need to rotate for transportation, to rest for stabilization, and to interlock for assembly. The solver leverages the potentials of varying densities of concrete to drive the geometric COM to a new target position, thus ensuring the calculated movements. This multi-variable calculation is verified with built prototypes that test the assembly approach.

The *Walking Assembly* prototype incorporates the COM solver with a fully three-dimensional curvature continuous motion geometry as well as interlocking assembly geometry

(Figure 2). The purpose of this prototype is to embody the intelligence of COM location in relation to the element's COC so it can spin, rotate, and tilt safely, therefore making it transportable and adjustable on site. Further, all elements utilized braking regions and variable curvature in the cross section of the motion geometry for stability. The assembly geometries incorporate dado connections into the element overlap as seen in Figures 3 and 4. The additional interlocking surfaces aid in the final alignment of the elements and account for the element's rotational draft during assembly.

Each of the smaller elements is roughly 1.2 m wide and 1.5m tall, ranging in depth from 0.3 m to 0.5 m. They range in mass from 420 kg to 700 kg and can easily be positioned by a single person. A stair is incorporated into a series of smaller elements (Figures 5-6) so that a person can climb and continue the assembly of a larger element twice the size. This element is 1.75 m by 0.5m by 3.0 m and weighs over 1.770 kg but is just as agile as the smaller elements (Figure 7).

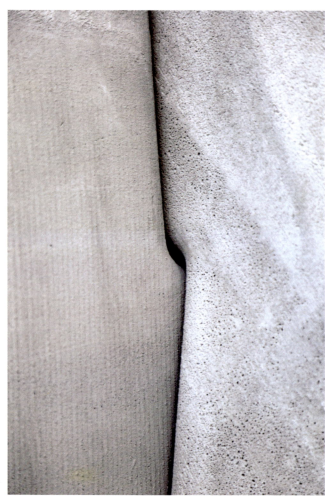

3　Detail view of the top assembly detail that aides in alignment

4　Interior view of the corner assembly detail

The resulting prototypes are incredibly massive solid cast concrete elements that can walk and assemble effortlessly (Figure 8). The introduction of innovative concrete technologies was fundamental to enable versatility in geometrical design and achieve the target performance from the displacement of the COM. The success of these prototypes points to the possibility where computation, coupled with novel concrete technologies, can expand the reach of, for example, tilt-up wall construction and reconsider the potential of mass in rapid and responsive deployable systems.

ACKNOWLEDGEMENTS

This research is produced in collaboration between Matter Design and CEMEX Global R&D. The recursion solver is generated through a custom definition that employs Anemone (theobject.co/anemone). The former, a plugin developed by Object to resolve recursion in Grasshopper (grasshopper3d.com), yet another a plugin developed by David Rutten for the Robert McNeel-developed program, Rhinoceros (rhino3d.com).

IMAGE CREDITS

All drawings and images by the authors.

5   Detail of the assembly geometries

6   Assembled units with an incorporated stair

REFERENCES

Abd Elrehim, Mostafa Z., Mohamed A. Eid, and Mostafa G. Sayed. 2019. "Civil Engineering: Structural Optimization of Concrete Arch Bridges Using Genetic Algorithms." *Ain Shams Engineering Journal.*

Brito, Jorge de, and Nabajyoti Saikia. 2013. *Recycled Aggregate in Concrete: Use of Industrial, Construction and Demolition Waste.* Green Energy and Technology Series. London, New York: Springer.

Brown, Jeffrey Blaine and Sabita Naheswaran. 2014. *Tiltwallism: A Treatise on the Architectural Potential of Tilt Wall Construction.* Mulgrave/Melbourne: The Images Publishing Group Pty Ltd.

Cupkova, Dana and Nicolas Azel. 2015. "Mass Regimes: Geometric Actuation of Thermal Behavior." *International Journal of Architectural Computing* 13(2): 169-93. doi:10.1260/1478-0771.13.2.169.

Dibner, Bern. 1991. *Moving the Obelisks: A Chapter in Engineering History in Which the Vatican Obelisk in Rome in 1586 Was Moved by Muscle Power, and a Study of More Recent Similar Moves.* Burndy Library Publication in the History of Science and Technology 7(6). Norwalk, Conn.

Hunt, Terry and Carl Lipo. 2012. *The Statues That Walked : Unraveling the Mystery of Easter Island.* Berkeley, Calif.: Counter Point Press.

Jewett, Jackson. 2018. *Design, Fabrication, and Testing of Plain Concrete Beams Using Topology Optimization.* Mech.E dissertation, Massachusetts Institute of Technology.

Liew, A., D. López López, T. Van Mele, and P. Block. 2017. "Design, Fabrication and Testing of a Prototype, Thin-Vaulted, Unreinforced Concrete Floor." *Engineering Structures* 137(April): 323-35. doi:10.1016/j.engstruct.2017.01.075.

7   Each element is calibrated to be maneuvered by a single person

8 *Walking Assembly* prototype

Brandon Clifford mines knowledge from the past to design new futures. He is best known for bringing megalithic sculptures to life to perform tasks. Clifford is the director of Matter Design and assistant professor at the Massachusetts Institute of Technology. As a designer and researcher, Clifford has received recognition with prizes such as the American Academy in Rome Prize, a TED Fellowship, the SOM Prize, and the Architectural League Prize for Young Architects & Designers. Clifford is dedicated to re-imagining the role of the architect. His speculative work continues to provoke new directions for the digital era.

Jo Lobdell is a partner at Matter Design where she is driven to bring inspiration and joy to the world through the lens of design. As a designer she uses play as a way to tackle how the body and mind can interact with objects and environments. Her focus is on the way in which color, pattern, and form operate together to express a narrative. Examples of this process can be seen in projects like the award winning Five Fields Play Structure, The Cannibal's Bath for MoMA's Young Architects Program, and The Cannibal's Cookbook that received a PRINT design award.

Tyler Swingle is research lead and project manager at Matter Design and holds a lecturer position at McGill University. In his work, he is committed to exploring the reciprocity between materials and computational methods and frameworks. As a part of Matter Design, this includes both ancient building techniques and new material technologies.

Davide Zampini has over 30 years of experience in the construction materials industry and is best known for pushing the limits of innovation in cement-based products and building solutions. Adopting a design- and industrially-driven innovation approach, Davide leads a multi-disciplinary and culturally diverse team at CEMEX's Center for Innovation and Technology. Through adaptive research and development conceived with versatility in mind, Davide's team at CEMEX in Switzerland develops novel functionalities in cement-based materials that incorporate customer-centered strategies and are designed to create solid emotional ties to a material that for ages has been considered "grey."

Janus
A Self-Erecting Colossus

Brandon Clifford
MIT/Matter Design

Jo Lobdell
Matter Design

Tyler Swingle
Matter Design

Davide Zampini
CEMEX Global R&D

1   Janus being performed at the American Academy in Rome

Megalithic era construction resolved an incredible feat of strength surrounding the transportation and erection of massive stones—fueled by carbohydrates and the limitations of the human body. In order to provide these incredible structures, megalithic civilizations were forced to impart intelligence of these actions into the elements themselves. This is evident in the Egyptian and Roman civilizations, particularly surrounding obelisks, structures that were transported horizontally and stood vertically without the energy consumption of mechanical cranes (Diebner 1991). While much is still uncertain about the ancient Egyptian and Roman methods, archaeologists have proven that the colossal statues of the Moai Rapanui were carved using a highly calibrated relationship between the curvature of the form and the center of mass (COM) of the object, enabling the Moai to march forward when tugged side to side (Hunt 2012). Today, contemporary construction is driven by fossil fuels, resulting in a default approach of dead-lifting heavy elements with cranes and other mechanical equipment. In the face of this reliance upon external devices, contemporary construction could learn a great deal from ancient civilizations about how to more intelligently deploy massive architectural elements with less energy.

As experiment, this research tackles the ancient problem of transporting and standing heavy elements of architecture. Building upon the knowledge gained in a previous research experiment titled *McKnelly Megalith* (Clifford 2016), *Janus* tests computation methods against problems surrounding solid cast concrete. When engaging the topic of casting instead of carving, questions emerge surrounding how to intelligently demold a

PRODUCTION NOTES

Designer:	Matter Design
Industry:	CEMEX Global R&D
Size:	2.25m x 1.3m x 1.3m
Mass:	2,000kg
Material:	Concrete
Date:	2018

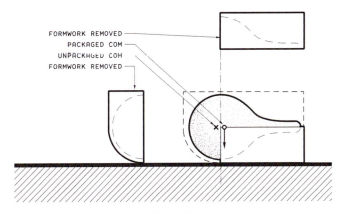

2   Unpacking the formwork to shift the COM to the tipping point

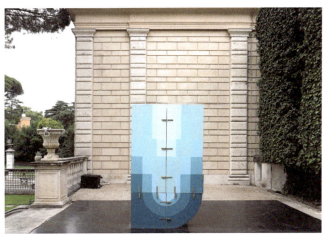

4   Janus in the vertical cast position

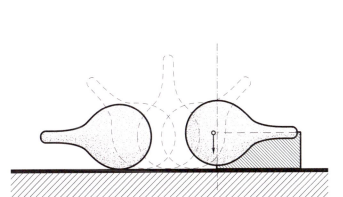

3   Releasing Janus from the formwork

5   Janus and formwork being rolled onto its back for demolding

massive concrete object without the reliance on external lifting devices. The challenge involves casting an object in a vertical position that can be repositioned in order to demold. Once demolded, the object should self-emerge from its own formwork and stand in a stable vertical resting position. Figures 2 through 5 demonstrate these various states.

This research incorporates solver computation to determine the location of the desired COM of a concrete object, considering the varying densities of the concrete and of the formwork in its various demolding states. The optimal COM allows the element, while still enclosed in its formwork, to roll onto its back so that the lower portion of the formwork can be demolded. In this horizontal position, enough mass has been removed from the formwork to relocate the center of mass of the element beyond the pivot of the edge of the formwork, enabling the element to stand itself up and emerge from the formwork.

Janus is the Roman god of thresholds, simultaneously looking to the past and the future. The ghost of *Janus* manifests as an animated double concrete sculpture on its original home and the current site of the American Academy in Rome—the Janiculum. *Janus* emerges from its own formwork and performs on stage in front of an audience of spectators. Working with composers, this collaboration merges sonic and physical animation to produce an hour-long living spectacle. During the performance, the audience is enveloped in spatial chatter that transitions from the noise of the crowd to a spirit-like whispering that draws the audience's attention to an apparently gift-wrapped object on stage.

Janus is designed through a series of monstrous contradictions. The graphic box references the Arch of Janus with a uniquely Roman color palette of pinks, oranges, and blues. The box slowly rolls onto its back, exposing itself as merely the lightweight formwork of a massive object inside.

6   Janus in the vertical standing position

Janus Clifford, Lobdell, Swingle, Zampini

7   Front elevation of the mural design

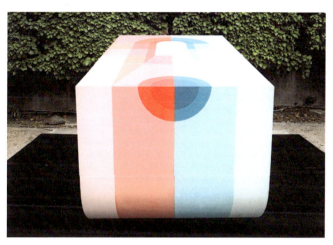

8   Mural continues as Janus rolls onto its back

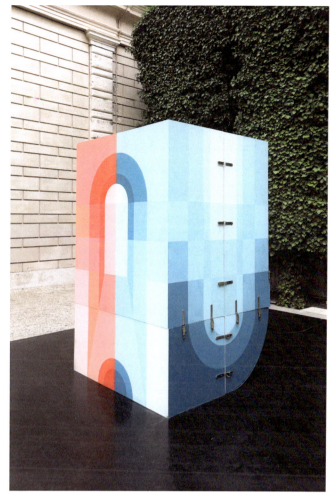

9   An image of the mural wrap and the side of the formwork enclosure

From this rigid box, a vital concrete object springs to life on its own. *Janus* wobbles on stage, breathing life into a solid sphere and hollowed ring sculpture until the momentum slowly fades and the wrecking ball of an object appears to hover on a single point for the amusement of spectators.

ACKNOWLEDGEMENTS

This research is produced in collaboration between Matter Design and CEMEX Global R&D. The performance is a collaboration with composers Federico Gardella and Simone Conforti. The formwork is provided by Odico Construction Robotics. *Janus* has been performed at the American Academy in Rome and at the Massachusetts Institute of Technology. Terez Lowry performed in the second performance.

IMAGE CREDITS

All drawings and images by the authors.

REFERENCES

Clifford, Brandon. 2016. "The McKnelly Megalith: A Method of Organic Modeling Feedback." In *Posthuman Frontiers: Data, Designers and Cognitive Machines, Proceedings of the 36th Annual Conference of the Association for Computer Aided Design in Architecture (ACADIA)*, edited by K. Velikov, S. Ahlquist, M. del Campo, and G. Thün, 440-449.

Dibner, Bern. 1991. *Moving the Obelisks: A Chapter in Engineering History in Which the Vatican Obelisk in Rome in 1586 Was Moved by Muscle Power, and a Study of More Recent Similar Moves*. Burndy Library Publication in the History of Science and Technology 7(6). Norwalk, Conn.

Hunt, Terry and Carl Lipo. 2012. *The Statues That Walked : Unraveling the Mystery of Easter Island*. Berkeley, Calif.: Counter Point Press.

10 Janus interacting with performers

11 Janus interacting with performers

Brandon Clifford mines knowledge from the past to design new futures. He is best known for bringing megalithic sculptures to life to perform tasks. Clifford is the director of Matter Design and assistant professor at the Massachusetts Institute of Technology. As a designer and researcher, Clifford has received recognition with prizes such as the American Academy in Rome Prize, a TED Fellowship, the SOM Prize, and the Architectural League Prize for Young Architects & Designers. Clifford is dedicated to re-imagining the role of the architect. His speculative work continues to provoke new directions for the digital era.

Jo Lobdell is a partner at Matter Design where she is driven to bring inspiration and joy to the world through the lens of design. As a designer she uses play as a way to tackle how the body and mind can interact with objects and environments. Her focus is on the way in which color, pattern, and form operate together to express a narrative. Examples of this process can be seen in projects like the award winning Five Fields Play Structure, The Cannibal's Bath for MoMA's Young Architects Program, and The Cannibal's Cookbook that received a PRINT design award.

Tyler Swingle is research lead and project manager at Matter Design and holds a lecturer position at McGill University. In his work, he is committed to exploring the reciprocity between materials and computational methods and frameworks. As a part of Matter Design, this includes both ancient building tech- niques and new material technologies.

Davide Zampini has over 30 years of experience in the construction materials industry and is best known for pushing the limits of innovation in cement-based products and building solutions. Adopting a design- and industrially-driven innovation approach, Davide leads a multi-disciplinary and culturally diverse team at CEMEX's Center for Innovation and Technology. Through adaptive research and development conceived with versatility in mind, Davide's team at CEMEX in Switzerland develops novel functionalities in cement-based materials that incorporate customer-centered strategies and are designed to create solid emotional ties to a material that for ages has been considered "grey."

Janus Clifford, Lobdell, Swingle, Zampini

12 Janus balanced on a single point at the American Academy in Rome

Precise Imprecision:
Flexible Construction with Robotics

Ester Hong-Fen Lo
Leon Yi-Liang Ko
University of Michigan,
Taubman College of
Architecture and Urban
Planning

1   Initial robotic stack casting experiment

FLEXIBLE FORMWORK

On September 8, 1897, Gustav Lilienthal hung sufficiently impermeable fabric in the catenary form between the beams to build a fireproof ceiling. This invention created the first customized natural geometry during the fabrication in situ (West 2017). In typical constructions, flexible formwork is difficult to implement, but its implementation expands the vision of formwork that generates complex arrangements. For instance, in recent works by Andrew Kudless (Kudless 2011) and Form Found Design (Sarafian 2017), flexible formwork integrates advanced technologies among various applications. Combining precedent ideas of robotic assembly, textile forming, and in situ plaster casting, *Precise Imprecision* demonstrates a new methodology: robotic stack casting.

METHODOLOGY

The technique of robotic stack casting combines dynamic performance and computational configuration to create natural shapes in digital practice. Materially, flexible form-fit presents customized form in what ordinarily would be considered a "precast units" environment. Parametrically, robotic assembly produces controlled data and diminishes labor-intensive manufacturing. Robotic stack casting integrates cast and construction practices simultaneously to bring out unique aesthetics and identity boundaries. The elastic form-fit pattern relates to the notions of dry-fitted Inca masonry. Compared with acts of measurement and carving in this ancient artifact, this flexible construction process accelerates the production of form-fitting.

PRODUCTION NOTES

Architect: Hong-Fen Lo, Yi-Liang Ko
Status: Completed
Material: Pleather Fabric, Plaster
Location: Ann Arbor, Michigan
Date: 2019

2   The drawing code of Precise Imprecision masonry digitizes robotic flexible formwork and assembly rules

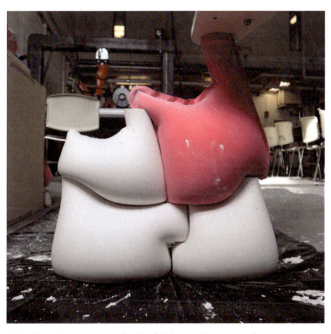

3   In the casting process, pleather fabric provides appropriate morphology without leaking

4   The customized end effector maintains the deformation of flexible formwork

COMPUTATION AND MORPH GRAMMARS

As an experiment, a full-scale prototype converges the similarity, transition, and contrast between the physical and digital worlds to evolve its private aggregation and numerical parameters. Based on recent work by Brandon Clifford and Wes McGee on digital Inca masonry (Clifford 2017), different shape, volume, and order outline three roles as Base, Fill and Keystone in the fabrication. For stimulating the dual wythe of curvature to Inca masonry, the Base, Fill and Through stones are redefined to cooperate with robotic construction and initial assembly, and the fabric formwork provides a combination of internal and external pressures. Converting the solid masonry into soft behavior, physical parameters between size, geometry, overlap, and arrangement influence both global and local systems. In order to digitize robotic stack casting, assembly rules and parameters generate a unique moment for drawing code which merges the deformation into the dramatic mass pattern.

FABRICATION

In the final studies, 116 units are shaped and aggregated in an efficient work flow by two KUKA robots with the customized end effector. As a versatile technique on site, the curved wall is split into two sections to increase the overall dimension. The base track, which aims to locate stones in the first layer, stabilizes the structure and extends the purpose of the form-fit seat; and the collaboration between robots investigates the potential of automatic adjustable construction without rigid formwork. The prototype displays the weakness of casting efficiency from robotic manufacturing and the impossibility of concrete in-stack casting, but it predicates a game beyond the gap between "precision" and "imprecision" in both analog and digital processes.

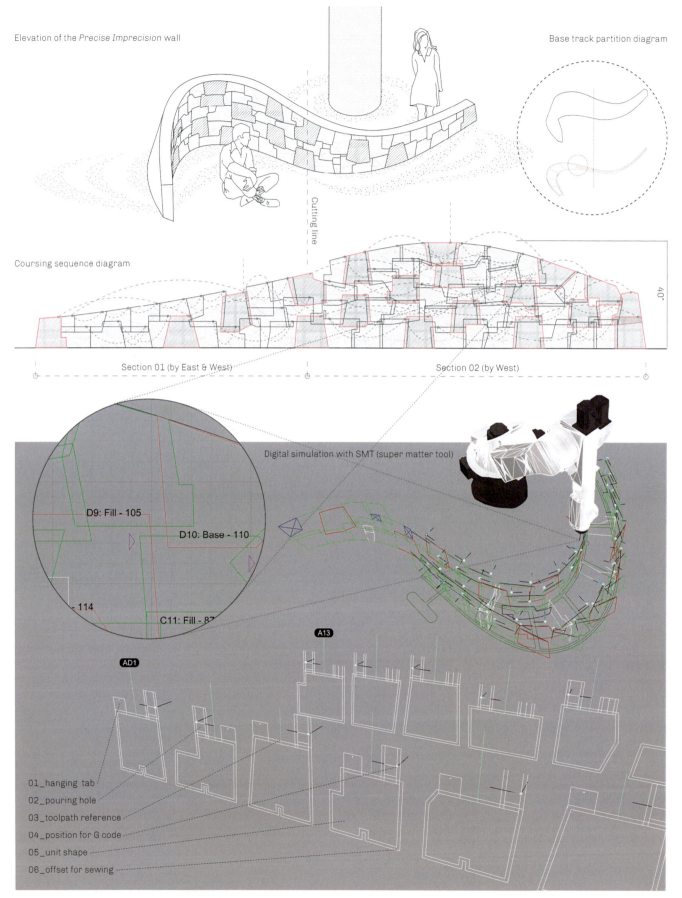

Elevation of the *Precise Imprecision* wall

Base track partition diagram

Cutting line

Coursing sequence diagram

40.0°

Section 01 (by East & West)

Section 02 (by West)

Digital simulation with SMT (super matter tool)

D9: Fill - 105

D10: Base - 110

- 114

C11: Fill - 87

A13

AD1

01_hanging tab
02_pouring hole
03_toolpath reference
04_position for G code
05_unit shape
06_offset for sewing

5   The digital configurations of *Precise Imprecision* cross the gap between physical and digital parameters, including feasible robots' toolpath,
     volume's calculation, mold's reference, shaping simulation

6   The building process of section 01 by two robots (East & West)

7   The building process of section 02 by one robot (West)

8   116 customized masses ready to be reassembled

9   Form-fit boundaries find individual identification on the environment and base track

PRECISION AND IMPRECISION

The definition of accuracy bounces between the collaboration of robots and fabrics. Precise robotic assembly causes inexact placement; imprecise fabric deformation creates accurate connections. This chaotic behavior relies on digital methodology and finds its position with little effort. *Precise Imprecision* addresses the digital and material tolerance and breaks the stereotype that precise manufacturing and robotic fabrication are inseparable. The research outlines the potential of combining generative coding and sensor feedback to establish an interactive, automatic building method. This autonomous behavior designs and constructs simultaneously through the process of data accumulation and revision.

ACKNOWLEDGMENTS

Precise Imprecision was made possible by the technical support from the FABLab at Taubman College, University of Michigan, and the funding support from the PCI Foundation. This project is a capstone design project in the MSDMT program which is led by advisor Prof. Glenn Wilcox. The robotic control utilizes Super Matter Tools (SMT) developed by Prof. Wes McGee as a plug-in interface for Rhinoceros 6. Additional support was received from Shan-Chun Wen and Julia Hunt.

FABLab: Asa Peller, Carlos Pompeo, and Rachael Henry

MSDMT Program: Prof. Catie Newell

10 Precise Imprecision is a pop-up installation which shapes a unique masonry wall in the courtyard

REFERENCES

West, Mark, Edward Allen, John Ochsendorf, Diederik Veenendaal, and Ronnie Araya Caceres. 2017. *The Fabric Formwork Book: Methods for Building New Architectural and Structural Forms in Concrete.* London: Routledge, Taylor & Francis Group.

Kudless, Andrew. 2011. "Bodies in Formation: the Material Evolution of Flexible Formworks." In *Integration through Computation: Proceedings of the 31st Annual Conference of the Association for Computer Aided Design in Architecture (ACADIA)*, edited by Joshua Taron, Vera Parlac, Branko Kolarevic and Jason Johnson, 98-105. Calgary/Banff, Canada: ACADIA.

Sarafian, Joseph, Ronald Culver, and Trevor S. Lewis. 2017. "Robotic Formwork in the MARS Pavilion: Towards the Creation of Programmable Matter." In *Disciplines & Disruption: Proceedings of the 37th Annual Conference of the Association for Computer Aided Design in Architecture (ACADIA)*, edited by Takehiko Nagakura, Skylar Tibbits, Mariana Ibanez, and Caitlin Mueller, 522–533. Cambridge, MA: ACADIA.

Clifford, Brandon and Wes McGee. 2018. "Cyclopean Cannibalism: a Method for Recycling Rubble." In *Recalibration: On Imprecision and Infidelity: Proceedings of the 38th Annual Conference of the Association for Computer Aided Design in Architecture (ACADIA)*, edited by Phillip Anzalone, Marcella Del Signore, and Andrew John Wit, 404-413. Mexico City, Mexico: ACADIA.

IMAGE CREDITS

All drawings and images by the authors.

11 Details of formation in *Precise Imprecision* wall

12 Details of solid and hollow form-fit boundaries

Ester Hong-Fen Lo is a Taiwanese architect/researcher of digital design and fabrication. She holds an M.S. degree in Digital and Material Technologies (DMT) from the University of Michigan Taubman College of Architecture and Urban Planning. As an experimentalist, Lo's research involves novel notions integrating design methodology, material performance, and advanced technology in digital practice. Prior to her time at DMT, she worked on multidisciplinary design projects, including architecture, exhibitions, interactive stage animation, and academic research. Lo has been honored from America and Delhi's Rethinking the Future (RTF) awards for her works.

Leon Yi-Liang Ko is a Taiwanese architect and an experimentalist of digital design and fabrication. He holds an M.S. degree in Digital and Material Technologies (DMT) from the University of Michigan Taubman College of Architecture and Urban Planning. As a researcher, he always interrogates the emerging relationships between architecture, engineering, material, and computation in the digital era. His research and practice centers on developing manufacturing methodology between advanced technology, material performance, and computational design as they relate to the built environment. Prior to attending DMT, he worked in multidisciplinary fields, including construction, landscape, architecture, and academic research.

Precarious Stand

Jinhui He
University Of Michigan

Xiaojie Cao
University Of Michigan

Tsz Yan Ng
University Of Michigan

Wes McGee
University Of Michigan

1   Rendering showing pavilion in green landscape

Precarious Stand explores the design and fabrication of a self-supporting dry-fit cantilever masonry system by controlling the centroids of the units' vertical compressive force. Concrete Masonry Units (CMU) are basic construction blocks that are ubiquitously used in our everyday world. This project challenges the singular nature of typical CMUs in its form and mode of assembly, by offering complex geometries as a fully assembled system, as well as customization for formwork production enabled by digital technology. Exploring the use of robotic hotwire cutting and ruled geometries, EPS foam molds were cut to cast the glass fiber reinforced concrete (GFRC) units.

Using Grasshopper plug-in for Rhino, the centroid balance, as in the force distribution of the masonry units, could be predetermined as part of the design process. Drawing from the project *Robotic Fabrication of Stone Assembly Details* by Ariza, Clifford, Durham, McGee, Mueller, and Sutherland where physics analysis was used to determine both the global and local equilibrium of a masonry compression assembly system, this project challenges concrete masonry units to assemble without the use of mortar but cantilever through the shaping of the units' centroid (Ariza et al. 2017). Early prototyping explored the prospect and extent of cantilever as sectional slices. By using its embodied weight, tapered shaping to the units, and choreographed sequence of assembly, the masonry system could be stacked without scaffolding or falsework during construction. To enable quick deployment, the design exploration also focused on masonry construction whereby mortar is not necessary, using male/female dry-fit jointing system and dowel connections

PRODUCTION NOTES

Designers: Jinhui He and Xiaojie Cao

Location: Ann Arbor

Date: 2019

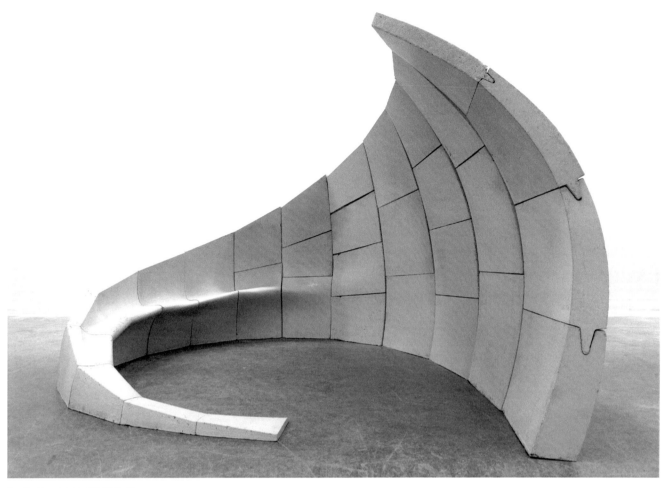

2   Final prototype at half-scale

for vertical racking. Connection tolerances were calibrated into the final design after a series of prototype testing to deal with both the hotwire cutting process and shrinkage from the cured concrete. Dry-fitting of the cantilevered system offers the opportunity to construct quickly and deconstruct without damage to the units. This suggests that the assembly system could be temporary, to be moved and rebuilt in another location.

The EPS foam formworks for concrete casting were produced using robotic hotwire cutting processes. Working with ruled surface geometries and limitations guided by the hotwire cutting process, the unique molds for the assembly were manufactured quickly and efficiently in terms of material use—all the mold pieces were cut in two days. Each mold was prepared with an epoxy coating, waxed, and release sprayed before casting. The molds could be reused as necessary.

The final design of an enclosure explores experiential effects when people are gathered within. The semi-circular sloped design of *Precarious Stand* welcomes and embraces individuals in the structure, and provides a temporary shelter for sitting and sun-shading. The final half-scale proof-of-concept aims to highlight the diverse and complex formal geometries that this molding process offers, especially when the system assembled will produce complex surface geometries with stable cantilevering.

REFERENCES

Ariza, Inés, T. Shan Sutherland, James B. Durham, Caitlin T. Mueller, Wes McGee, and Brandon Clifford. 2017. "Robotic Fabrication of Stone Assembly Details." In *Fabricate 2017*, edited by Bob Sheil, Achim Menges, Ruairi Glynn, and Marilena Skavara, 106-113. London: UCL Press.

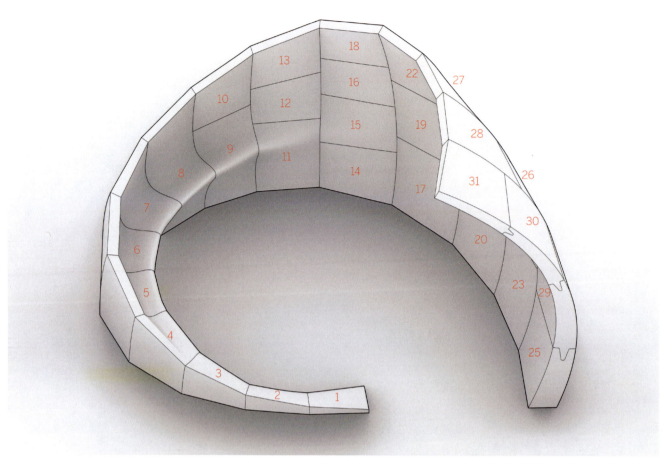

3   Panelization and order of assembly of units

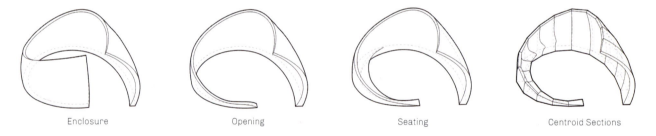

Enclosure   Opening   Seating   Centroid Sections

4   Form development for human interaction

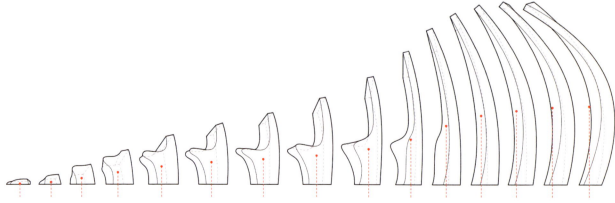

5   Controlling the centroid of each column of stacked units so that cantilevering could be achieved as the wall progressively bends

6   Prototype studies to test cantilevering limitation of the units and male/female joint connection tolerances

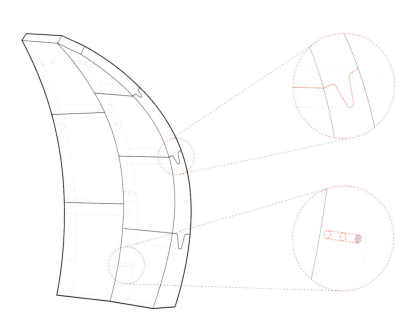

7   Connection details

8   Centroid aligned for each wall section

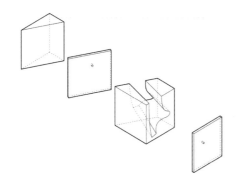

Hot Wire Cut Foam

CNC Cut Wood

Hot Wire Cut Foam

CNC Cut Wood

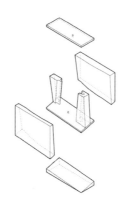

CNC Cut Wood

Hot Wire Cut Foam

Hot Wire Cut Foam

CNC Cut Wood

Hot Wire Cut Foam

Hot Wire Cut Foam

9   Exploded axon diagram of two typcial formwork for seat area and wall area.

10 EPS foam coating.

11 Assembled mold for casting.

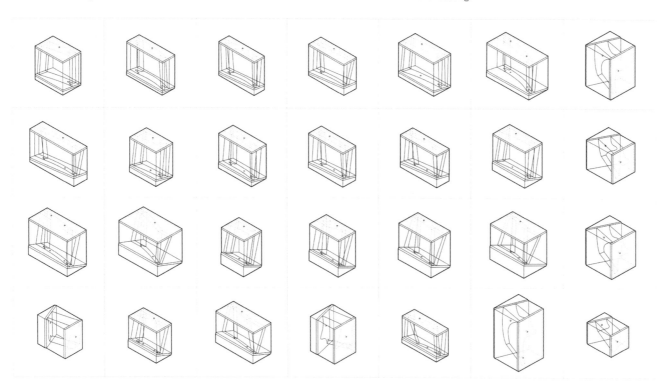

12 Matrix diagram of all molds used for the casting

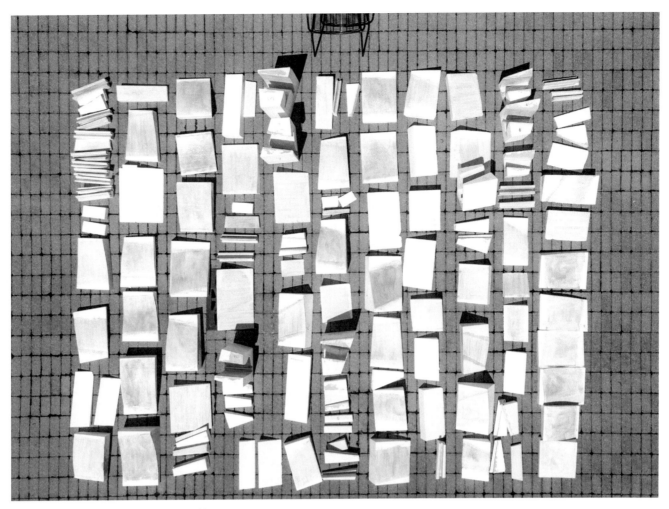

13 EPS foam formwork parts for entire assembly

ACKNOWLEDGMENTS

This project was produced for the year-long M. Arch thesis course *Concrete Labor* taught by Tsz Yan Ng. The fall seminar and winter semester design studio examined experimental concrete forming using advanced digital fabrication technology and computational design. The winter design studio is linked with Wes McGee's Advanced Digital Fabrication Seminar to further develop prototypes for testing. Partial funding for the project was provided by Taubman College.

IMAGE CREDITS

All drawings and images by the authors.

Jinhui He received his M. Arch from Taubman College, University of Michigan in 2019, with special focus typology studies via computational design and digital technology. He is currently working at Solomon Cordwell Buenz (SCB) as Designer.

Xiaojie Cao received her M. Arch degree from Taubman College, University of Michigan in 2019 and B.S. from University at Buffalo in 2017 where she received the Alpha Rho Chi Medal and was awarded the Design Excellence Award for outstanding studio work. She is currently working at Studio Daniel Libeskind as Designer.

Tsz Yan Ng is Assistant Professor in Architecture at Taubman College, University of Michigan. She was the Walter S. Sanders Fellow at the University of Michigan (2007-08) and the Reyner Banham Fellow at the Unversity of Buffalo (2001-02). Ng's practice includes architectural designs and installations in visual art. Common to both practices are projects that deal with questions of labor in its various manifestations, with special focus on techniques in clothing manufacturing and concrete forming.

Wes McGee is Associate Professor and the Director of the FabLab at Taubman College, University of Michigan. His work revolves around the interrogation of the means and methods of material production in the digital era, through research focused on developing new connections between design, engineering, materials, and manufacturing processes as they relate to the built environment.

KNEUCRETE
CNC Knits for programmable hybrid formworks

Shan Chun Wen
University of Michigan

Maryam Aljomairi
University of Michigan

Misri Patel
University of Michigan

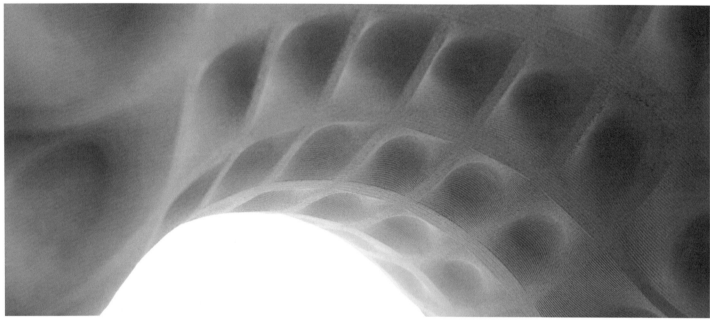

1   Inverted and self-supported full scale prototype, the curvature and corrugation induced by the control of knit structures, Ann Arbor, USA, 2019.

Kneu-crete aims to interrogate and establish a material dialogue between CNC-knitted inflatable form-works and concrete, attempting to redefine the role of concrete within formwork— where it acts as an active contributor rather than a passive one. The resulting data-material and formwork-concrete dialogs become driving agents for form-finding and slumping control within the casting process as opposed to traditional shaping of concrete with rigid molds.

The research investigates computational and physical methods simultaneously to generate and under-stand doubly curved, flat, or ruled surfaces. The main challenge of applying flexible fabric formwork into real construction practices is control and translation— translating the desired digital geometry into a relaxed flat geometry and then into a tensioned geometry. This integration of computational design and physical experiments aims to develop a viable workflow (Figure 2) that enables data to flow between digital and physical models along with potential design solutions. Initial studies described in this project use digital simulations (Figure 3) and physical experiments to understand and anticipate the material dialogue within the kneu-crete system while creating a taxonomy that indexes procedural slumping within CNC-knitted inflatable formwork through material programming at a micro-level.

The computational method is used to develop the textile component of the system, both in design and fabrication. In the digital simulation, a design workflow is developed to separate the computational task into two parts, global and local deformation, to make the simulation process more efficient. The acquired information from the two simulated resolutions (micro/macro deformations) provide numerical data detailing the type of action to be executed by the CNC-Knitting machine such as stitch structure, stitch type, stitch length, and overall knit dimensions (Figure 4, 5).

PRODUCTION NOTES

Designer: Shan Chun Wen
            Maryam Aljomairi
            Misri Patel
Status: Complete
Material: GFRC
Location: Ann Arbor, MI
Date: 2019

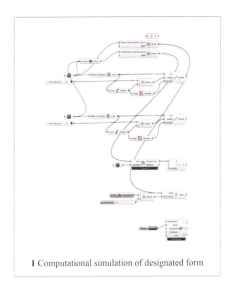

1 Computational simulation of designated form

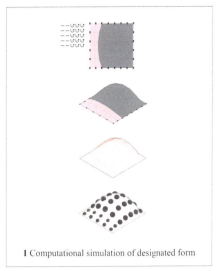

1 Computational simulation of designated form

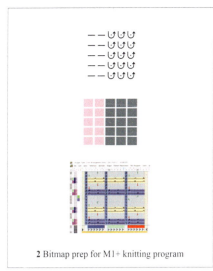

2 Bitmap prep for M1+ knitting program

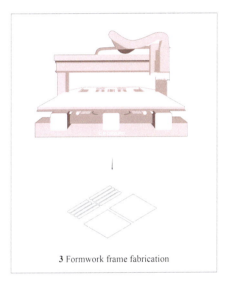

3 Formwork frame fabrication

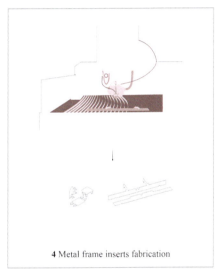

4 Metal frame inserts fabrication

5 Knit + insert inflatables

6 Place knit

9 Inflate Knit

7 Tension knit

10 Spray GFRC

8 Sandwich knit + water proof

11 Peel

12 Scan Pieces for comparative analysis

2 Order of operation, indicating steps of design and fabrication workflow.

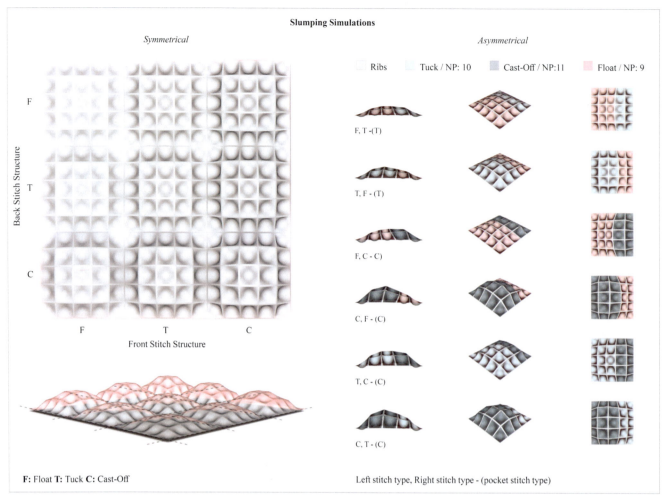

Slumping Simulations

Symmetrical

Asymmetrical

Ribs   Tuck / NP: 10   Cast-Off / NP:11   Float / NP: 9

Back Stitch Structure

F
T
C

Front Stitch Structure
F   T   C

F, T -(T)
T, F - (T)
F, C - C)
C, F - (C)
T, C - (C)
C, T - (C)

F: Float **T:** Tuck **C:** Cast-Off

Left stitch type, Right stitch type - (pocket stitch type)

3   Preliminary tensile knit structure simulations: symmetrical and asymmetrical slumping using varying stitch structures.

The feasibility of this system is explained and studied through the design and analysis of nine distinct CNC-knitted textiles and glass fiber reinforced concrete panels (Figure 8), where each panel explores the capacity of different stitch structures and integration of stitch lengths at a cellular level to influence the overall form and topology of the surface. This series of prototypes that aims to depict the potentials of the hybrid system places materiality as a priori agent and generator of complex forms and control. By measuring the simulation outcome with scans of a physical experiment, the data emerged into a set of knowledge that bridges the gap between the digital and the analog. This process helps in the creation of a feedback loop to better understand and digitally foresee material behavior under different specified conditions, such as types of yarn, stitch structure, gravity, and weight (Figure 11).

The other facet of this research addresses the development and the application of physical methods. Utilizing weights and the inherent tensile behavior of elastic yarns, pre-stress was applied to the textile component in addition to the weight of the concrete to fix the three-dimensional formwork. The variation in the three-dimensional outcome was essentially a result of the knit structure, the interconnection of differentiated material properties, and external uniform weights across a given region.

This programmable formwork challenges the presumed configuration of concrete casting. Architectural qualities emerge from the fine grains produced technologically by the CNC Knitting machine and the contrasting material nature of concrete. The scale and nature of the surface offer a significant opportunity for development of methodologies that harmonize the material process with digital and robotic workflow. The ability to respond to variables from materials and environment, gravity, weight, tensile strength, as well as the control of the symmetrical and asymmetrical slump, engender a new understanding towards building the foundations of digital materials discourse.

Project Title Author last names, separated by commas

Ribs ■ Pockets   Ribs ■ Pockets

4   Diagrams illustrating knit details of pocket and rib.

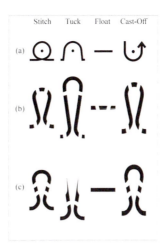

5   Left: Comparison of stitch structures, (a)programming icon, (b)front view, (c)back view. Right: Diagrams illustrating knit structures distribution.

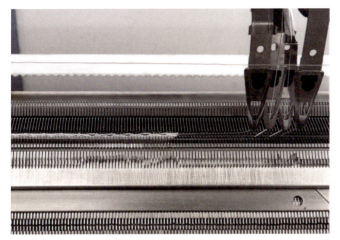

6   Yarn transfer between two needle beds as ribs to form pockets.

7   Close up of knit formwork with pneumatic system.

ACKNOWLEDGMENTS

We'd like to thank Tracey Weisman for her generous collaboration and assistance with the CNC knitting machine; this project would not have been possible without her contributions. Tracey received her MArch from the University of Michigan and is currently a researcher in Sean Ahlquist's lab.

This research was conducted as part of the capstone project under the supervision and guidance of Glenn Wilcox, Associate Professor of Architecture at Taubman College of Architecture at the University of Michigan, where he teaches courses in architectural design, generative design computing, and digital fabrication.

We are thankful to the Rackham Graduate Student Research Grant, and the PCI (Precast Concrete Institute) for funding this research and the support from Kerkstra Precast and JVI Industries. The project was developed through the use of a large-scale industrial CNC knitting machine, part of the FabLab at the Taubman College of Architecture and Urban Planning, University of Michigan.

IMAGE CREDITS

Figure 1,3, 9-11: Shan Chun Wen, Maryam Aljomairi, 2019

Figure 2: Maryam Aljomairi, Shan Chun Wen, Tracey Weisman, 2019

Figures 4-6: Maryam Aljomairi, 2019

All other drawings and images by the authors.

Shan Chun Wen is a digital and architectural designer interested in computational design and digital fabrication. His work concentrates on digital design and geometry optimization. He received his MSc. of Architecture in Digital and Material Technologies at

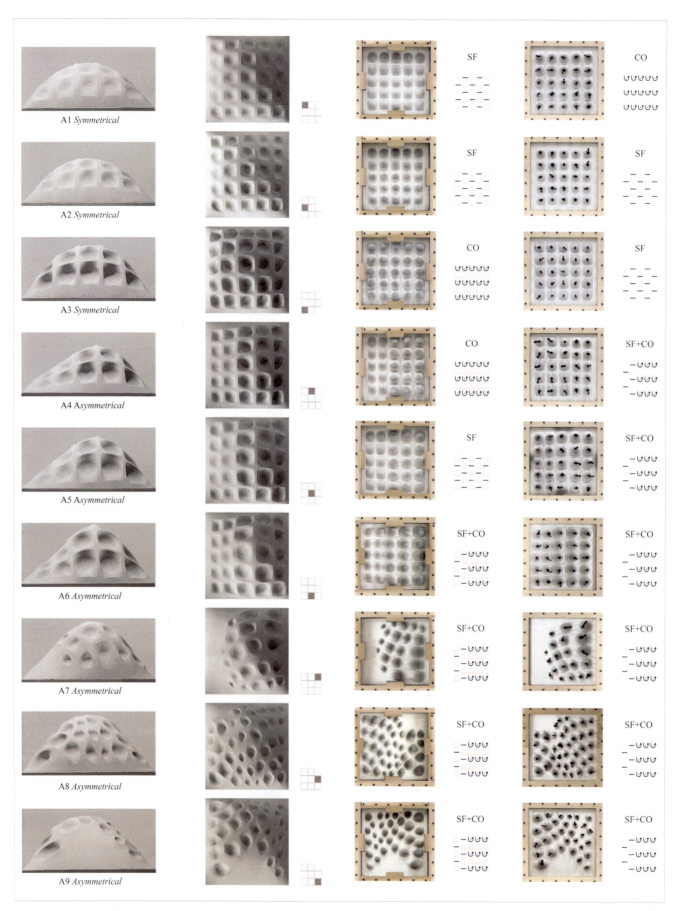

8 Comparative study of symmetrical vs. asymmetrical slumping under different stitch structures and stitch lengths.

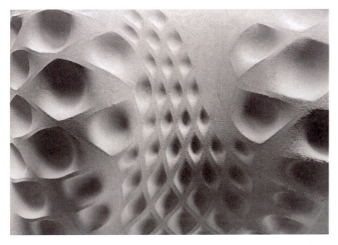

9 Top view of asymmetrical double slump : the patterned tensile strength differentiates the depth and size of the concrete corrugations.

10 Side view of asymmetrical double slump: the three parts tension formwork results in hills and valley.

11 Close-up showing knit structure imprint.

12 Two full scale KNEUCRETE:reversed structure and patterned concrete.

the University of Michigan, where he received the Merit-Based-Scholarship in the MS program. His design experience spans across industrial, landscape, interior, and architectural design. He participated in national and international design workshops lead by ACADIA, Yun-Tec, TKU, AECOM, and ETH, and the scale of his projects ranges from architectural construction to IoT products. Currently he is employed at Quarra Stone.

Maryam Aljomairi is a Bahraini architect and researcher. Her work aims to integrate novel fabrication techniques with computational design and material systems. In 2018, Maryam was awarded with a Fulbright Graduate Scholarship to pursue a MSc. of Architecture in Digital and Material Technologies at the University of Michigan, where she served as a research assistant to Catie Newell. Her work has been exhibited and published at the Venice Architecture Biennale, RIBA President Medals, A' Design Award, ArchDaily, and the National Museum of Bahrain. She acquired professional experience at Studio Anne Holtrop and is currently employed at Diller Scofidio + Renfro.

Misri Patel is an architect from Mumbai, India. She earned her MSc.Arch in Digital and Material Technology from Taubman College during which she was a research assistant to Sean Ahlquist. She completed her B.Arch from NMIMS BSSA in Mumbai where she was the recipient of Certificate of Merit. Prior to graduate school, she gained experience at LOT-EK, New York, and her work was exhibited at Venice Biennale, and Center for Architecture in New York City. Currently, she is a researcher with Catie Newell and Wes McGee at Taubman College and will serve as Ballard International Fellow at the CoAD, Lawrence Technological University.

Paper Folding to Foldable Composites

Joseph Choma
Design Topology Lab
Clemson University

1   Folding fiberglass along curved creases

INTRODUCTION

This research seeks to move beyond origami—the art of folding paper—by embracing material and structural constraints. Traditionally, origami is dominantly composed of hidden under-tucked folds, which is not an efficient use of material or ideal for resisting structural loads. Once a folded plane has a material thickness with the intent of carrying loads and specific orientation to gravity, it is no longer 'just origami', but a folded structure. That said, one would think folded structures have a long historical lineage within the field of architecture. However, most structures which we casually label as 'folded' are not folded at all, but are folded plate structures, where discrete planar elements are connected at some dihedral angle (Choma 2018). This research develops a technique to literally fold fiber-glass—like folding paper by hand—at the architectural scale.

The concept of foldable composites is straightforward: take a dry fiber reinforcement fabric, mask off seams to create fold points, infuse the unmasked fabric with resin, and cure the resin. This results in a composite laminate with uncured, soft seams that allow the entire structure to be folded for easy transport and installation on site. After the entire laminate is installed, the dry seams can be infused with resin to solidify the whole structure (Choma 2018). Key features of the fabrication technique include the potential for numerous variations, no fasteners or molds, decrease in manufacturing costs through a reduction in production time and zero material waste, high portability and flat-packing capabilities, and the possibility to design stronger lightweight structures. Foldable composites have

PRODUCTION NOTES

Principal: Joseph Choma

Team: Sarah Nail
             Harrison Novak
             William Marshall
             Claire Hicks
             Joseph Scherer

Sponsors: Composites One
             Vectorply
             Polynt-Reichhold
             United Initiators
             Windsor Fiberglass

Date: 2018

80   ACADIA 2019

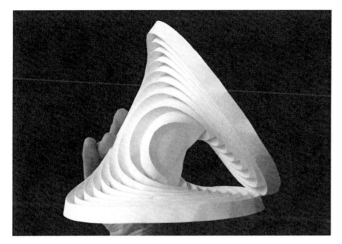

2   Folded paper model composed of twenty concentric circles

3   Folded fiberglass composed of twenty concentric circles

4   The crease width is calibrated to allow enough degrees of freedom

numerous potential applications ranging from architecture, packaging, aerospace, product design to the automotive industry. The research presented advances the current state of foldable composites by further developing the fabrication technique to allow fiberglass to fold along curved creases. As an initial test, twenty concentric circles are folded on an 8 ft diameter fiberglass disc. It took just 3 minutes to fold the flat disc into the three-dimensional saddle. Beyond this exploration, a full-scale wall panel and column have been fabricated out of a flat sheet of fiberglass.

Folding is a systematic method that transforms planar material into three-dimensional rigid structures. Depending on the organization of folds, structures can be flat-packed for ease of transport. By beginning with a flat plane, there is the potential to reduce production costs associated with manufacturing parts with curvature. Additionally, there are numerous variations possible with one systematic method. Within this research, computation-based simulation and analysis are used to design stronger lightweight structures.

Simultaneously, more efficient methods for manufacturing parts are being developed in direct dialogue with industry sponsors and collaborators. The research is motivated by the possibilities associated with translating paper folding into materials which have the potential to scale-up. Foldable composites will allow a new range of structures that have yet to be physically realized.

TWENTY CONCENTRIC CIRCLES

In 1927, a student within Josef Albers' studio at the Bauhaus folded a series of concentric circles on a piece of paper (Wingler 1969). As the paper was folded, alternating between mountain and valley folds, a saddle-shape emerged. By increasing the number of concentric circles from eight to twenty, a new range of geometric freedom emerges. It no longer has to remain symmetrical, but could be pushed and pulled according to outside forces.

Moving beyond folding concentric circles out of paper, a technique has been developed to allow fiberglass to fold along curved creases. Typically, paper models have a

5   The 8 ft long wall has a structural depth of approximately 1 ft

Paper Folding to Foldable Composites Choma

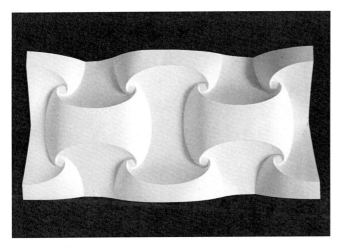

6 The tessellated crease pattern is folded out of paper

7 The tessellated crease pattern is folded out of fiberglass

8 A close up of one of the rotational nodes

particular relaxed state that we can observe after letting go of the model. Fiberglass does not need to have a relaxed state, any position can be frozen and fixed. Within this research, the process begins with a sheet of dry fiber reinforcement fabric, which is selectively coated with resin. After the foldable structure is positioned, resin can be applied to the curved creases to rigidify the structure. Through the inherent cross-stitch design of the fiber reinforcement fabric infused with resin, the material itself is capable of supporting the multidirectional residual stresses of the folded form. Although the structure is at the scale of a large object, it suggests the potential for a larger inhabitable structure.

ROOF OR WALL

The crease pattern was inspired by the work of David A. Huffman (Demaine et al. 2011). In particular, this author developed a means to array Huffman's initial square with ellipses by systematically mirroring the component. Through computational analysis, it was discovered that if the tessellation is not iteratively reflected, the surface is not foldable. Parametrically, the pattern can also be calibrated to control a specific structural depth along the surface.

Typically, when looking at a crease pattern, an individual sees a series of mountain and valley folds. However, this tessellated crease pattern could be architecturally interpreted as a reflective ceiling plan, where each square is the location of columns meeting a roof.

The width of the panel is 8 feet. Although it was initially imagined as a roof structure, the same design could be applied to make a wall panel. In the photographs, the piece is standing without any additional supports. The fiberglass piece was folded with just two people out of one continuous flat sheet.

COLUMN

The lightweight column is 8 feet tall and can effortlessly be carried by one person. The column was designed based on intuitive structural and aesthetic criteria. More specifically, the curved creases 'kiss' and mirror along vertical lines.

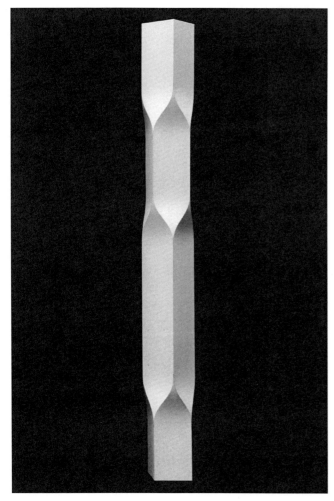

9 The small-scale column is folded out of paper

10 The full-scale column is folded out of fiberglass

Typically, single creases behave like hinges, such that if not fixed with resin, the structure will deform along the crease. With this particular design, the crease transitions from behaving as a hinge to that of a bi-stable structure which 'pops' into place, similar to a curved tape spring (Seffen et al. 2000). This behavior must be specifically designed into the crease pattern such that the equilibrium shape is achieved.

Since all the creases are mountain folds, it is easy for an individual to fold the entire column. The crease pattern was deliberately designed to have five faces to allow one face to overlap with another. Chopped strand mat was placed between the two overlapping panels.

Although the column was imagined as a lightweight foldable structure, the column could also be used as a stay-in-place formwork for a concrete column, here the fiberglass could also provide additional tensile reinforcement. Alternatively, with just a few adjustments it could become a reusable formwork. Aspects of this research into foldable composite structures are currently patent-pending.

ACKNOWLEDGMENTS

Throughout the process, a handful of research interns assisted in the fabrication of various artifacts. In Summer 2018, Sarah Nail, William Marshall, Claire Hicks, and Joseph Scherer helped fabricate 'Twenty Concentric Circles'. In Fall 2018, Sarah Nail and Harrison Novak helped fabricate 'Roof or Wall' and 'Column'.

Lastly, this research would not have been possible without the generous support of industry sponsors: Composites One, Vectorply, Polynt-Reichhold, United Initiators, and Windsor Fiberglass. In particular, special thanks to Karen Zullo (Composites One), Jordan Haar (Vectorply), Rick Pauer (Polynt-Reichhold), and David Riebe (Windsor Fiberglass).

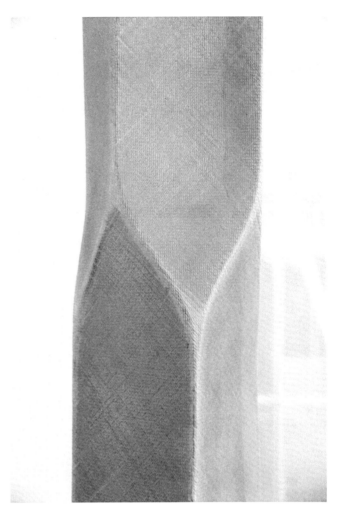

11 Looking up the folded fiberglass column

12 Detail of the curved creases along the column

REFERENCES

Choma, Joseph. 2018. "Foldable Composites for Architectural Applications." In *Origami 7, Volume One: Design, Education, History, and Science*, edited by R. Lang, M. Bolitho and Z. You, 135-150. St Albans: Tarquin.

Demaine, Erik D., Martin L. Demaine, and Duks Koschitz. 2011. "Reconstructing David Huffman's Legacy in Curved-Crease Folding." In *Origami 5: Fifth International Meeting of Origami Science, Mathematics, and Education*, edited by P. Wang-Iverson, R. Lang, and M. Yim, 39-52. Boca Raton, FL: CRC Press.

Seffen, K. A., Z. You, and S. Pellegrino. 2000. "Folding and Deployment of Curved Tape Springs." *International Journal of Mechanical Sciences* 42(10): 2055-2073.

Wingler, Hans M. 1969. *The Bauhaus: Weimar, Dessau, Berlin, Chicago*. Cambridge, MA: The MIT Press.

IMAGE CREDITS

All images by the author

Joseph Choma Founder of the Design Topology Lab and an Associate Professor of Architecture at Clemson University. He is the author of *Morphing: A Guide to Mathematical Transformations for Architects and Designers* (Laurence King Publishing, 2015) and *Études for Architects* (Routledge, 2018). He has received awards from both the American Institute of Architects and the American Composites Manufacturers Association. In recent years, he has given invited lectures at the ETH Zurich, Cornell University, Georgia Tech and taught a workshop at Carnegie Mellon University. Choma completed graduate studies in design and computation at Massachusetts Institute of Technology.

ORIGAMI CONCRETE
Robotic Folding Fabrication

Roger Hubeli
Syracuse University

Julie Larsen
Syracuse University

1   Detail of twisted lattice form (APTUM, May 2019)

ABSTRACT

Origami Concrete investigates a parametrically controlled fabrication method for prefabricated concrete building elements through the use of an 'origami' folding technique that uses adjustable formwork configurations and 'foldable' concrete mixes. With the use of fiber reinforced Ultra-High-Performance Concrete (UHPC) mixes, CNC milling, and robotic arms, we create geometries with novel formwork that begins as a flat surface and is folded up into varied forms during the curing process. Where traditional prefabricated concrete elements require elaborate formwork and reinforcement for each unique desired form, the variability of the method bridges the formal potential of digital modeling with fabricating those geometries using very little formwork to achieve the complex forms.

INTRODUCTION

The fabrication process transforms parametric modeling into scripts for the robotic arm in order to fold the formwork into a variety of configurations (Figures 2, 3). With the proposed 'folded' formwork techniques, we derived the formal explorations from the performative qualities of 'origami' folding techniques (and its sister technique 'kirigami') that begin as flat paper surfaces and are folded into complex forms. The 'origami concrete' techniques create a variety of forms from a singular formwork because the technique can be incrementally folded up and down. The two prototypes explore the technique to fabricate a 'twisted' lattice frame and a 'rolled' hollow column (Figures 4, 5).

PRODUCTION NOTES

Architect:	APTUM
Industry Partner:	Cemex Global R&D
Status:	Ongoing
Location:	Autodesk, Boston, MA
Date:	2019

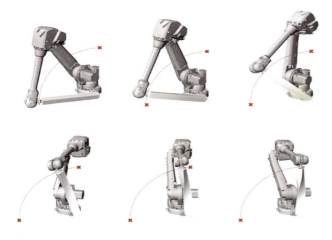

2   Diagram of robotic simulation for twisted form

3   Diagram of rolled column formwork: from flat to rotated upright

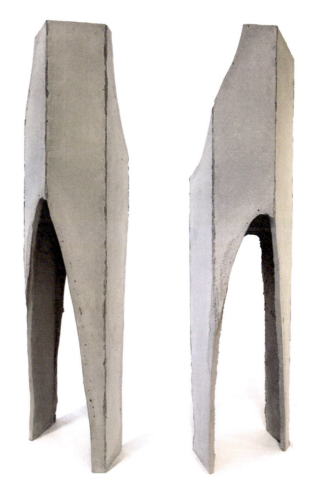

4   Series of rolled columns; Test 1 and Test 2 (APTUM, June 2019)

BACKGROUND

"Folding" in concrete construction has been used as a fundamental structural principle to increase the strength and stability of structural elements without having to increase the amount of material used or strengthening it. Although there are many 'folded' structures made of concrete, there has always been a schism between the material and the technique. Contrary to sheet metal, concrete is not a two-dimensional material that can easily be 'folded' but rather, is a composite of a liquid mix that is poured around a pre-formed formwork that takes a "folded" shape but isn't literally folded.

ARGUMENT

The benefits to the 'origami' construction method are three-fold. First, to make many forms, the method uses considerably less formwork and material because the same formwork is used for many pours. Second, a singular formwork can be computationally controlled and altered after each pour to create a series of dynamically varied elements that vary in height, width, or depth. Third, unlike traditional concrete that cannot be 'folded' due to becoming too brittle once cured, the concrete mix is capable of moving and holding its shape while the formwork is transformed during curing.

METHODS

To explore a range of techniques, an 'Origami Element Catalogue' (OEC) is used to define formal ambitions and a construction strategy for a given element (Figure 7). Depending on the type of 'fold' (creasing, rolling, twisting, etc.) of the formwork, specific parameters in Grasshopper are controlled in the script, such as height, width, depth, scale, distance between edges, middle and corner points, or surface alignments. The computational forms were developed with TACO, in conjunction with Kangaroo, and then translated to ABB Robot Studio (Figures 2, 10). With TACO, the movement of the formwork is adjusted to account for the occurring deformation of the formwork itself during the process of folding. Once the script is fixed, the flat formwork is manually assembled from CNC-milled or waterjet-cut elements. The robotic arm is only used

5   Three twisted origami forms assembled together (APTUM, June 2019)

6   Step-by-step robotic process of twisted formwork and concrete cast

7   Origami Element Catalogue (OEC)

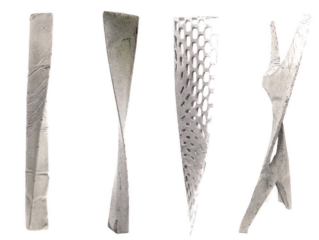

8   Twisted concrete forms - Test 1, 2, 3, and 4 (APTUM, June 2019)

to move the formwork from a flat position to the final folded position to ensure accuracy in the final geometry. After the concrete is poured into the flat formwork, it is folded into the final position after only 60 minutes of curing (Figures 6, 9). The form remains in the formwork overnight and is demolded in order to reuse the formwork.

RESULTS
The prototypes consist of a twisted latticework and a rolled column that can be aggregated into a waffle system (Figures 5, 11). Origami Concrete has proven that the mix is viable for the folding formwork technique, and the prototypes were successfully cast into geometries directly translated from the computational forms.

CONCLUSION
The questions explored in the Origami Concrete research reflects how new fabrication techniques make it possible to reconnect with the tradition of ubiquitous precast methods for various building elements. The complex relationship between digital form, mix and fabrication helps formulate new fabrication strategies for computational form but also challenges the economies of labor, material flow, and production. The variability of the process defies the typical standardization of prefabricated elements, when using robotic technology, to achieve variability and complexity in concrete form-making.

ACKNOWLEDGMENTS
This project would not be possible without our collaborators, Davide Zampini and his team at CEMEX Global R&D (most notably Alex Guerini and Matthew Meyers). We would like to thank Dean Michael Speaks at the School of Architecture at Syracuse University for his support. And lastly, we appreciate the hard work and dedication of our Research Assistants at Syracuse University: Michael Aiardo, John Mikesh, Jinsung Kim, and Haoquan Wang.

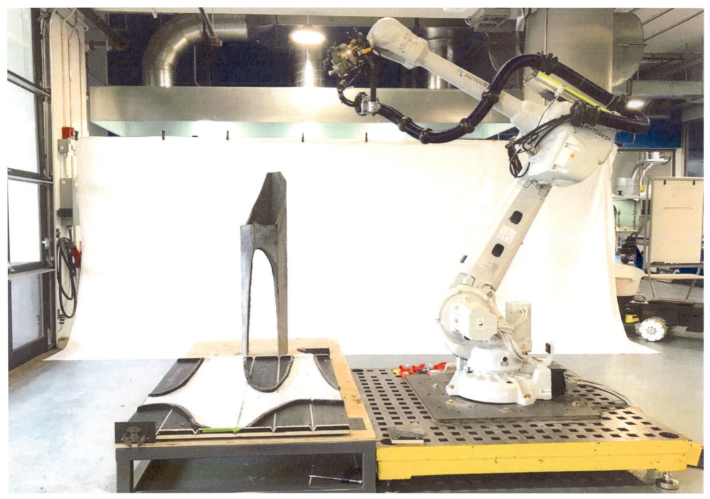

9 Robotic arm with flat formwork and final rolled concrete column (APTUM, June 2019)

REFERENCES

Culver, Ronald, Trevor S. Lewis, Joseph Sarafian. 2017. "Robotic Formwork in the MARS Pavilion: Towards the Creation Of Programmable Matter." In *ACADIA 2017: Disciplines + Disruption, Proceedings of the 37th Annual Conference of the Association for Computer Aided Design in Architecture*, 522-533.

Jackson, Paul. 2016. *Folding Techniques for Designers: From Sheet to Form*. London: Laurence King Publishing.

Peck, Martin. 2014. "Building Material and Products". In *Modern Concrete Construction Manual: Structural Design, Material Properties, Sustainability*, 36-41. Munich: DETAIL. For an abbreviated overview of the recent development of UHPC concrete mix design in relationship to architecture.

Portland Cement Association (PCA). n.d. "Ultra-High Performance Concrete." Accessed August 5, 2019. https://www.cement.org/learn/concrete-technology/concrete-design-production/ultra-high-performance-concrete. UHPC is also known as reactive powder concrete (RPC).

Wierzbicki-Neagu, Madalina. 2005. "Unfolding Architecture – Study, Development and Application of New Kinetic Structure Topologies." In *Smart Architecture: Integration of Digital and Building Technologies: Proceedings of the 2005 Annual Conference of the Association for Computer Aided Design in Architecture*, 246-253. ACADIA. Savannah, Georgia: Savannah School of Architecture and Design (SCAD).

Windeck, Georg. 2016. "Evolutionary Structural Optimization," In *Construction Matters*, 80. Brooklyn, NY: Powerhouse Books.

IMAGE CREDITS

All drawings and images by the authors.

Origami Concrete Hubeli, Larsen

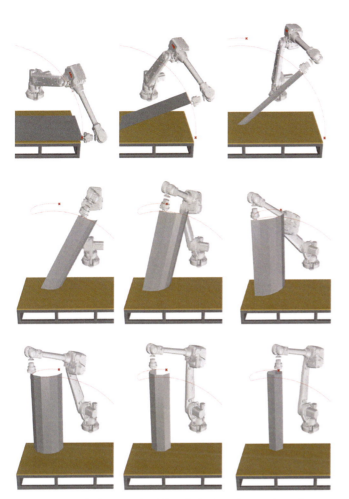

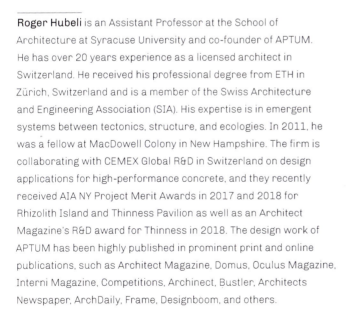

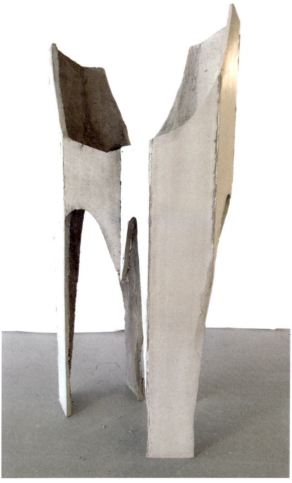

10 Diagram of robotic arm scripted for rolled column formwork rotation

11 Four assembled rolled origami columns (APTUM, May 2019)

Roger Hubeli is an Assistant Professor at the School of Architecture at Syracuse University and co-founder of APTUM. He has over 20 years experience as a licensed architect in Switzerland. He received his professional degree from ETH in Zürich, Switzerland and is a member of the Swiss Architecture and Engineering Association (SIA). His expertise is in emergent systems between tectonics, structure, and ecologies. In 2011, he was a fellow at MacDowell Colony in New Hampshire. The firm is collaborating with CEMEX Global R&D in Switzerland on design applications for high-performance concrete, and they recently received AIA NY Project Merit Awards in 2017 and 2018 for Rhizolith Island and Thinness Pavilion as well as an Architect Magazine's R&D award for Thinness in 2018. The design work of APTUM has been highly published in prominent print and online publications, such as Architect Magazine, Domus, Oculus Magazine, Interni Magazine, Competitions, Archinect, Bustler, Architects Newspaper, ArchDaily, Frame, Designboom, and others.

Julie Larsen is an Associate Professor at the School of Architecture at Syracuse University and co-founder of APTUM. She has over 20 years experience as an architect and is an associate member of AIA NY. She received her professional degree from Columbia University in 2002. Her expertise is in the role of digital fabrication as it applies to multiple scales; from material technology to ecological and infrastructural applications. Julie is the co-founder of APTUM, along with Roger Hubeil, an award-winning design practice that focuses on material research and its influence on architecture. Their most recent research, teaching, and professional design work revolves around digital fabrication and tectonics and their potential to mediate between architecture, systems, and ecologies. Their award-winning Thinness Pavilion was exhibited at the California College of the Arts (CCA) in San Francisco as part of the 'Designing Material Innovation' exhibition and symposium in 2017. Rhizolith Island was recently exhibited at the Floating Cities Exhibition at Woodbury University's WUHO Gallery in 2019, curated by Professor Anthony Fontenot.

Melting

Shelby Elizabeth Doyle
Iowa State University

Erin Linsey Hunt
Iowa State University

Augmenting Concrete Columns
with Water Soluble 3D Printed Formwork

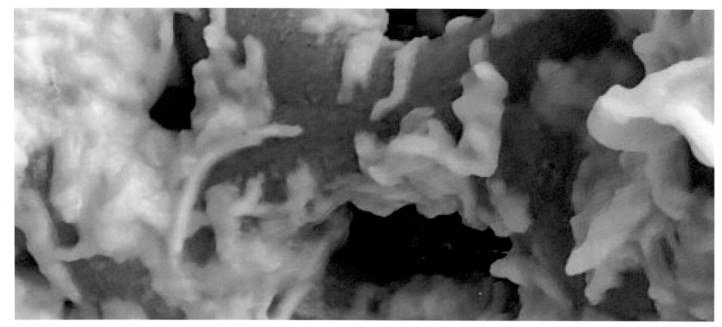

1   Image of PVA formwork dissolving off of a cast column

OVERVIEW

Melting is a continuation of prior research conducted in the paper "Dissolvable 3D Printed
Formwork: Exploring Additive Manufacturing for Reinforced Concrete" (Doyle & Hunt 2019).
The paper proposes simultaneously printing two systems—polyvinyl alcohol (PVA) formwork and steel PLA tensile reinforcement—to produce a water-soluble concrete formwork
with integrated reinforcement. One conclusion of the paper is that the complete elimination
of formwork may continue to be more preferable than the introduction of biodegradable
or water-soluble formworks, and that the most promising application for these methods
might be the augmentation of traditional formwork. The prototypes explored here use the
methods developed in "Dissolvable 3D Printed Formwork" to augment typical concrete
construction methods with moments of unique geometry that would be difficult to fabricate
using other concrete formwork methods (Asprone 2018).

CUSTOM 3D PRINTED FORMWORK

The custom 3D printed formwork was produced using a LulzBot TAZ 6 (build volume
of 280 mm x 280 mm x 250 mm) utilizing the Dual Extruder v3 tool head (Figure 2). The
polyvinyl alcohol formwork was 200 mm in diameter and height. The simultaneously
printed PLA steel reinforcement diameter was 12 mm. A constraint of the form was the

2   Custom PVA formwork and steel PLA rebar printing on a LulzBot TAZ 6

3   Interior image of a cast column

forty-five-degree angle limitation of Fused Deposition Modeling (FDM) printing. Angles of greater than 45 degrees would cause loss of print adhesion and require the generation of supports, which the designers chose to avoid to conserve filament (Jipa 2017). The print time for each mold was 45 hours and the formwork took 40 hours to dissolve in 70 degree Celsius water. In addition to being submerged in water, cleaning by hand with a brush was required to remove remaining PVA.

PROCESS + OBSERVATIONS

Three prototypes were developed that combined traditional formwork fabrication methods with the proposed 3D printed augmentations.

FORM A

The top and base design of this column was created by bounding the 3D printed PVA formwork. The boundary was then used to find the curves that touched the top and bottom faces; these curves were polar-arrayed and merged into an outer and center curve to create the

extruded profile, a method that was an attempt to create a smooth transition between the two formwork methods. Subsequently, the profiles were CNC-routed from polystyrene insulation foam. Additional custom caps at the top and bottom were CNC-routed as formwork to hold the 1/2" rebar vertically in position and to connect the two formwork methods. The top layer of CNC-routed formwork had additional apertures to allow the Hydraulic Expansion Cement (HEC) to be poured (Figure 5). Although this method allowed for greater formal cohesion and customization, it took nearly four hours to CNC route a single prototype; moreover, the formwork was destroyed upon removal and could not be reused, limiting it as a replicable strategy. This column used two-thirds of a board of polystyrene insulation foam costing twenty dollars.

FORM B

Form B iterations used an eight-inch diameter standard sonotube augmented with PVA formwork. In addition to the sonotubes, four custom CNC-routed polystyrene insulation foam caps were created to hold the center off-the-shelf

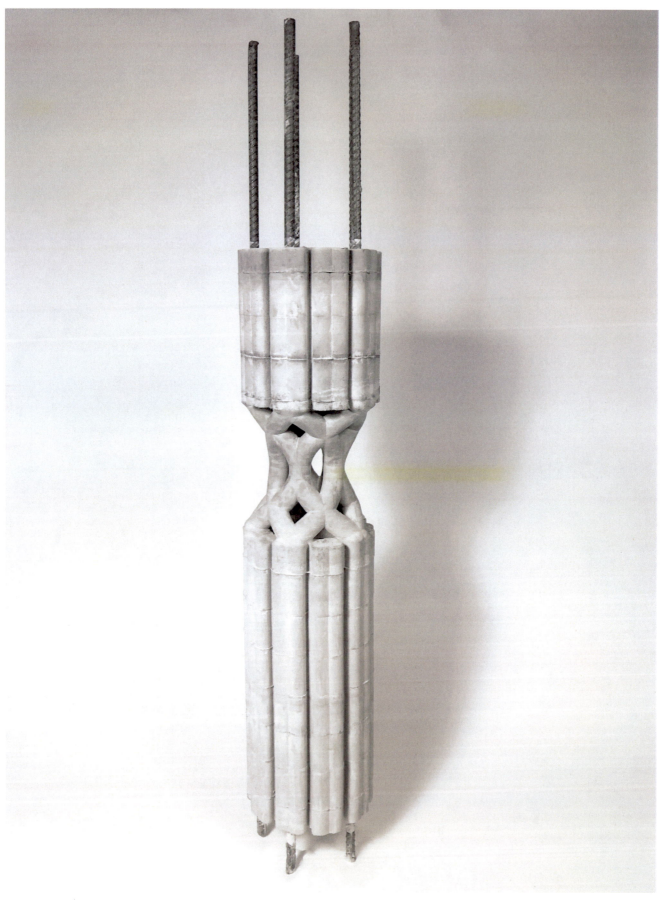

4   Resulting HEC cast column

5   Left to right: Diagram of Form A column formwork, rendering of column, and elevation denoting the path of the reinforcement

PVC pipes (used to create a hollow cast), 1/2" rebar, and the 3D printed formwork. The CNC-milled caps allowed for the addition of custom edge qualities such as a chamfer or fillet to create continuity between the 3D printed formworks and the sonotube formworks (Figure 6). Two prototypes were created using this method and a single sonotube costing nine dollars, allowing for a cheaper and faster method than using only water-soluble formwork. Form B-1 had filleted edges (Figure 9) and Form B-2 had chamfered edges (Figure 10), resulting in different resolutions of the connection between formwork types. These caps were not damaged upon removal allowing for future reuse. Form B-1 was cast using Quikrete Fast-Setting Concrete with the aggregate sifted out of the mix, resulting in a less polished surface finish than Form B-2, which was cast using two-parts fine sand one-part cement and one-part water.

NEXT STEPS + CONCLUSIONS
After curing for twenty-eight days, each of the columns will be subjected to crushing test per ASTM C39/C39M to compare the augmented columns with unreinforced

concrete and standard steel reinforcement columns of the same dimensions.

Future tests will be calibrated for shorter print times. The LulzBot TAZ 6 Dual Extruder v3 tool head has a standard layer height of 0.22 mm and a nozzle diameter of 0.5 mm. The constraints of this tool head resulted in long print times due to the need for infill to allow the print to self-support. In future tests a larger diameter nozzle could be used to only print a single shell, a modification that would not only reduced print time but also a more rapid rate of PVA dissolution.

PVA was selected expressly for its water-solubility, rather than pursuing any number of materials that could serve as formwork. The work shown here demonstrates that PVA—having served as a proof-of-concept—is likely not the appropriate material for future full-scale investigations. For the purposes of this research PVA stands in for a speculative future where non-toxic, compostable, and/or water-soluble construction materials serve as formwork

 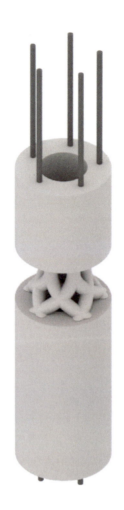 

6   Left to right: Diagram of Form B-1+2 column formwork, rendering of column, and elevation denoting the path of the reinforcement

or self-contained architectural elements. These materials will serve a pre-determined purpose, for a specific length of time, then degrade through exposure to environmental conditions, such as rain, resulting in the structure being reabsorbed into the surrounding ecosystem.

REFERENCES

Asprone, D., F. Auricchio, C. Menna, V. Mercuri. 2018. "3D printing of reinforced concrete elements: Technology and design approach." *Construction and Building Materials* 165: 218-231.

Jipa, A., B. Dillenburger, M. Bernhard. 2017. "skelETHon Formwork: 3D Printed Plastic Formwork for Load-Bearing Concrete Structures." In *SIGraDi 2017: XXI Congreso de la Sociedad Ibero-Americana de Gráfica Digital*, 345-352.

Doyle, S.E. and E.L. Hunt. "Dissolvable 3D Printed Formwork: Exploring Additive Manufacturing for Reinforced Concrete." In *Ubiquity and Autonomy: Papers of ACADIA 2019.*

IMAGE CREDITS

7   Form B-1 column cast in Quikrete Fast-Setting Concrete
    with the aggregate sifted out

8   Form B-2 column cast using two-parts fine sand one-part cement
    and one-part water

Shelby Elizabeth Doyle, AIA is Assistant Professor of Architecture at Iowa State University College of Design and co-founder of the ISU Computation & Construction Lab (CCL), which works to connect developments in computation to the challenges of construction through teaching, research, and outreach. The central hypothesis of CCL is that computation in architecture is a material, pedagogical, and social project. This hypothesis is explored, through the fabrication of built projects and materialized in computational practices. The CCL is invested in questioning the role of education and pedagogy in replicating existing technological inequities and in pursuing the potential for technology in architecture as a space of and for gender equity. Doyle received a Fulbright Fellowship to Cambodia, a Master of Architecture from the Harvard Graduate School of Design, and a Bachelor of Science in architecture from the University of Virginia.

Erin Linsey Hunt was the ISU Computation & Construction Lab Associate from 2017-19 where she oversaw operations and conducted research. Her research interests include construction applications for additive manufacturing technologies, specifically 3D printing. She was an Undergraduate Research Assistant with the ISU CCL and she holds a Bachelor of Architecture degree from Iowa State University. She is pursuing a Master in Design Studies in Technology at the Harvard Graduate School of Design.

MUD Frontiers / Zoquetes Fronterizos

Ronald Rael
The University of California
Berkeley/Emerging Objects

Virginia San Fratello
San Jose State University/
Emerging Objects

1   Local clay samples collected from El Paso, Texas and Juarez, Mexico (Photo © Dina Edens-Perlasca)

MUD: MOBILITY, UBIQUITY AND DEMOCRACY

MUD Frontiers addresses Mobility, Ubiquity and Democracy within the field of robotic additive manufacturing.

During the last thirty-five years, additive manufacturing has become commonplace within the realm of academic research as a tool for creating models and full scale working prototypes and, in very rare instances, it is used as a method of manufacture by specialist to fabricate custom componentry for buildings. However, additive manufacturing is still not close to being a commonplace or ubiquitous method of manufacture within the larger building industry due to the expense associated with the purchases of heavy, industrial 3D printers and professional robot arms. Additionally, many materials such as resins, bulk filament and pellets, and proprietary powders are also expensive when used for large format printing and in instances where these materials must be shipped long distances. Finally, additive manufacturing requires expertise in 3D modeling and coding, which means additional costs and time must be spent mastering advanced software applications. For many end users, these obstacles have precluded the use of additive manufacturing as a way of building.

2   3D Printed Brownware (Photographer: Olalekan Jeyifous).

3   3D Printed Brownware (Photographer: Olalekan Jeyifous).

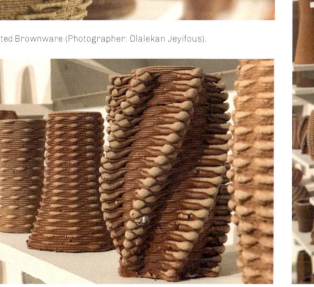

4   3D Printed Brownware (Photographer: Olalekan Jeyifous).

MOBILITY: ROBOTIC 3D PRINTING

The MUD Frontier project addresses these challenges through the development of a mobile and lightweight, robotic 3D printing set-up that can easily be transported to the field or jobsite. The robotic 3D printer can be combined with a continuous flow hopper that can print wall sections and enclosures up to a 2200mm diameter circle and 2500mm tall, structures considerably larger than the printer itself. The printer can be picked up by 2 people (it weighs less than 100 pounds) and relocated in order to continue printing.

UBIQUITY: MUD AND CLAY

The printer is used to 3D print local muds and clays from the print site and surrounding region. The mud and clay in many instances are free, as they can be dug directly from the ground or surrounding region where the walls and enclosures are being printed. Phase I of the MUD Frontier project took place in El Paso, Texas where earthen architecture and clay pottery of the Mogollon culture (A.D. 200 - 1450) define the archeological history of the region.

Excavated pit houses and above ground adobe structures defined the historic architecture of the region, and by A.D. 400 this region witnessed the development of a distinctive, indigenous coil-and-scrape pottery tradition known as Brownware. Local clays were gathered from eight sites throughout the region and used to print 170 ceramic vessels and a 3D printed adobe structure. The structure and vessels were produced to connect the forefront of digital manufacturing with the traditional coiled pottery techniques, and subterranean and adobe architecture of the borderland regions between Texas, New Mexico, and Chihuahua.

DEMOCRACY: SOFTWARE

Custom software, called Potterware, is used to design the walls and enclosures printed by the robotic 3D printer. The software is an intuitive design app, that runs in the cloud, for 3D printing that attempts to democratize because it features easy to use sliders and automatically generates printable gcode files, alleviating the need to learn any 3D modeling software. Objects, walls, and enclosures, at the

5   MUD Frontiers as part of the "New Cities, Future Ruins at the Border" exhibit at the Rubin Center for the Visual Arts at the University of Texas at El Paso

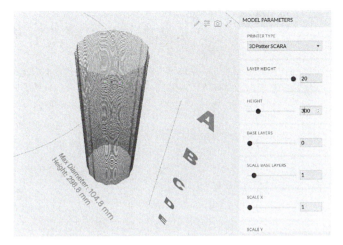

6   Potterware: Layer height and overall height

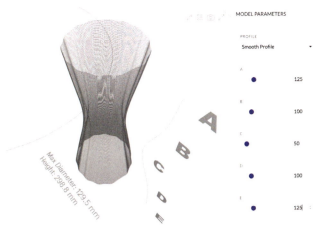

7   Potterware: Diameter dimensioning

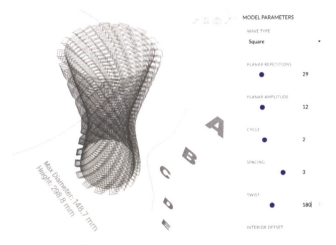

8   Potterware: Wave type

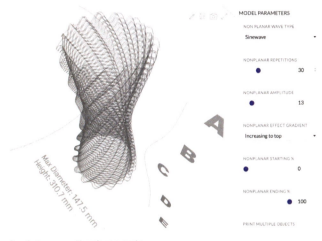

9   Potterware: Nonplanar mode

scale of rooms, can be designed and ready for printing within minutes.

The MUD Frontier project unearths and reexamines ancient building traditions and materials using 21st century technology and craft coupled with local skills to create emerging and new traditions.

ACKNOWLEDGMENTS

Emerging Objects: Ronald Rael, Virginia San Fratello, Loggman Arja, Sandy Curth

Rubin Center for the Visual Arts: Melissa Barba , Kerry Doyle, Daniel Szwaczkowski

The Univervisty of Texas at El Paso: Vincent Burke, Dina Edens-Perlasca and the ceramics students

Texas Tech University: Ersela Kripa, Stephen Mueller and the architecture students

3D Potter: Danny Defilici

REFERENCES

Rael, Ronald and Virginia San Fratello. 2018. *Printing Architecture: Innovative Recipes for 3D Printing.* New York: Princeton Architectural Press.

Wall Text, Brochure, *Ancient Borderland: The Jornada Mogollon*, El Paso Museum of Archeology, El Paso, Texas.

Emerging Objects. n.d. "POTTERWARE." Accessed July 28, 2019. www.emergingobjects.com/project/potterware_litev2/.

IMAGE CREDITS

Figure 1: © Dina Edens-Perlasca
Figure 2, 3, 4: © Olalekan Jeyifous
All other drawings and images by the authors.

10 MUD Frontiers as part of the "New Cities, Future Ruins at the Border" exhibit at the Rubin Center for the Visual Arts at the University of Texas at El Paso

Ronald Rael

Ronald Rael is the Chair of the Department of Architecture, in the College of Environmental Design, at the University of California Berkeley where he founded the printFARM Laboratory (print Facility for Architecture, Research and Materials). He is an applied architectural researcher, design activist, author, and thought leader in the fields of additive manufacturing and earthen architecture. He is the author of *Borderwall as Architecture: A Manifesto for the U.S.-Mexico Boundary* (University of California Press 2017), an illustrated biography and protest of the wall dividing the U.S. from Mexico, featured in a recent TED talk by Rael, and *Earth Architecture* (Princeton Architectural Press, 2008) a history of building with earth in the modern era to exemplify new, creative uses of the oldest building material on the planet. With San Fratello he co-authored *Printing Architecture: Innovative Recipes for 3D Printing.*

Virginia San Fratello

Virginia San Fratello is an architect, artist, and educator. She is an Associate Professor in the Department of Design at San Jose State University in Silicon Valley where she is also Director of the Interior Design Program. San Fratello recently won the International Interior Design Educator of the Year Award and her creative practice, Rael San Fratello (with Ronald Rael), was named an Emerging Voice by The Architectural League of New York and also received the ACADIA digital practice award in 2016. She is also a winner of the Metropolis Magazine Next Gen Design Competition. The work of Rael San Fratello has been published widely, including in Interior Design Magazine, The New York Times, Wired, MARK, Domus, Metropolis Magazine and PRAXIS and is recognized by several institutions including The Museum of Modern Art (MoMA), SFMOMA, and The Cooper Hewitt Smithsonian Design Museum.

11 MUD Frontiers under construction

12 Close up view of mud being extruded from the mobile 3D Printer

CeramicInformation Pavilion

Christian J. Lange
The University of Hong Kong

Donn Holohan
The University of Hong Kong

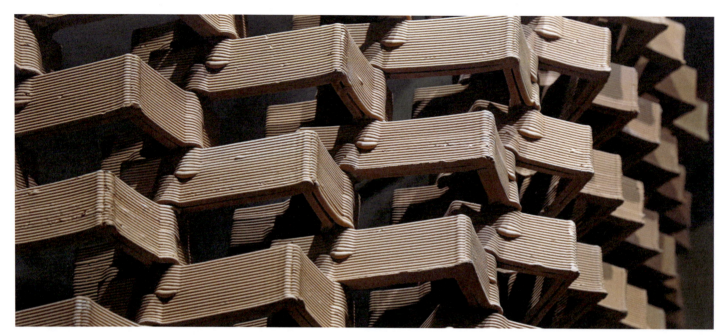

1   Detail view of brick assembly

RETHINKING STRUCTURAL BRICK SPECIALS
THROUGH AN INDEXICAL ROBOTIC 3D PRINTING METHOD

The *CeramicInformation* pavilion is the second outcome of an ongoing research project that attempts to revitalize the material system of the brick special through the development of an intelligent 3D printing method that works in conjunction with a layman assembly procedure.

In the past decade, 3D printing technology has become increasingly advanced and has made its way into architecture. Within this field there has also emerged a research trajectory that focuses on utilizing the technology to reimagine ceramic brick specials for architectural production. Recently, work by Ronald Rael and Virginia San Fratello with "Cabin of Curiosities" (Rael and San Fratello 2017) and the "Ceramic Morphologies" project of the Material Processes + Systems Group at Harvard GSD (Bechthold et al. 2018) have demonstrated the opportunities presented by the non-standard module.

By developing a model suitable for complex global geometries, this research project seeks to build on emerging work and aims to utilize the potentials offered by today's computational and fabrication tools to develop a system that can rely on its own structural material capacity. Referencing a range of modular interlocking brick systems, the project provides a versatile solution, one that is capable of adapting more precisely to a wide range of spatial conditions. Specifically, the following objectives were defined for this part of the ongoing

2   DIW process with linear ram extruder attached to ABB 6700

3   Printing process of a single brick

4   Selection of continuously differentiated bricks

research: to develop an intelligent brick special utilizing robotically controlled ceramic 3D printing technologies with a generic flatbed printing method that can achieve curvilinear form in the global design; and to develop a brick assembly system that works without intricate jigs or specialized tools during the assembly process, which would, therefore, be informed by local spatial relationships between the neighboring bricks.

The research pavilion which was part of the latest edition of the Shenzhen Bi-City Biennale on Architecture and Urbanism (UABB) in 2017 had roughly a footprint of 2.5 by 2.5 meters and measured 2.2 meters in height. The continuously differentiated components were manufactured over 20 days before the lightweight elements were shipped to the site and assembled in 5 days into the multifaceted wall by laymen. Approximately 1.5 million lines of robot code were generated, with each brick containing an average of 1400 individual target-points, and 882 individual brick specials were printed utilizing a set up that consisted of an industrial robot in conjunction with an automatic clay

extruder. Around 700 kg of standard low fire terracotta clay was used for the production of the bricks. The average printing time for each brick was about six minutes. The bricks were fired at 1125 degrees Celsius to achieve a structurally sound result. After firing each brick weighed approximately 600 grams, close to one-quarter of the weight of a standard brick.

Generic bricks are relatively neutral and uniform. They do not have a distinct direction for their assembly, nor do they have any articulation on their surfaces. As robotic fabrication is exceptionally versatile, there was a great deal of freedom for the design of the brick specials in this project. However, since clay as a material system requires very consistent environments during the drying and firing process, and complex shapes are harder to control, the geometry was kept relatively simple to a C-shape. The design team eventually decided to develop a brick that had two different geometric sides which varied in depth and width and focused more on the performative aspects within the global assembly of the project.

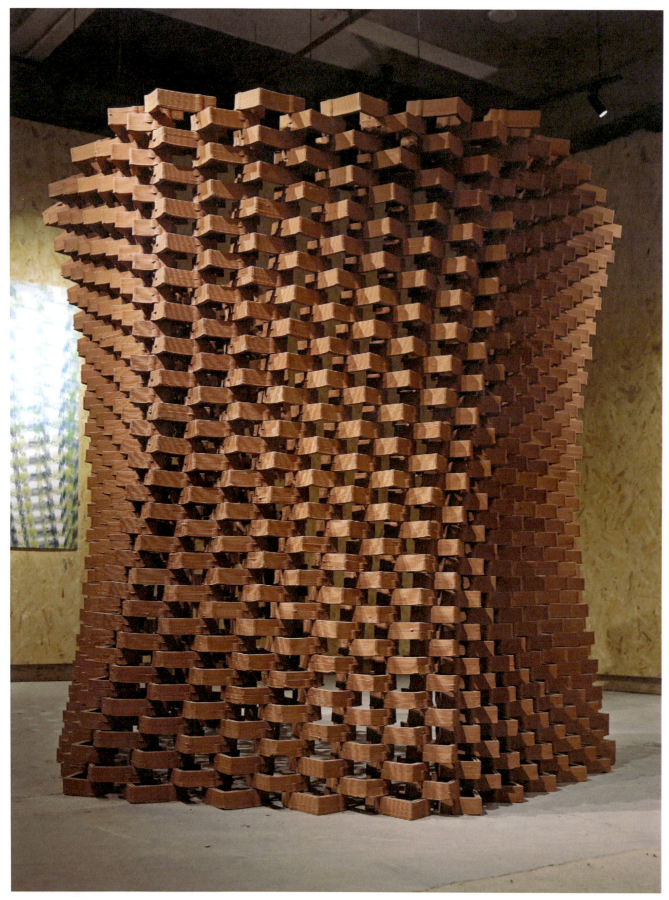

5   Pavilion in exhibition space, front view

CeramicInformation Pavilion Lange, Holohan

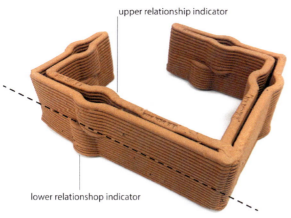

upper relationship indicator

lower relationshop indicator

6   Detail shot of brick special

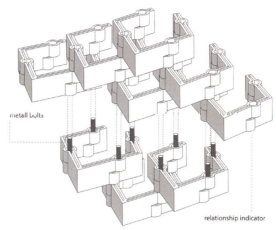

metall bolts

relationship indicator

7   Brick relationship concept

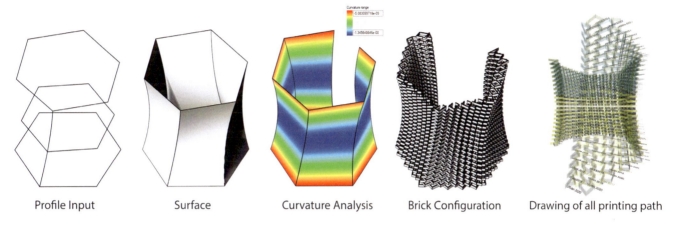

| Profile Input | Surface | Curvature Analysis | Brick Configuration | Drawing of all printing path |

8   Concept diagram

On the one hand, the geometric configuration helps to distinguish the inside from the outside, while on the other hand, it allowed for continuously differentiated transparencies in the global system to occur and for experimenting with light and shadows in a new way. The brick pattern within the global system was based on a traditional running bond that transformed from dense to sparse configurations along the perimeter of the pavilion, generating varying degrees of transparencies between the inside and the outside and resulting in unexpected shadow effects. As the global form of the pavilion required each brick to be unique, the critical aspect within the design of the brick was to develop a system that allowed not only for the indication of its precise position, but also for its relationship to neighboring bricks. Inspired by notching methods within timber construction that allow for the accurate assembly and tight fit of the components without any jigs, the team developed a system based on four integrated vertical holes in the outline of the c-shaped brick that work as relationship indicators for the running bond. These indicators were placed where the bricks overlapped in the running bond, and, in part, functioned to replace the traditional mason's plumb line and level and turned out to be quite accommodating during the assembly process by providing enough tolerance to assemble the system precisely.

While most digital workflows in contemporary practice seek to work with a high degree of precision, this project is an example in which material performance plays an important role to disturb that digital precision. Clay, as a building material in conjunction with the DIW printing method, has the unique behavior to develop unexpected outcomes during production. In the case of this pavilion, the drooping artifacts that occurred at the relationship indicators, and where no supporting material was present during printing added a unique aesthetic detail to the project. Though the project is based on a numerically controlled set-up, the outcome of this detail is strikingly organic. The precision in the making of bricks through algorithmic protocols influences and even triggers material imprecisions in the perception of the brick. If historically ornamentation is achieved through either the interplay of geometries or the mimicry of natural patterns, the ornamentation in this case is based on numbers, material, and gravity.

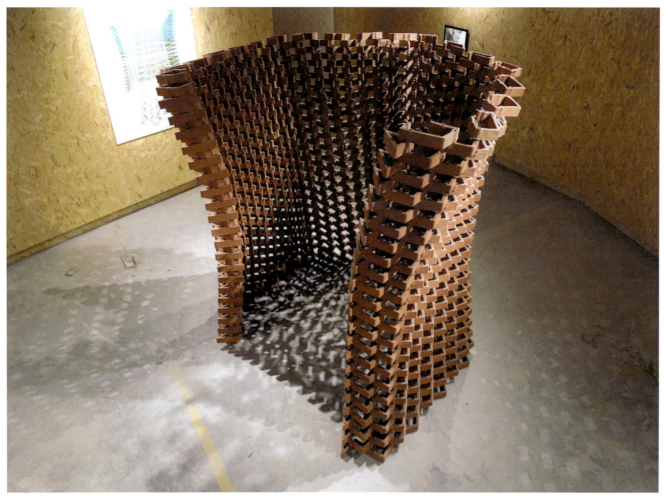

9 Pavilion in exhibition space, top view

ACKNOWLEDGMENTS

This project was part of the Shenzhen Bi-City Biennale of Urbanism\Architecture 2017/18.

Project Design: Christian J. Lange & Donn Holohan

Production and Assembly Team:
Mono Tung, Kristy Chow, Pamela Maguigad

REFERENCES

Bechthols M., Z. Seibold, K. Hinz, J.L. Garcia del Castillo y Lopez, N. Alonso, S. Mhatre. 2018. "Ceramic Morphologies." In *ACADIA 2018: Recalibration, On Imprecision and Infidelity, Proceedings of the 38th Annual Conference of the Association for Computer Aided Design in Architecture (ACADIA)*, 351-358.

Rael, Ronald and Virginia San Fratello. 2017. "Clay Bodies: Crafting the Future with 3D Printing." *Architectural Design* 87(6): 92-97.

Rael, Ronald and Virginia San Fratello. 2018. *Printing Architecture.* New York: Princeton Architectural Press.

10 Exterior articulation of bricks

11 Interior articulation of bricks

Christian J. Lange is a founding partner of Rocker-Lange Architects, a research and design practice based in Hong Kong and Boston. He is a registered German architect and Senior Lecturer in the Department of Architecture at the University of Hong Kong, where he teaches architectural design and classes in advanced digital modeling and robotics. A strong emphasis in his work is the implementation of computation and novel fabrication methods in the design and construction process. His work and research has been published internationally and is featured in over 30 exhibits, including the Venice Biennale and the Hong Kong & Shenzhen Bi-City Biennale.

Donn Holohan Donn Holohan is a designer and educator based in Hong Kong and Ireland. His work is primarily based on the potentials of emerging technology not only as it relates to the practice of architecture, but also to the question social and environmental sustainability. A founding partner of multidisciplinary design studio Superposition, he is also currently working as Assistant Lecturer at the University of Hong Kong, where his teaching focuses on empowering designers to effectively engage with emerging technologies through an increased understanding of both material and technical aspects of design.

FLOCK \\ proof of concept

Jeffrey L. Day, FAIA
University of Nebraska

1   FLOCK at The Little Gallery in Omaha, Nebraska (Photo © 2016 Colin Conces)

A Low-Resolution Wood Structure Designed with High-Precision Software

Advanced timber construction is a topic of great interest to architecture and the building industry due to its versatility and sustainable performance. Conventional light timber frame construction relies on redundant studs and "dumb" fasteners (nails). Current research focuses on mass-timber construction using glue-laminated beams and cross-laminated timber; however, these systems depend on sophisticated manufacturing facilities and a significant amount of adhesive or fasteners. FLOCK explores an alternative, post-tensioned system to support a free-standing timber structure using no adhesives, no fasteners, and simple fabrication techniques. Combining the advanced geometric controls afforded by parametric software with standard production of repeated, low-precision, ubiquitous components, the project achieves formal complexity via simple means.

The FLOCK pavilion transitions from a 10'-0" x 10'-0" square at the base to a 7'-0" diameter circle at the top with an entrance on one side. The structure comprises a bolted 4" wide-flange steel base, stacked short lengths of 2x6 lumber, and a steel ring at the top. Cables anchored to the steel base extend through slots in the lumber and are tensioned with swaged fittings above the top ring. Wood components consist of two types: a standard slotted 2x6 (limited set of lengths determined by the parametric model) and a shaped 2x6 (a "twig"). The pavilion is freestanding and does not require attachment or bracing to the surrounding walls or floor.

PRODUCTION NOTES

Architect: Min | Day (now Actual Architecture Company)

Client: The Little Gallery

Status: Completed

Site Area: 100 sq. ft.

Location: Temporarily installed at The Little Gallery in Omaha, Nebraska, in 2016, now permanently reinstalled at the Bemis Center for Contemporary Arts, Omaha.

Date: 2016

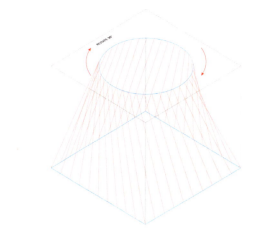

3   A 30-degree twist between the base and the top tension ring produces an apparent rotation due to the angle of the cables (in red)

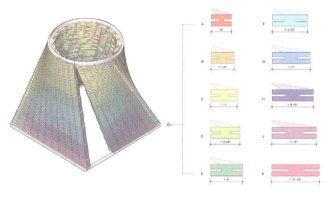

2   Stacked, slotted boards held loosely in place by cables tensioned between steel frames at top and bottom (Photo © 2016 Colin Conces)

4   A Grasshopper definition controls board sizes and locations

FLOCK challenges the expectation that advanced design computation and digital fabrication results in projects built with fine tolerance and high precision. Instead, FLOCK is a low-resolution construction designed with high-precision software. The inherent looseness of the system permits the use of average or even low-quality wood, allows room for error in the shaping and placing of wood parts, and yields an unexpected lack of control at the scale of the individual part while providing evident control of the overall form.

FLOCK responds to two factors: 1. the computational process used to derive the form, and 2. material and cost constraints accepted as given. Thus, FLOCK embodies programmed imprecision between controlled parameters and zones of unruliness (the slippage of wood blocks, for example). The dynamic and loose appearance of the built form reflects a conflict between the low-resolution and imprecision of material constraints (2x6 lumber) and the high-precision capacity of the parametric model. The project expands the discourse on digital fabrication into an area left unexplored by designers such as Gramazio &

Kohler. At first look, Gramazio & Kohler's work is similar in its formal manifestation and part-to-whole relationships, but the means to achieve these complex stacked surfaces require highly sophisticated equipment. Though exploring construction innovation broadly, many of their stacking projects combine robotic assembly with static attachment systems such as adhesives and nails. FLOCK is by contrast a narrowly-applicable prototype but one that may have relevance in particular circumstances.

The Hookah Den in Office dA's Mantra Restaurant is similar in appearance, but different by method. Using techniques from apparel design, the architects derived a complex vessel-like form with sartorial references that, similar to FLOCK, uses stacked plywood "bricks". Unlike Gramazio & Kohler's work, the Hookah Den is manually assembled. The architects used 2-dimensional patterns as jigs, but the pieces are fastened with screws. In contrast, FLOCK's contribution is in the self-jigging of the cable array and the looseness of the assembly, both affording flexibility for expansion and contraction. The use of steel rods to tension

5   Outside corner detail showing the transition from a square to a circular profile (Photo © 2016 Colin Conces)

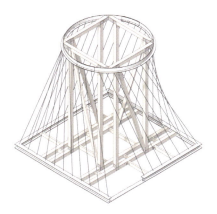

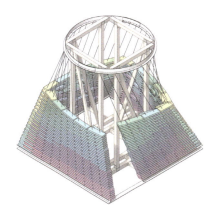

6   A bolted scaffold holds the steel base and top tension ring in place while cables are tensioned and 2 x 6 wood members installed

7   Slotted 2x wood members installed over cables following a detailed location map, cables further tensioned, and scaffold removed when complete

8   Wide flange steel base, scaffold, and first row of 2 x 6 wood members

9   Base detail at corner (Photo © 2016 Colin Conces)

a loosely-stacked wood structure was pioneered by Peter Zumthor in his Swiss Sound Box, but here, the limited set of parts arrayed in strict repetition never deviates from the norm. Though limited to ruled surfaces, FLOCK has potential for a wider range of complexity via the shape of its steel rings.

Where precise control yields loose and imperfect formal results, an inversion of expectations occurs. The orthodoxy of digital fabrication tells us to expect narrow tolerances, refinement, and high precision allowing for increases in formal complexity. Instead, FLOCK produces a relatively forgiving and imprecise construction that still performs as required.

ACKNOWLEDGMENTS

The following people contributed to this project: Kristen Smith, Grasshopper definitions, design lead; Jacob Doyle, construction modeling and management; Dennis Krymuza, construction supervision; Polynomial, steel fabrication; Benjamin Corotis, structural engineering; E.B. Min, co-principal-in-charge with Jeffrey L. Day for the original design for Santa Clara University. Modifications and permanent installation at the Bemis Center for Contemporary Arts in 2018 by Actual Architecture Co. + FACT. Thank you to Teresa Gleason of The Little Gallery.

REFERENCES

Gramazio Kohler Architects. n.d. "Gramazio Kohler Architects." Landing Page. Accessed May 1, 2019. http://www.gramaziokohler. com.

Piskorec, Luka, David Jenny, Stefana Parascho, Hannes Mayer, Fabio Gramazio, and Matthias Kohler. 2019. "The Brick Labyrinth." In *Robotic Fabrication in Architecture, Art and Design 2018*, edited by Jan Willmann, 489-500. Switzerland: Springer.

NADAAA. n.d. "Mantra Restaurant, Renovation of Former Old Colony Trust Bank, Boston, Massachusetts." NADAAA.com. Accessed May 1, 2019. http://www.nadaaa.com/portfolio/mantra-restaurant/.

Zumthor, Peter. 2000. *Swiss Sound Box: A Handbook for the Pavilion of the Swiss Confederation at Expo 2000 in Hanover.* Basel: Birkhäuser.

10 Interior face showing standard wood members and special members with projections called "twigs" (Photo © 2016 Colin Conces)

IMAGE CREDITS

Figures 1, 2, 5, 9, 10-12: Photographer © Colin Conces, 2016.
All other drawings and images by the architects.

Jeffrey L. Day, FAIA is the Douglass Professor of Architecture
and Landscape Architecture at the University of Nebraska-Lincoln
and founding principal of Actual Architecture Company. At UNL
Jeff runs FACT, an interdisciplinary design\build studio that
engages non-profit clients and communities in collaborations that
span design, research, and construction. In 2018, after 15 years
practicing as a founding principal of Min | Day (San Francisco &
Omaha), Jeff reorganized the Omaha office as Actual Architecture
Co., an internationally recognized architecture and design firm
based in Omaha, Nebraska and operating around the world with
expansive vision. www.actual.ac

11 Interior view, looking up (Photo © 2016 Colin Conces)

12 FLOCK with furniture by the architects (Photo © 2016 Colin Conces)

Zippered Wood:
Small Material Moves
can Bend Large Systems

Blair Satterfield
University of British Columbia

Alexander Preiss
University of British Columbia

Derek Mavis
University of British Columbia

Graham Entwistle
University of British Columbia

1   Stick Formed Wall: a prototype assembly for the integration of Zippered Wood into traditional light wood framing

Light frame construction with wood is flexible, adaptable, cheap, renewable, and requires very little skill to assemble. It is a dominant system for good reason and has changed little in over a century. Global real estate speculation is driving demolition and new construction, causing large quantities of quality used lumber to be wasted. In response to this our research strives to create contemporary computational form from waste stream timber. The method we have developed entitled Zippered Wood is a novel take on wood joinery and deformation in which digitally-generated, formally-specific joint patterns are cut into boards that are joined to produce predictably precise bends. This method creates complex bending and twisting without formwork. Simulation software and geometric analysis mediate between digital models and fabrication. This technology is targeted at disrupting light wood framing through the unconventional redeployment of its most basic component, the 2x4.

In the wake of global capital, existing light wood frame buildings are being demolished and replaced with new structures. This cycle of demolition and construction produces an incredible amount of wood waste. Often, reclaimed wood from existing buildings is of superior quality compared to contemporary lumber. Zippered Wood presents an opportunity to capitalize on the bending capacity of reclaimed wood. Upcycling allows a single piece of wood to exist within two radically different structural identities. Using this method with reclaimed materials increases its lifespan, while vastly increasing the formal capacity of the material.

2　Manually-kerfed 2x4 with varying angles

3　Zippered Wood 2x4 demonstrating twisting and bending

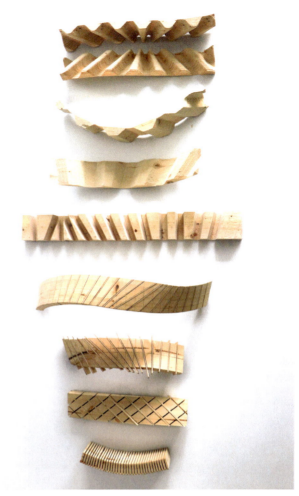

4　Zippered Wood evolution from manual kerfing to CNC-milled pairs

This research maintains codependency between material properties and digital simulation. Bending and twisting in wood are governed by the material behavior of wood grain. By deploying digital physics simulation, this research allows a designer to manipulate this phenomenon in the abstract. A series of geometric analysis algorithms have been developed that translate simulated twists or bends into unique joint patterns. Robotic milling transcribes these coded joints into reclaimed stock, removing the need for formwork or skilled assembly. After milling, corresponding pairs are assembled by the simple application of adhesive and pressure. Form is a result of the cumulative displacement occurring between all faces of the internal joint pattern. Zippered Wood uses a material informed digital processes to convert standard 2x4s into formally sophisticated building components. Refinements are underway for the algorithmic analysis, fabrication, and adhesive assembly methods that promise to reduce production time and aid in the scalability of the system.

The future development of this work will focus on refining production and developing strategies that introduce twisted members in light wood framing. The team is testing methods to drastically reduce production time using saw blades and laser relief. Another issue is the presence of knots. When a veneer contains a knot it is prone to cracking, this is minimized by locating the milling area such that knots are within teeth. Currently methods are in development that analyze the face grain of the 2x4 and place a cut pattern in the optimal location relative to these knots. Further, the process might be improved by automating glue up with a mechanism that applies glue, pressure, and radio frequency curing to extrude a complete zippered member.

As the construction industry changes perhaps the role of the architect will be redefined as the master fabricator when form and fabrication converge. In this new role architects would benefit from an understanding of material systems. The Zippered Wood process is offered as an example. This project uses subtractive forming and material deformation to convert standard 2x4s into formally

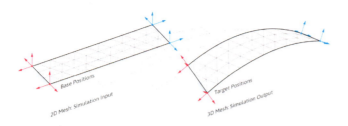

5 Simulation of a developable surface in Kangaroo

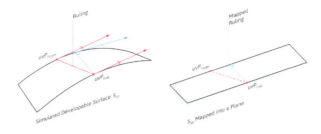

6 Reverse engineering of surface rulings

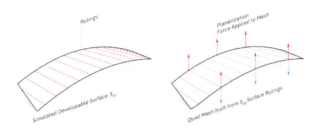

7 Quad mesh built from surface rulings and planarization of mesh

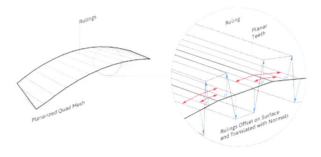

8 Construction of planar teeth from surface rulings and planar mesh

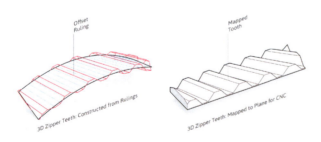

9 Mapping of Zippered Wood joint teeth to 2D plane for CNC milling

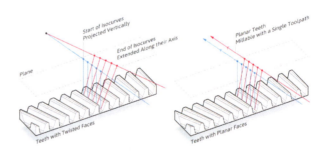

10 Planar teeth capitalize on single toolpath milling to increase efficiency

Zippered Wood Satterfield, Preiss, Mavis, Entwistle

11 Demonstration of Zippered Wood assembly: milled pairs are soaked in water and clamped while drying to retain their shape

12 Laser micro kerfing increases flexibility in a macro-kerfed system

13 Tight radii are made possible through laser micro kerfing

sophisticated building components. Our approach generates form using material behavior and geometry, advancing techniques from analog production to digital, and from precision fitting to precision displacement.

ACKNOWLEDGMENTS

This research is made possible by support from UBC SEEDS (Social Ecological Economic Development Studies) Sustainability Program, and The Foundation for the Carolinas.

IMAGE CREDITS

All drawings and images by the authors.

Blair Satterfield is a co-founding principal with Marc Swackhamer of the research design collaborative HouMinn Practice. HouMinn's work has been featured in many publications, including Dwell and Fast Company, and has garnered prestigious awards such as the ACSA National Design Award, 2014 & 2008 R&D Award from Architect magazine, 2014 Core77 Design Award for Environments, and the Best in Environments award from ID Magazine. Satterfield is an Associate Professor and chair of the architecture program at the University of British Columbia, where he teaches design studios and coordinates design media courses. He is also the director of HiLo Lab, a UBC SALA based collaborative research initiative that reckons with three interrelated ideas: the use of second stream materials in construction, providing designers and the broader community with greater access to digital design and fabrication processes, and the design and application of energy and material efficient methods for construction.

14 Speculative pavilion demonstrating Zippered Wood

Alexander Preiss is a recent graduate from the Master of
Architecture program at The University of British Columbia and
holds a Bachelor of Architectural Studies from Carleton University.
He is a research assistant at UBC SALA HiLo Lab, where he
develops innovative processes that translate between material
behavior, digital simulations, and robotic fabrication. His personal
research pursues alternative structures in design methodologies
that deploy computation to enrich design intent.

Derek Mavis is in his third year of the M.Arch program at the
University of British Columbia (UBC), Canada, and has been a
research assistant at UBC's HiLo Lab since May 2018. He earned
his BA in Greek and Roman studies from Carleton University in
Ottawa, Canada. He enjoys working in both the Digital and Analog
environments of the lab's research. Derek has a background in
carpentry, robotic design, and fabrication and is interested in the
development of different fabrication methods and tools, and how
they can be exploited by designers. He also enjoys a fine whiskey.

Graham Entwistle is a workshop and digifab technician at the
University of British Columbia's School of Architecture and
Landscape Architecture. He has a background as a furniture
designer/maker and has a BFA in Industrial Design from the Rhode
Island School of Design. He is interested in the interplay between
the experience of making and understanding.

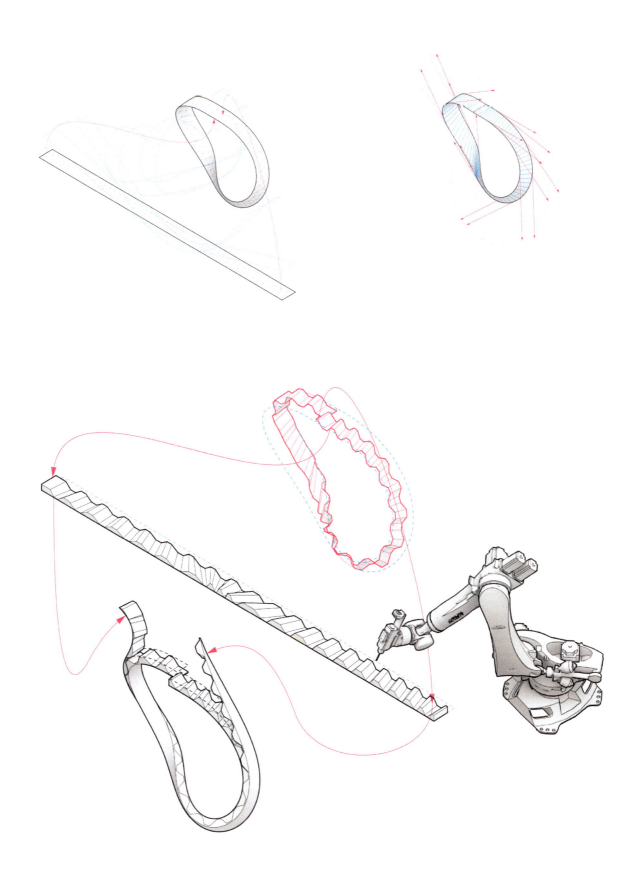

15 Zippered Wood workflow: simulation, fabrication, and assembly

Plaisiophy

Christoph Klemmt
University of Cincinnati/
Orproject

Rajat Sodhi
Orproject

1   Plaisiophy nighttime view (Shovan Gandhi © Orproject)

PAVILION FOR AN INDIAN WEDDING

The project Plaisiophy is a wedding pavilion on the private grounds of a client in India. While the local climate does not require a shielding from the elements during the wedding season, the main aim of the pavilion is to define different spaces for the guests to arrive and for the bride and groom to meet them, as well as to provide an atmospheric setting for the event.

The structure was therefore conceived as a timber gridshell (Liddell 2015, Chilton and Tang 2016) that touches the ground in different locations to form walls in order to separate those spaces. A large canopy forms the main entrance welcoming the visitors, while the bride and groom greet their guests in front of a screen in the center of the pavilion. The surface of the triangulated gridshell then forms a flowing veil to create this geometry.

GRIDSHELL GEOMETRY

Albeit mirrored, as a result of the floating, non-repetitive geometry, all the timber members have different lengths and every node is unique. The timber members with a cross section of 95mm x 37.5mm were oriented to be normal to the underlying mesh geometry. As a result, not only do the angles vary at which the members arrive at every node—the yaw axis in aviation terms—but also the pitch and the roll axes (Clancy 1978). Some of the yaw angles between adjacent beams are very small, while some of the roll angles are large, resulting in clashes of the beam geometries even in locations relatively far from the center of a node. Combined with a limited budget and limited digital fabrication technologies

PRODUCTION NOTES

Architect: Orproject
Client: Private
Status: Completed
Area: 97.5 m²
Location: New Delhi, India
Date: 2018

2   Plaisiophy detail (Shovan Gandhi © Orproject)

in India, led to the design of a node system beyond existing methods (Rabagliati et al. 2014) that handled the geometric constraints while still being able to be feasibly manufactured.

NODE DESIGN

Taking those constraints into account, the nodes were designed to be made from mild steel, to be assembled and subsequently welded from separate components that were all CNC-cut from flat steel plates. The center of each node forms a steel tube of 75mm length, oriented along the normal of the underlying mesh geometry at the center of the node. This tube is capped by two steel circles of a larger diameter than the tube, that have CNC-cut slots at their edges that define the yaw axis positions of the adjacent beams. Vertical steel plates are inserted into those slots. While those plates now align in the yaw axis with the beams, they need to be individually angled in order to also align with the beam's pitch angle. In order to meet the beams at the required roll angle, the plates slide into accordingly angled slots in a vertical end plate of the beam, with the

angle of the slot taking up the difference between the roll angle at the node and the roll angle of the beam. The end plate of the beam has a further central plate welded to it in a T-arrangement that slots into the timber beam itself and is attached by bolts. Lastly, in order to avoid clashes of the beam geometries of narrowly angled adjacent beams, the plates that are protruding from the node are extended until the beam geometries clear each other.

CONSTRUCTION

Plaisiophy was constructed from 309 nodes and 1146 timber beams. The methodology of digital fabrication for the node's steel components—that were then manually welded and manually connected to the timber beams— proved a successful combination for utilizing India's existing construction sector. Although using unskilled labor especially in computational technologies, the methodology managed to avoid any geometric errors and led to a high precision outcome down to every detail.

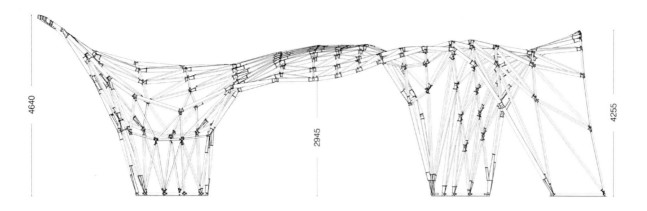

4640

2945

4255

3　Plaisiophy side elevation (© Orproject)

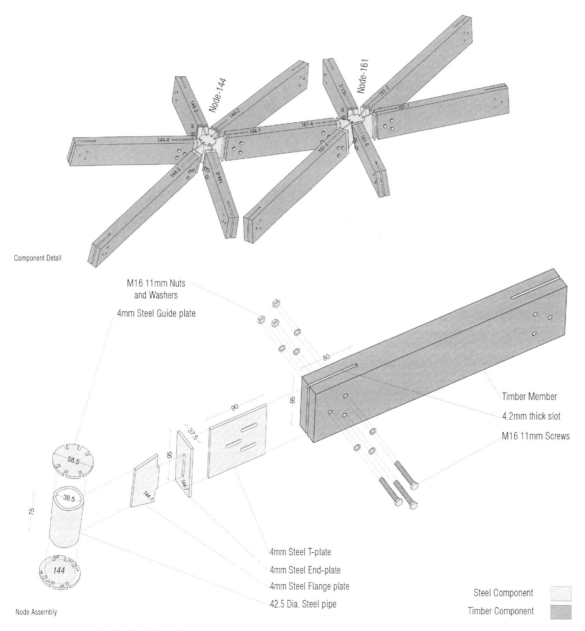

Node-144

Node-161

144-3

144-2

144-1

144-4

144-5

144-6

161-3

161-4

161-5

161-6

161-2

161-1

Component Detail

M16 11mm Nuts
and Washers

4mm Steel Guide plate

80

90

95

37.5

95

144-1

58.5

38.5

75

144

Timber Member

4.2mm thick slot

M16 11mm Screws

4mm Steel T-plate

4mm Steel End-plate

4mm Steel Flange plate

42.5 Dia. Steel pipe

Steel Component

Timber Component

Node Assembly

4　Plaisiophy connection details (© Orproject)

5　Wedding reception (© Orproject)

6　Plaisiophy front view (Shovan Gandhi © Orproject)

7　Plaisiophy actively used (© Orproject)

REFERENCES

Chilton, John and Gabriel Tang. 2016. *Timber Gridshells: Architecture, Structure and Craft*. London: Routledge.

Clancy, Laurence J. 1978. *Aerodynamics*. London: Pitman Publishing.

Liddell, I. 2015. "Frei Otto and the development of gridshells." *Case Studies in Structural Engineering*, 4: 39-49.

Rabagliati, Jonatha, Clemens Huber, Dieter Linke. 2014. "Balancing Complexity and Simplicity." In *Fabricate 2014: Negotiating Design & Making*, edited by Fabio Gramazio, Matthias Kohler, and Silke Langenberg, 45-51. London: UCL Press.

IMAGE CREDITS

Figures 1, 2, 6, 8, 9: Shovan Gandhi © Orproject
All other drawings and images by the authors.

Christoph Klemmt received his diploma from the Architectural Association in London in 2004. He is partner at Orproject and Assistant Professor at the University of Cincinnati, where he founded the Architectural Robotics Lab.

Rajat Sodhi received his diploma from the Architectural Association in London in 2007 and the DRL masters in 2009. He has lectured and given workshops at the AA, University of Westminster and the Indian Institute of Technology in New Delhi.

8   Plaisiophy side view (Shovan Gandhi © Orproject)

9 Plaisiophy nighttime detail (Shovan Gandhi © Orproject)

Styx

Igor Pantic
Architectural Association/
UCL Bartlett

Christoph Klemmt
University of Cincinnati/
Orproject/University of
Applied Arts Vienna/
Architectural Association

Andrei Gheorghe
University of Applied Arts
Vienna

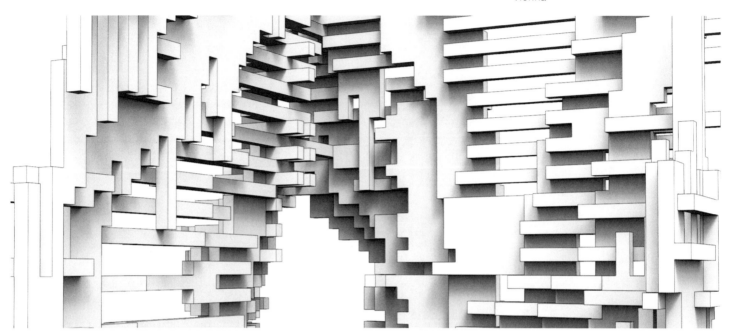

1   Discrete cellular growth, details

DISCRETE VS DISCRETIZED

Processes of growth have been computationally simulated in discrete environments, such as Cellular Automata or Diffusion Limited Aggregation (Witten and Sander 1981, Wolfram 1983, Gardner 1970), or free-form in 3d space, such as Differential Growth or Cellular Growth simulations (Lomas 2014, Bader et al. 2016). While the first often creates geometries that are difficult to control and therefore difficult to use for architectural design, the second often produces highly complex forms that are difficult to construct at a larger scale. We, therefore, propose the utilization of free-form Cellular Growth simulations that are afterwards discretized in a second step for constructability. This was tested with a large scale prototype that was constructed during the AA Visiting School at the Angewandte Vienna.

COMPUTATIONAL METHODS

The computational simulations are based on individual cells that occupy space. They proliferate through cell division that is commonly triggered at marginal cells. The cells reposition and arrange themselves according to intercellular behaviors that are acting between adjacent cells and according to globally acting forces. The proliferation and rearrangement of a small amount of cells then leads to the generation of a larger cell accumulation that exhibits specific geometric traits according to behavioral rules.

PRODUCTION NOTES

Architects: Igor Pantic
              Christoph Klemmt
              Andrei Gheorghe

Client: AA Visiting School at the
             Angewandte Vienna

Status: Completed

Site Area: 10 m²

Location: Vienna, Austria

Date: 2018

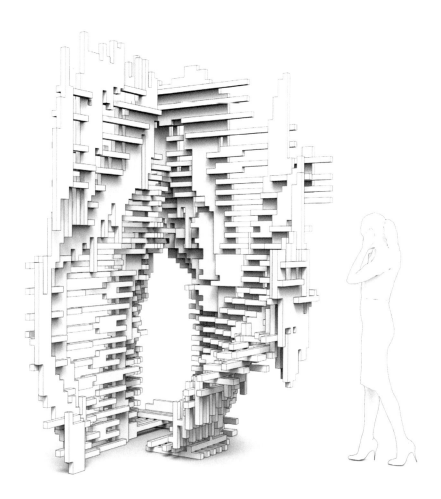

2   Styx, rendered view of prototype design

DISCRETIZATION

The geometries resulting from the growth simulations are difficult to construct due to their complexity. We, therefore, integrated a discretization into the algorithm (Retsin 2016, Sanchez 2016). While the underlying calculations still happen free-form in space, the cells are then positioned within a regular square grid with an edge length close to the average distance between neighboring cells. Within this grid, repetitive components are placed through the populated voxels, with each component occupying a row of adjacent voxels. Different possible lengths of the components can be predefined.

The components can be arranged locally along the X, the Y or the Z direction. The alignment can be defined globally or according to the local cell arrangement. Additional rules were integrated to control varying densities of the components, with dense and sparse areas defined by additional attractors in space. This was used to create different patterns and textures within the component agglomeration.

PROTOTYPE CONSTRUCTION

A physical prototype was constructed from 40mm x 40mm timber sticks, corresponding to the edge length of the grid of 40mm. 720 individual components were used in lengths of 320mm, 480mm, 640mm, 800mm, 960mm, 1280mm, 600mm, 2080mm and 2240mm. The components were cut and assembled by hand with wood screws, with the alignment controlled by wooden spacers. Microsoft HoloLens and Fologram (Jahn et al. 2018), an Augmented Reality plug-in for Rhino and Grasshopper, were used during the construction process to display the complete structure and to define the length and the location of the component that was to be attached next. This led to an economic and efficient construction that was completed by the group within two days.

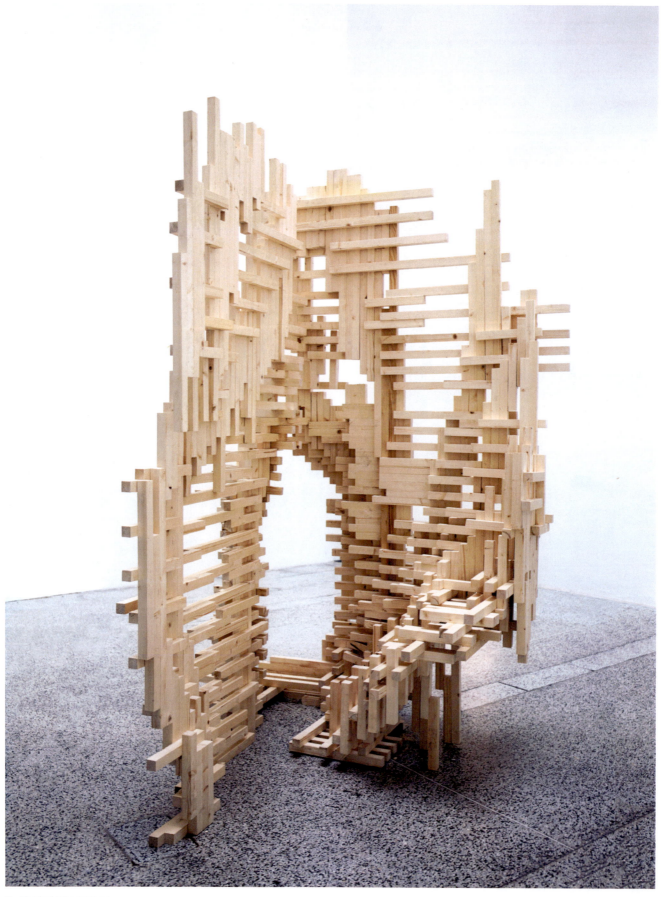

3   Physical 1:1 prototype

4   Discrete cellular growth simulation: (top) Cells, Cell Neighborhood, Occupied Volumes; (bottom) Voxelized Normals, Occupied Voxels, Component Placement

ACKNOWLEDGMENTS

The project was constructed as part of the AA Visiting School at the Angewandte Vienna 2018. Teaching Assistants: Alexandra Moisi, Nasim Nabavi, Saba Nabavi, Adam Sebestyen.

REFERENCES

Bader, C., W.G. Patrick, D. Kolb, S.G. Hays, S. Keating, S. Sharma, D. Dikovsky, B. Belocon, J.C. Weaver, P.A. Silver, and N. Oxman, 2016. "Grown, printed, and biologically augmented: An additively manufactured microfluidic wearable, functionally templated for synthetic microbes." *3D Printing and Additive Manufacturing*, 3(2): 79-89.

Gardner, M. 1970. "Mathematical Games: The fantastic combinations of John Conway's new solitaire game 'life'". *Scientific American* 223: 120–123.

Jahn, G., C. Newnham, M. Beanland. 2018. "Making in Mixed Reality: Holographic design, fabrication, assembly and analysis of woven steel structures." In *Proceedings of the 38th Annual Conference of the Association for Computer Aided Design in Architecture (ACADIA)*, 88-97.

Lomas, A. 2014. "Cellular forms: an artistic exploration of morphogenesis." In *ACM SIGGRAPH 2014 Studio*. ACM: New York.

Retsin, G. 2016. "Discrete and Digital. A Discrete paradigm for Design and Production," edited by Kory Bieg. In *2016 TxA Emerging Design + Technology Conference Proceedings*.

Sanchez, J. 2016. "Combinatorial design: Non-parametric computational design strategies." In *Posthuman Frontiers: Data, Designers, and Cognitive Machines, Proceedings of the 36th Annual Conference of the Association for Computer Aided Design in Architecture (ACADIA)*, 1-13.

Witten Jr., T.A., L.M. Sander. 1981. "Diffusion-Limited Aggregation, a Kinetic Critical Phenomenon." *Phys. Rev. Lett*, 47: 1400.

Wolfram, S. 1983. Statistical Mechanics of Cellular Automata. *Reviews of Modern Physics* 55(3): 601-644.

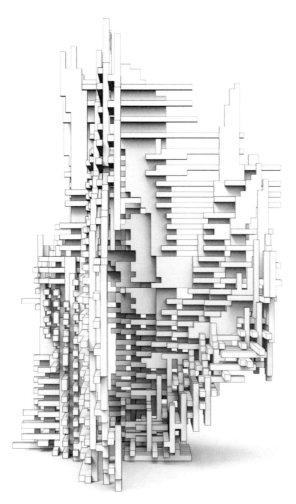

5   Prototype design, front view

6   Prototype design, back view

IMAGE CREDITS
All drawings and images by the authors.

Igor Pantic received a Master's Degree from the AA DRL. He is a Teaching Fellow at the UCL Bartlett School of Architecture and was co-director of the AA Visiting School Vienna.

Christoph Klemmt received his diploma from the Architectural Association in London in 2004. He co-directed the AA Visiting School Vienna, and he is partner at Orproject and Assistant Professor at the University of Cincinnati, where he founded the Architectural Robotics lab.

Andrei Gheorghe graduated with distinction from the Harvard GSD and received his doctorate from the University of Applied Arts Vienna. He is teaching as an Assistant Professor at the University of Applied Arts Vienna and directing the Angewandte Architecture Challenge.

7   Physical 1:1 prototype

Bryx

Christoph Klemmt
University of Cincinnati/
Orproject

Igor Pantic
UCL Bartlett

1   Bryx, details

DISCRETE CELLULAR GROWTH

Computational architectural design and research has had a longstanding interest in time-based simulations (Andrasek 2012, Snooka 2013, Stuart-Smith 2014). However, often the complexity of the resulting geometries has caused difficulties for a feasible construction, and only a few projects have been realized. We, therefore, propose the integration of a discretization into the simulations, which allows a construction from identical repetitive components.

Bryx, the presented project, is based on a Cellular Growth simulation that mimics the development of form based on cell proliferation as it occurs in natural organisms. The resulting geometries are voxelized and then constructed from prefabricated components that align with the voxel grid. Various forces acting on the cell accumulations during the growth, as well as the resulting geometries, have been explored and influenced the design of the physical 1:1 prototype. While the overall geometries of the free-form and the voxelized outcomes align, the discretization results in distinct patterns at the smaller scale of the voxel.

COMPUTATIONAL METHODS

Cellular Growth algorithms simulate the iterative development of form based on accumulations of individual cells that are usually programmed as point clouds (Lomas 2014, Bader et al. 2016). Starting with a small amount of cells, their repetitive division leads

PRODUCTION NOTES

Architect:	Christoph Klemmt & Igor Pantic
Client:	CAADRIA 2018
Status:	Completed
Site Area:	10 m²
Location:	Tsinghua University, Beijing
Date:	2018

2   Discrete Growth (top): Cell Accumulation, Range of Influence, Cell neighborhood, (middle) Cell Connections, Division Triggers, Voxel Grid, (bottom) Occupied Voxels, Component Placement, Components

to an expansion of the overall structure. Different inter-cellular behaviors as well as global forces are acting on the cells and cause them to reposition according to their local cell neighborhood. The settings of those forces can be used to control the geometric behaviors as well as the overall arrangement of the cell accumulations.

The resulting geometries exhibit a high degree of free-form complexity that is costly to construct at an architectural scale. To address this aspect, we integrate a voxelization into the growth logic as the system for a geometry rational-ization. In line with the discrete paradigm, the voxelization then allows for the placement of repetitive multi-voxel components that lead to a feasible and cost-effective construction (Retsin 2016, Retsin and Jimenez Garcia 2016, Retsin et al. 2017, Sanchez 2016).

DISCRETIZATION
The space subdivision utilizes an underlying grid of alter-nating pyramids and tetrahedra that are all based on a single edge length. Every cell always occupies one voxel within the grid. One physical component occupies eight adjacent voxels in a line and, therefore, has the geometry of an extruded equilateral triangle. A component is then placed through every occupied voxel, with additional rules of orientation and clash detection. The growth process, voxelization, and component placement are executed itera-tively and influence each other during the development of the form.

PROTOTYPE CONSTRUCTION
The prototype was constructed from 450 identical aluminum components that each occupied the eight neigh-boring voxels. The components were prefabricated and extruded using a custom die design that allowed for an attachment of end caps at those faces that connected to an adjacent component. The components were then connected by means of an epoxy resin that allowed for tolerances to be taken up. The assembly of the complete structure by twelve students was possible in less than twelve hours.

3   Bryx, side view

Bryx Klemmt, Pantic

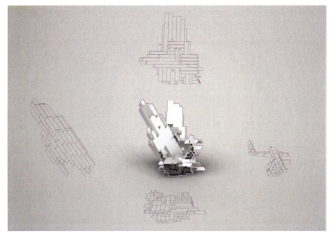

4   Construction segments

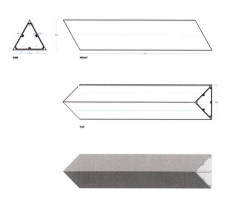

6   Component design

5   Bryx, top view

7   Custom die for aluminium extrusion

The use of prefabrication and identical components for the construction proved very cost and time efficient. A labelling of the components was not required, and the placement within the grid led to a simple positioning of each new component. While curvature and free-form geometry are lost at the scale of the voxel, the discretization results in its own distinct geometric patterns.

ACKNOWLEDGMENTS

Constructed as part of a workshop for the CAADRIA 2018 conference at Tsinghua University, Beijing. Special Thanks to Prof. Xu Weiguo and Yu Lei for the invitation and organization. Teaching Assistant: Ning Tang.

REFERENCES

Andrasek, Alisa. 2012. "Open Synthesis//Toward a Resilient Fabric of Architecture." *LOG* 25: 45-54.

Bader, C., W.G. Patrick, D. Kolb, S.G. Hays, S. Keating, S. Sharma, D. Dikovsky, B. Belocon, B., J.C. Weaver, P.A. Silver, Neri Oxman. 2016. "Grown, printed, and biologically augmented: An additively manufactured microfluidic wearable, functionally templated for synthetic microbes." *3D Printing and Additive Manufacturing* 3(2): 79-89.

Lomas, A. 2014. "Cellular Forms: An Artistic Exploration of Morphogenesis." In *ACM SIGGRAPH 2014 Studio; Proceedings of the 41st International Conference and Exhibition on Computer Graphics and Interactive Techniques.* New York: ACM.

Retsin, Gilles. 2016. "Discrete Assembly and Digital Materials in Architecture." In *Complexity & Simplicity; Proceedings of the 34th eCAADe Conference, University of Oulu, Finland, 22-26 August 2016,* edited by Aulikki Herneoja, Toni Österlund and Piia Markkanen, 143-151.

Retsin, Gilles and M. Jimenez Garcia. 2016. "Discrete Computational Methods for Robotic Additive Manufacturing." In *ACADIA 2016: Proceedings of the 36th Annual Conference of the Association for Computer Aided Design in Architecture,* edited by Kathy Velikov, Sean Ahlquist, and Matias del Campo, 332-341. Ann Arbor: University of Michigan.

8　Bryx, front view

Retsin, Gilles, M. Jimenez Garcia, and V. Soler. 2017. "Discrete Computation for Additive Manufacturing". In *Proceedings of Fabricate 2017*, edited by Achim Menges, Bob Sheil, Ruairi Glynn, Marilena Skavara, 178-183. London: UCL Press.

Sanchez, Jose. 2016 "Combinatorial design: Non-parametric computational design strategies." In *ACADIA 2016: Posthuman Frontiers: Data, Designers, and Cognitive Machines, Projects Catalog of the 36th Annual Conference of the Association for Computer Aided Design in Architecture*, edited by Kathy Velikov, Sandra Manninger, and Matias del Campo, 1-13. Ann Arbor: University of Michigan.

Snooks, Roland. 2013. "Self-organised bodies." In *Architecture in Formation: On The Nature of Information in Digital Architecture*, edited by P. Lorenzo-Eiroa and A. Sprecher, 264-267. London: Routledge.

Stuart-Smith, Robert. 2014. "Qualitative Affects of Building Life Cycle: The Formation of Architectural Matter." In *Cities for Smart Environmental and Energy Futures*, 101-113. Berlin/Heidelberg: Springer.

IMAGE CREDITS

Photographer: Xiao Yang.
All drawings and images © by the authors.

9 Bryx, details

10 Bryx, details

Christoph Klemmt received his diploma from the Architectural Association in London in 2004. He is partner at Orproject and Assistant Professor at the University of Cincinnati, where he founded the Architectural Robotics lab.

Igor Pantic received a Master's Degree from the AA DRL. He is a Teaching Fellow at the UCL Bartlett School of Architecture and was co-director of the AA Visiting School Vienna.

Lost House

Joel Lamere
University of Miami/GLD

Cynthia Gunadi
University of Miami/GLD

1   View of unique, parametrically-defined nodes creating branching structures (© 2018 Christopher Schuch)

PRODUCTION NOTES

Architect: GLD
Status: Built
Site Area: 400 sq. ft.
Location: Dorchester, MA
Date: 2018

Lost House is a project that wants it both ways: it embraces the vast range and exuberant output afforded through digital tools, while acknowledging the constraints and material conditions of the moment. It resists the common drive to announce itself as purely digital, or autonomous, aiming instead for a more ambiguous reading of a malleable object tempered by the ubiquitous conventions of building practice in the world as it is. As such, Lost House proposes a hybrid strategy that leverages both off-the-shelf components and digital fabrication to innovate on ubiquitous light wood framing systems. The project joins dimensional lumber with customized nodes, creating branching connections, and in doing so inverts the convention of concealing such framing—instead, the project celebrates the joint and sub-assembly in a manner more often seen in heavy timber construction. The end result demonstrates a new method of light framing that can produce highly efficient network structures, as it expands the formal and geometric possibilities of these materials.

Built on a now vacant, city-owned lot in an economically depressed residential neighborhood, Lost House plays with forgotten domestic histories of the site, while proposing a new, communal space. A website accompanying the object details this history: a house built in 1894 is continuously occupied until the 1970s, when it is foreclosed upon and demolished. The project, in telling this tale and inviting the neighborhood to use the benches at its heart, asks visitors to imagine an afterlife for such spaces. As the city waits on developers to see exploitable value in the property—now forty years and counting—Lost House endorses unapologetic communal appropriation.

2   Frontal view showing white-painted, iconic house form (GLD)

3   Rear view, dimensional lumber and nodes (© 2018 Elyse Pono)

4   Interior clearing with communal bench (© 2018 Christopher Schuch)

The physical artifact reflects this complex history in its ambiguity. Its global form evokes an iconic house when viewed frontally, but loses this familiarity as one walks through and around it, illustrating the hybrid system's formal malleability. The paint scheme also serves to support this transformative nature: painted white only on the surfaces facing Washington Street, the joint detail is effectively hidden from the front view, then revealed when viewed from other angles.

The branching structural system is produced through a transformation of a conventional Kagome truss. The system is highly malleable, with unique connective nodes that are parametrically-defined and optimized for digital fabrication. Given an input boundary volume, and specified column locations, a computational process negotiates the two: vertical columns bifurcate within a plane, then trifurcate to pack into structurally well-behaved truss cells at the top. As the system progresses vertically, the linear members halve in cross-sectional area; 2x8 columns become 2x4s, 2x2s, then chamfer stock, reflecting the decreasing axial

load traveling through the dimensional lumber members. Though able to adapt to an infinite range of global geometries, the system always meets the ground in vertical columns, which interfere minimally with the occupation and use of space below the structured canopy.

The nodes are designed to produce surface continuities between adjacent dimensional lumber members, re-emphasizing the project's hybrid nature; the ruled surfaces are unabashedly digital and figured, but in service of resolving the ubiquitous rectangular cross-section of conventional building components. Each is flip-milled from laminated marine plywood on a CNC router, allowing for a materially uniform connection detail that eschews mechanical fasteners in favor of glued-in plywood splice plates. Self-stable "trees" were sub-assembled off-site, while on-site connection of the trees produced overall structural stability.

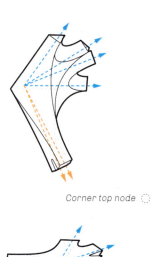

Corner top node ⬚

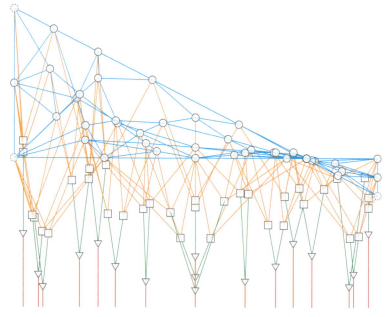

Network and node key

Triple top node ◎

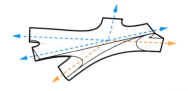

Top node ◯

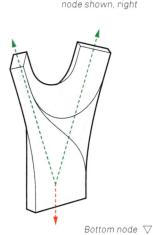

Middle node ☐

34 variations on middle node shown, right

Bottom node ▽

5 Drawings of node types

Lost House Lamere, Gunadi

7   Detail view of middle node (© 2018 Christopher Schuch)

6   Detail view of nodes showing variations (© 2018 Christopher Schuch)

8   Detail view of nodes showing variations (© 2018 Christopher Schuch)

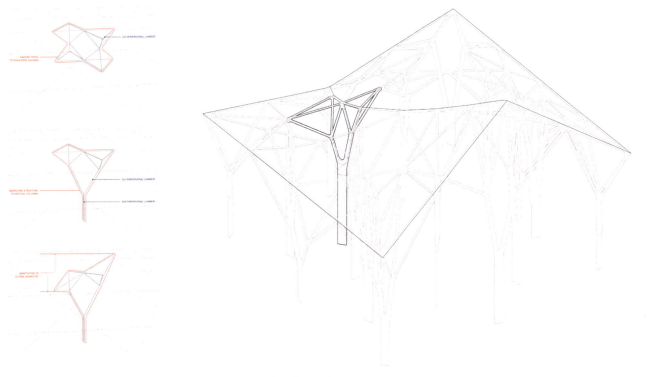

9   Video stills showing structure.   10   Axon highlighting self-stable "tree"

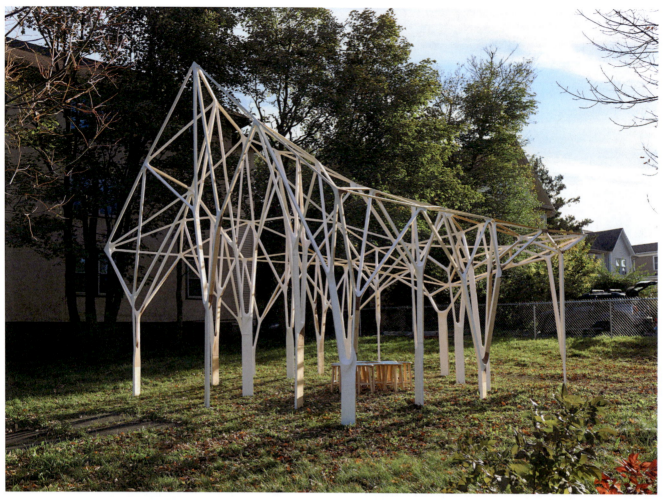

11 Three-quarter view (© 2018 Christopher Schuch)

12 View looking up at front peak (© 2018 Christopher Schuch)

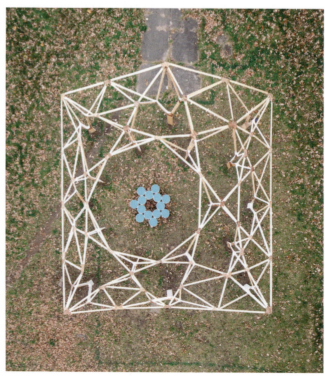

13 Aerial view (© 2018 Elyse Pono)

Lost House Lamere, Gunadi

14 Aerial view showing Lost House in context of the Four Corners neighborhood, Dorchester, Massachusetts (© 2018 Elyse Pono)

ACKNOWLEDGMENTS

Project Team: Joel Lamere, Cynthia Gunadi, Alexandre Beaudouin-Mackay, Marisa Waddle

With thanks to Rabeeya Arif, Chris Dewart, Jaya Eyzaguirre, Nare Filiposyan, Nico Guida, Trevor Hilker, Kristin Imre, Effie Jia, Alex Kobald, Melika Konjicanin, Ruoyu Lan, Thaddeus Lee, Katherine Paseman, David Register, Erin Register, John Skibo, Yutan Sun, Joseph Swerdlin, Evellyn Tan, and Matt Wagers.

Project partners include Four Corners Main Street, United Neighborhood Association, Greater Chamberlain Neighborhood Association, Pine Street Inn, the Boston Arts Commission, the Boston Department of Neighborhood Development, and Now+There.

IMAGE CREDITS

Figure 1, 4, 6-8, 11-12: © Christopher Schuch, 2018
Figures 3, 13-14: © Elyse Pono, 2018
All other drawings and images by the authors.

Joel Lamere is an Assistant Professor in the University of Miami School of Architecture. He was formerly the Homer A. Burnell Chair at MIT, where he had been teaching courses in architectural geometry, design and representation since 2007. His research critically explores the forms and other outcomes facilitated by the expanding palette of materials available to architecture, proliferating digital fabrication techniques, and evolving simulative design environments. The internationally-exhibited installation work of his design practice GLD, co-founded in 2010, is pre-occupied with radically thin structures produced through curved folding, composites, and linear networks.

Cynthia Gunadi, RA, NCARB, is a licensed architect in the state of MA with over ten years of professional design experience, with projects ranging in scope and scale from residential renovations to campus design and master planning. She currently teaches undergraduate design studios at the University of Miami School of Architecture. Before co-founding GLD, she was a senior member of Hashim Sarkis Studios, where she headed architecture and urban design projects located in the US and the Middle East.

NECTARY
Modular Assembly System

Manuel Jimenez Garcia
MadMDesign / Nagami

1 Nectary assembled at Digital Design Weekend 2018, Victoria and Albert Museum London (Photo © 2018 Victoria and Albert Museum)

Nectary is a modular system able to create an infinite number of morphological variations. Based on four different robotically 3d printed elements, it can be assembled into a plethora of spaces by following structurally driven combinatorial algorithms. From furniture to architecture, Nectary emerges as a three-dimensional pattern where porosity and color dynamically change to offer a unique spatial experience.

This project promotes a universal system that could be assembled without the use of large sets of heavy machinery. It is based on four modules which can be connected into a variety of structures by non-expert users.

A custom-made software allows the definition and nature of the object to be configured, establishing combinatorial processes that shift from a table to a bench, to a shelving system or even to larger structures, becoming columns, facades or other kinds of architectural elements. The rotation of each element is balanced both tectonically and experientially. The software defines a combination between a fully emergent system and a modular interface, in which users can control the growth of the structure from high-level rules (such as typology, maximum dimensions or growing tendencies) to local interventions in a single piece, an interface that engenders the exploration of different combinations while having structural guidelines to assure the viability of the assembly.

PRODUCTION NOTES

Architect: Manuel Jimenez Garcia

Client: Victoria and Albert Museum

Location: London

Date: 2018

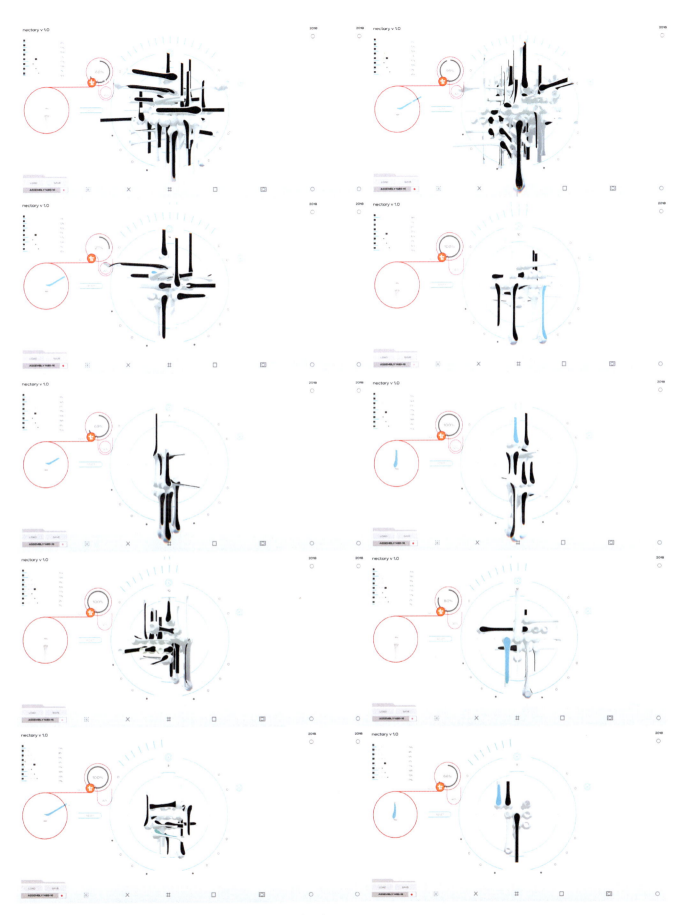

5 Nectary Assembly Software screenshots (Diagram © 2019 Nagami Design)

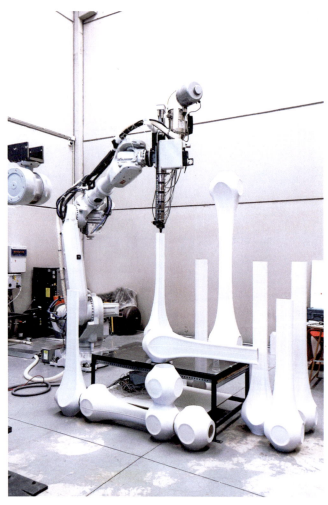

3 3d printing Nectary modules at Nagami in Avila, Spain (© 2018 Nagami)

4 Nectary assembly process at V&A London (© 2019 Manuel Jimenez Garcia)

The pieces are robotically 3d printed at Nagami Design, the practice founded by Manuel Jimenez Garcia. The use of this technology for a discrete modular system can seem a priori contradictory. However, the versatility of 3d printing methods, as well as their ability to dramatically reduce the production chain, has recently positioned them as a competitive solution for serialized product manufacturing, especially for the production of short editions that would otherwise require large initial investments. Furthermore, the construction industry is adopting 3d printing technologies to reduce material waste, outlining new paths beyond the initial promise of infinite formal variation.

At the same time the material, geometric, and technological constraints in large scale FDM 3d printing have proven difficulties of onsite manufacturing. The utopian idea of 3d printing entire buildings in one go starts to loose strength against the prefabrication of parts in a controlled environment.

Nectary capitalizes on the previously outlined advantages of 3d printing methods, situating itself as a product in constant flux, in which both new combinations and new types could emerge at no extra cost.

The system was first exhibited as a stand-alone installation at the sculpture gallery of the Victoria & Albert Museum (London) in September 2018. A second assembly was showcased at the Experimental Architecture Biennale (Prague) in June 2019, exhibition hosted by Galerie Jaroslava Fragnera. The product will become available in 2020, as part of Nagami Design collection. Future development of the system includes the addition of elements to be used as lost formwork in large scale concrete structures, expanding the possibilities of this system beyond its use in domestic spaces.

5   Nectary assembled at V&A London (© 2019 Manuel Jimenez Garcia)

10 Nectary disassembled at V&A London (© 2019 Manuel Jimenez Garcia)

ACKNOWLEDGMENTS

Design: Manuel Jimenez Garcia and MadMDesign

Robotic 3d printing: Nagami Design

Software developed with quadricular.ai

Design and fabrication team: Manuel Jimenez Garcia,
Ignacio Viguera, Miguel Angel Jimenez Garcia,
David Rubin de Celix, Luis De la Parra, Vicente Soler

Installation team: Roberto Garcia Velez, Alvaro Lopez,
Christos Chatzakis, Daniel Gonzalez, Marina Dimopoulou,
Man Nguyen, Ngai Wu, Han Hsun Hsieh, Daniel Rodriguez,
Manuel Jimenez Garcia

IMAGE CREDITS

Figure 1: © 2018 Victoria and Albert Museum, London (UK)

Figure 2: © 2018 Nagami Design

Figure 3: © 2018 Nagami Design

Figure 4-10: © 2018 Manuel Jimenez Garcia

Figure 11, 12: © 2019 Manuel Jimenez Garcia

11 Nectary at Galerie Jaroslava Fragnera (© 2019 Manuel Jimenez Garcia)

12 Nectary at Galerie Jaroslava Fragnera (© 2019 Manuel Jimenez Garcia)

Manuel Jimenez García is the co-founder and principal of madMdesign, a computational design practice based in London, and the co-founder of Nagami, a robotic manufacturing startup based in Spain. His work has been exhibited worldwide in venues such as Centre Pompidou (Paris), V&A Museum and Royal Academy of Arts (London). Alongside his practice, Manuel is a lecturer at The Bartlett School of Architecture UCL. He is Program Director of Architectural Computation, co-founder of Design Computation Lab, design tutor of RC4 at the M.Arch AD and curator of the Plexus Lecture Series.

Nagami Design is a design brand that explores the future of product design in a new technological era. Founded in Ávila (Spain), in 2016 by Manuel Jimenez García, Miki Jimenez García and Ignacio Viguera Ochoa, the company brings 3d printing and robotic manufacturing to large-scale products, with a wide range of customisation possibilities.

Research and innovation are at the core of Nagami's projects, which are developed in collaboration with internationally renowned architects, designers, and artists such as Zaha Hadid Architects, Ross Lovegrove, Daniel Widrig, and Davide Quayola, as well as with emerging talents who can embrace new technologies to materialise groundbreaking products.

Where Do the Twigs Go?

Faysal Tabbarah
American University
of Sharjah

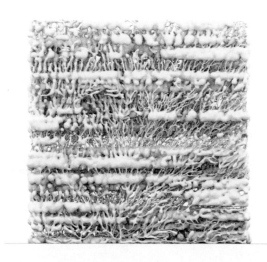 

1   Versions of digitally produced twigs and digitally simulated paper pulp showing striated patterning

INTRODUCTION

Where do the Twigs Go? is a 3,000 sq ft spatial construct made primarily of scavenged palm fronds, leaves, and recycled paper pulp. This project is part of an ongoing body of work that deploys painterly attitudes and workflows into a contemporary practice focusing computational design methodologies that is critical of highly standardized modes of sustainable design production.

In the seminal book Principles of Art History: The Problem of the Development of Style in Later Art, Swiss art historian Heinrich Wolfflin's identifies a material shift from the linear to the painterly in European representational art styles in the period between the Late-Renaissance and the Baroque. Wolfflin defines the painterly as embodying limitlessness and merging, receding, open, and lacking in linear hierarchy. This represents an antagonistic and direct shift from clarity, tangibility and solidity of the linear style prevalent in Late Renaissance representational art (Wolfflin 1950, Tabbarah and Ibrhaim 2018). Today, this alludes to ambiguous part-to-whole relationships. Thus, this project deploys the painterly at a time of increased democratization of computational design tools, and highly standardized sustainable design production at a time of increased climate crisis.

PRODUCTION NOTES

Client: Dubai Design Week
Status: Completed
Site Area: 3,000 sq. ft.
Location: Dubai, UAE
Date: 2018

2   View of the interior of a pavilion space showing the thickened wall in elevation

3 A prototype showing scavenged twigs and sprayed paper pulp binder

4 A prototype showing scavenged twigs and sprayed paper pulp binder

PROJECT BRIEF

The project brief aimed to create five discrete temporary exhibition spaces, each measuring approximately 500 square feet. As such, the overall project is conceived as a series of five spaces acting as a single and varied spatial landscape. The dynamic composition and the relationship between each of the five spaces, and the exhibitions they host, defines an activated public space where an overall common curatorial narrative can potentially emerge.

Each differentiated spaces is defined by textured wall surfaces constructed through the layering of natural (i.e. scavenged palm fronds and leaves) and synthetic materials (i.e. recycled paper pulp) to create an almost natural condition that challenges visitors' assumptions about material, structure, and construction. The textures recede on the interior of every individual space to allow exhibited material to become primary.

RESEARCH AND PROCESS

The project engages with the ubiquity of technology through developing a digital/analogue workflow that moves circularly between scavenging plant matter, 3D-scanning, physical prototyping, and digital simulations to produce composite material systems that exhibit ideas of painterliness through challenging traditional part-to-whole logics.

Materially, the structuring of the textured wall surfaces with both natural and recyclable synthetic materials emerged by asking a child-like question: Where do the twigs go? This was asked to rethink the life span of materials used in the construction of temporary events. Here, the potential second life of plant matter emerges between the time they are harvested, and the time they turn to compost in the form a thickened yet porous structural wall.

Where Do the Twigs Go? Tabbarah

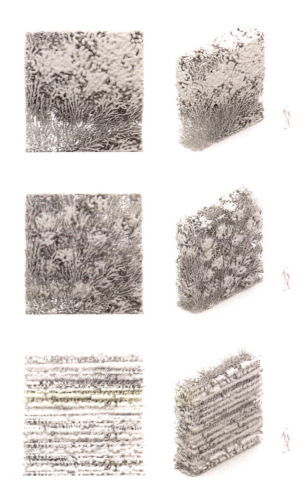

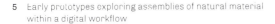

5   Early prototypes exploring assemblies of natural material
    within a digital workflow

6   Digital twigs and simulated paper pulp showing striated and gradient
    patterning
    that communicate to the contractor specific design intentions such
    as densities, porosities and thicknesses

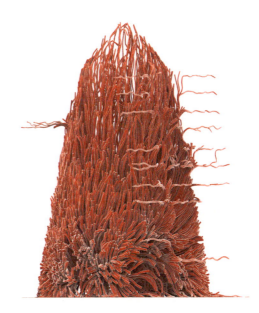

7   Early prototypes exploring assemblies of natural material within a digital workflow into a wall condition; these methodologies were developed
    and later integrated the paper pulp simulation seen in Image 6, making them both a design and communication tool

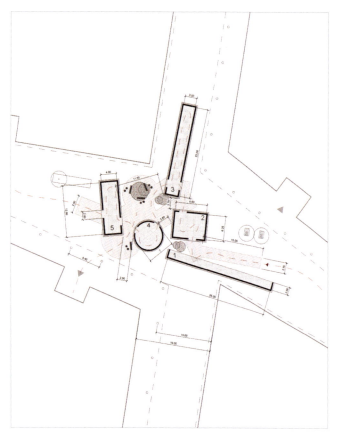

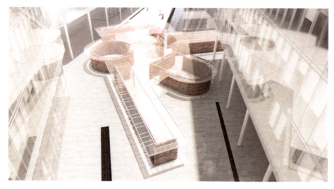

9   Top view render showing the 5 radically different pavilions and roof; the roof is made of simple 4x4 pine wood framing system with recycled advertising banner material

8   Plan diagram showing the 5 different pavilions and how the different proportions create a varied curatorial experience

10   Spatial render showing an impression of how the walls work together to create a varied curatorial experience

11   The landscape of a waste management facility where the plant matter was scavenged

12 Early prototyping studies showing the white wood frame and mesh infra-structure that supports the organic palm material

13 Early prototyping studies showing the paper pulp binder sprayed onto a panel with organic palm material

14 Early prototyping studies showing process of spraying the paper pulp binder on the organic material

15 First full thickened wall construction that includes different color tests and binder recipes

16 Thickened free-standing wall and skylight (Cartel/Sergey B, 2018)

17 Audience interacting with a viewing cone and projection designed by exhibitors within this pavilion (Jalal Abu Thina, 2018)

18 Pavilion image showing thickened free-standing wall, skylight, roof, entry and the white surfaces of the interior space, which alternate between white, (exterior) red, and black depending on interior exhibits (Cartel/Sergey B, 2018)

The process integrated the digital assembly of 3D-scanned plant matter with simulations of sprayed paper pulp. Initial steps included finding wall assembly patterns from a myriad of plant matter types before simulating the different paper pulp recipes. This was deployed in the design phase and became a tool to communicate to the contractor. specific design intentions such as densities, porosities, and thicknesses.

Each pavilion is composed of thickened wall surfaces (7 x 9.8 x 0.2 ft) that assemble together to create the spaces. The elements that make up each wall include: 1. Scavenged palm fronds and leaves found at a leading waste management facility in Sharjah, United Arab Emirates (U.A.E), close to where the final construction took place; 2. Paper pulp made from recycled newspapers; 3. White-wood frame; 4. Metal wire mesh. No mechanical connections exist between the plants and the metal mesh as the paper pulp acts as the binder.

At the end of its short, seven day life, all elements of the project were composted or recycled.

ACKNOWLEDGEMENTS
This project was conducted as part of the collaborative Architecture + Other Things. Project team members include Mohamed Rowizak.

The plant material was collected from Bee'ah, a leading environmental management company in thr UAE.

REFERENCES
Tabbarah, Faysal and Ibrahim Ibrhaim. 2018. "Painterly Structures." In Project *Proceedings for ACSA 106: Ecological Imperative, 2018*. Colorado: University of Denver Colorado. A version of this introduction was written in this previous paper co-authored paper.

Wolfflin, Heinrich. 1950. *Principles of Art History: The Problem of the Development of Style in Later Art*. New York: Dover Publications.

IMAGE CREDITS
Figure 16, 18: Cartel/Segrey B, 2018
Figure 17: Jalal Abu Thina, 2018
All other drawings and images by the authors.

Faysal Tabbarah is an Associate Professor of Architecture at the College of Architecture, Art and Design at the American University of Sharjah. He is also co-founder of Architecture + Other Things. His research investigates the relationship between environmental imaginaries, technology, and architectural production in the Middle East and North Africa.

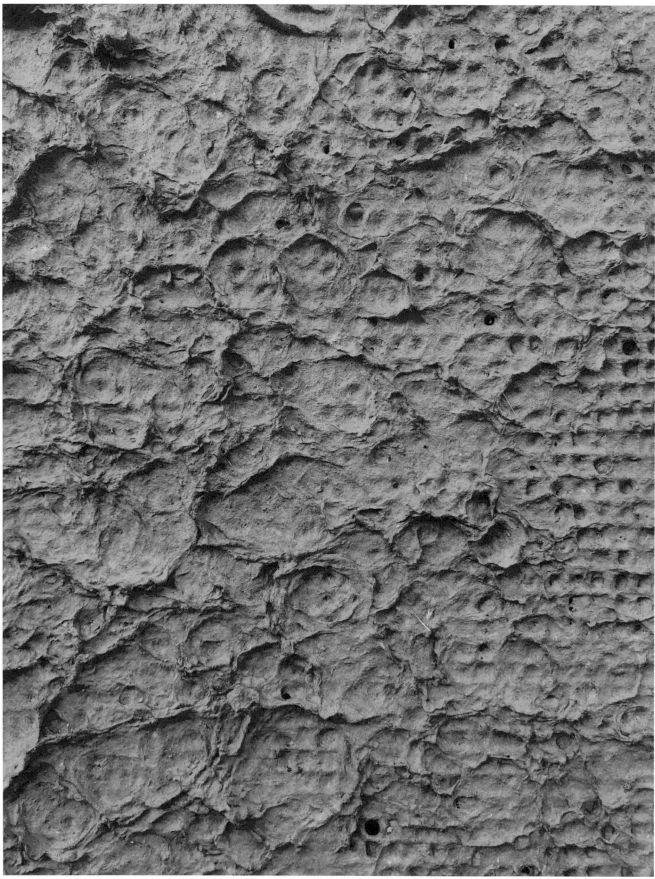

19 Close-up of internal wall texture; this texture was designed to allow for the displayed work in the interior of the pavilion space to be the center of attention, while the wall surfaces recede

Where Do the Twigs Go? Tabbarah

20 Close-up of external wall texture

Spatial Felted Structure

Anat Uziely
Chun-Nien Ou Yang

1   Production of the Spatial Felted Structure; the model exhibits the fabrication process developed throughout the study

EXPLORATION OF WOOL AND NEW FABRICATION METHODS

The tactile qualities of materials are central to the way one interacts with their environment. The main aim of the research is to reintroduce a novel role for soft materials in the architectural realm. The project focuses on a widely used, yet rarely glorified material: wool fibres. Wool is a natural, sustainable, and biodegradable fibre (IWTO 2014). The study seeks to re-examine wool's inherent ability to consolidate and transform into felt and explores the potential of wool as a bonding agent and of felting process as a binding operation using advanced fabrication tools. Skipping costly and labour-intensive production phases, the new material practice intends to form a methodology whereby wool is employed in diverse scenarios, to enrich architectural space and enhance its tangible qualities.

Felting of animal hair has a versatile history. After reviewing traditional and commercial felt manufacturing and exploring the potential of felting as a binding procedure by small-scale hand-crafted models, the next exploration step was the translation of these findings to an automated process. Robotic needle-felting was the first phase, followed by hydroentanglement, a well-established method in the production of synthetic fibres in the nonwoven industry. Hydroentanglement technology follows a principle similar to the mechanical entanglement of needle-felting, replacing engineered needles with water jets (Crawshaw & Simpson 2002).

PRODUCTION NOTES

Title: Spatial Felted Structure

Materials: Plywood, Wool Fibres

Dimensions: 140/300cm

Exhibition Location: London

Date of exhibition: December 2018

2 Felting as Binding, Hand Needle Felting: 3x3cm plywood, wool fibres

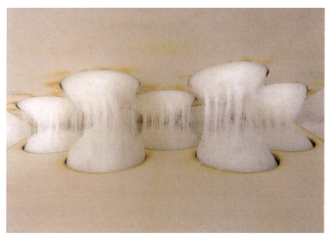

3 Automation, Robotic Needle Felting: 20x20cm plywood, wool fibres

4 Hydroentanglement: Toolpath 2cm Grid, 3mm plywood, wool fibres

The first trial included a fibrous web and a piece of MDF that served as backing. The outcome was a complete surprise. Instead of entangling the fibres with themselves, the machine forced the wool fibres deep into the MDF. The composite achieved by the procedure was different from the expectations but opened a door for further investigation.

The novel hydroentanglement process embeds wool fibres into rigid materials. It does not condense and transform all the fibres into felt, and depending on the toolpath, it entangles the fibre in certain points while retaining the raw distinctive tactility of the wool. The study included the sampling of numerous backing materials such as plastics, metal meshes, plywood, and hardwoods that yielded diverse results. In addition, studies extended to testing various joinery strategies, including one approach where flat wool 'seams' formed soft, flexible joints, and another that explored three-dimensional wool connections and fixing plywood members in predefined angles.

The Spatial Felted Structure produced as a demonstrator model exhibits the fabrication process developed through-out the study. and yielded a double-sided structure comprised of fifteen birch plywood members connected solely via the waterjet procedure. Plywood was selected as the substrate due to its self-supporting ability and grain consistency. One façade displays wool strip connections that reveal the plywood substrate, while the other side is completely covered with wool. The product's height is restricted due to the machine working area, but there is no limit to its length, as horizontally it can be continuously joined with more wool. In the two edges of the structure, members are fixed at 90 degrees, a strategy that assists in stabilising the structure and presents the potential of volumetric joints alongside flexible connections.

Generating the pattern of the fibre entanglement was one of the study's discoveries, whereby in addition to its functional role, the toolpath became a decorative feature. The method enables designing different graphic patterns that play upon the inherent qualities of wool. The intricate weave-like

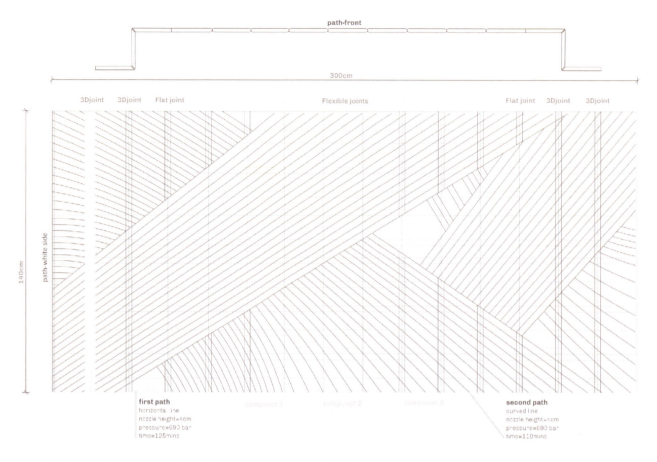

path-front

300cm

3Djoint　3Djoint　Flat joint　　　　　　　　Flexible joints　　　　　　　Flat joint　3Djoint　3Djoint

140cm

path white side

first path
horizontal line
nozzle height=40cm
pressure=680 bar
time=125mins

component 1　　　component 2　　　component 3

second path
curved line
nozzle height=40cm
pressure=680 bar
time=110mins

5　Toolpath design for the wool covered façade features a pattern informed by the fibre length and the desired connections between the plywood members

6　The Spatial Felted Structure before assembly; due to the waterjet machine dimensions, the structure had to be divided into three components

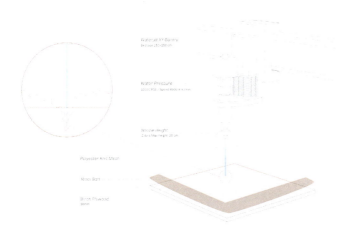

7 Hydroentaglement: Waterjet Binding , Parameters, and Constraints

9 Hydroentanglement: Processing Volumetric Joinery, plywood, wool fibres

8 Hydroentanglement: Sampling Soft Joinery, plywood, ash, oak, wool fibres

10 Hydroentanglement Outcome: 3D Joint, plywood, wool fibres

pattern generated as a whole then deconstructed to multiple paths in a specific order to attain the anticipated impression. The manufacturing method developed throughout the project offers a new perspective in regards to the introduction of soft materials into the architectural space.

ACKNOWLEDGMENTS

The study pursued as part of our Master Thesis at The Bartlett School of Architecture UCL (2017-2018). We thank the Design for Manufacture program tutors and directors: Giulio Brugnaro, Matthijs la Roi, Prof. Stephen Gage, Prof. Bob Sheil, Dr. Christopher Leung, Peter Scully, B-Made staff, and our Thesis Project Supervisor Dr. Jane Scott.

REFERENCES

Burkett, M. E. 1979. *The Art of the Felt Maker*. Kendal: Abbot Hall Art Gallery.

Simpson, W. S. and G. H. Crawshaw, eds. 2002. *Wool: Science and Technology*. Cambridge: Woodhead Publishing.

IWTO. n.d. "Health & Wellness." International Wool Textile Organisation, Our Work, Health & Wellness. Accessed July 28, 2019. www.iwto.org/work/health-wellness.

IMAGE CREDITS

Figure 15: © 2018 Sean Pollock

All other drawings and images by the authors

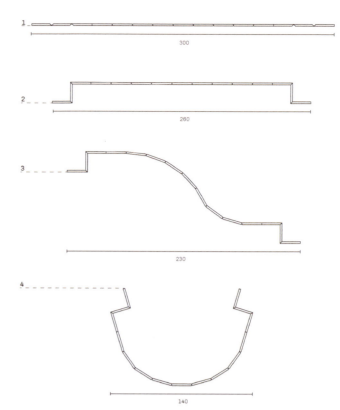

1. Initial layout for the waterjet joining process
2. Fixed edges to stabilise structure
3. Optional curved layout
4. Optional rounded layout

11 Spatial Felted Structure Design: optional layouts where the wool strips façade reveals the plywood substrate

12 Spatial Felted Structure, Wool Covered Façade, 180x300cm, Wool fibres, 18mm Plywood, Steel Base, 15 Exhibition, 2018, London

13 Spatial Felted Structure, Wool Strips Façade, 15 Exhibition, 2018, London

14 Spatial Felted Structure, Pattern Enhances Material Tactility

15 Spatial Felted Structure, 140x300cm (© 2018 Sean Pollock)

Anat Uziely is an Israeli designer, born in 1988. She attended Bezalel Academy of Art and Design in Jerusalem, Parsons School of Design in New York, and finally The Bartlett School of Architecture UCL, where she recently graduated from the Design for Manufacture MArch program. Intrigued by materials, handcrafts, and novel fabrication processes, her holistic practice spans the scales of projects, from architecture through product design.

Chun-Nien Ou Yang is a Taiwanese architectural designer who has working experience in interior and architectural design. She has completed a bachelor degree of architecture in Taiwan and studied MArch Design for Manufacture in The Bartlett School of Architecture UCL, thus expanding her research on material and digital fabrication.

Resonant Stacks

Lee-Su Huang
University of Florida

Gregory Thomas Spaw
American University of Sharjah

Jakob Marsico
Carnegie Mellon University

1   The completed Resonant Stacks installation on site at dusk (Jakob Marsico © 2016 SHO Architecture)

EXPERIENCE

Resonant Stacks consists of two monolithic glowing towers emitting deep resonating harmonies. Simultaneously a visual and aural interactive experience, the towers are opaque and densely white during the day, and at night, they are lit from within as light patterns morph in response to the generative sound composition.

EXPLANATION

Each of the curved towers contains a lighting system, a series of microphones, and a speaker system. The exterior is shrink-wrapped in white industrial plastic—opaque in the day, and a smooth, glowing, translucent surface at night. Peeking from the top of each tower is a metal stack, recalling the aesthetic of the location's historical industrial past. Visitors "play" the towers like instruments, singing or humming into two interaction points placed at different heights on each stack, and the tone, timbre, and volume of their voices are synthesized and incorporated into the perpetually changing light and sound patterns of the Stacks. Though each stack has distinct sound and visual characteristics, they are also deeply connected. When the voices of the visitors at each tower harmonize, the towers reflect that harmony with specific light patterning. Likewise, the patterning changes when the contributing sounds are dissonant. The resulting experience is one in which visitors are encouraged to not only interact with the installation itself, but also to communicate with one another through both digital and analog means.

PRODUCTION NOTES

Designers:	SHO Architecture + Ultra Low Res Studio
Client:	Georgetown Business Improvement District
Status:	Completed
Site Area:	225 sq. ft.
Location:	Georgetown, Washington, D.C.
Date:	2016

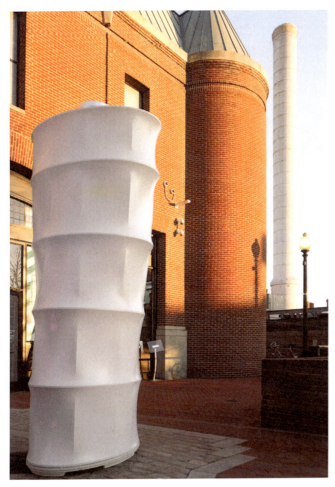

2   The project's two stacks were inspired by the surrounding neighborhood's historical industrial past (Lee-Su Huang © 2016 SHO Architecture)

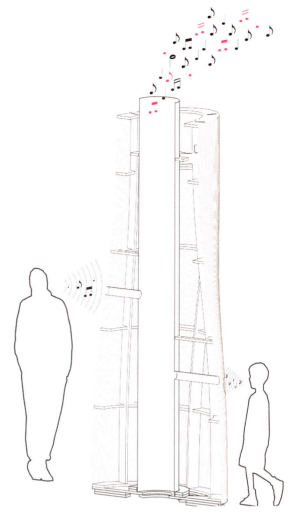

3   Diagram with project elements and interaction (© 2017 SHO Architecture)

The site for this installation is a urban canyon-like pathway, and incorporating natural rythmic sounds was an intended response to these artificial surroundings. The hard surfaces (brick walls and pavement) around the installation add a layer of reverberation to the sound design, which pairs beautifully with droney, resonating sounds.

TECHNICAL AND SOUND DESIGN

The microphones, lights, and speakers are all controlled by a central computer system, which sends and receives data to and from the towers via CAT5 and audio cables.

Every layer of sound in this project, whether visitors' voices or the generative sound and light composition that runs in the background when visitors are not interacting with the piece, is the result of synthesis using a bank of resonant filters. The baseline self-generating sound is composed of three layers: a looping recording of Gregorian chants that are filtered to wipe out articulation, leaving only resonant traces of the original vocalizations; a field recording of snow falling on trees, the "natural rhythm" track; and white noise. The frequencies of the filter banks in layers two and

three are driven by a generative chord building algorithm to always be in tune with each other and in the same key and mode as the chant track.

As part of the interactive portion of the piece, as visitors sing or hum into microphones, their voices too are analyzed and broken down into harmonic components, and pass through a pitch analysis node that identifies the frequencies and amplitudes of the five strongest overtones of the incoming voice and then populates a new resonant filter bank with those value sets. That resonant filter bank is thus "excited" to create a completely synthesized resonating voice, and this user-derived reverberation attacks strongly then slowly decays, creating a sense of sound drifting away in wind. These same voice components are also used to drive the generative lighting patterns that move across the surfaces of the towers. Once a new voice is identified and the resulting resonant sound synthesized, the lighting control system is programmed to cause a "light explosion" starting at the microphone location and emanating outward before dissipating at the same rate as the user's sound.

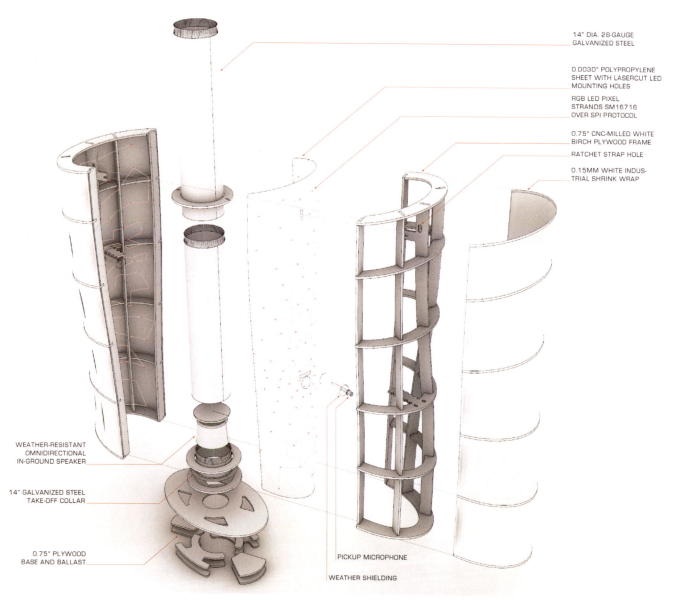

14" DIA. 28-GAUGE
GALVANIZED STEEL

0.0030" POLYPROPYLENE
SHEET WITH LASERCUT LED
MOUNTING HOLES

RGB LED PIXEL
STRANDS SM16716
OVER SPI PROTOCOL

0.75" CNC-MILLED WHITE
BIRCH PLYWOOD FRAME

RATCHET STRAP HOLE

0.15MM WHITE INDUS-
TRIAL SHRINK WRAP

WEATHER-RESISTANT
OMNIDIRECTIONAL
IN-GROUND SPEAKER

14" GALVANIZED STEEL
TAKE-OFF COLLAR

0.75" PLYWOOD
BASE AND BALLAST

PICKUP MICROPHONE

WEATHER SHIELDING

4　Exploded axonometric drawing documenting material systems, layers and components (© 2019 SHO Architecture)

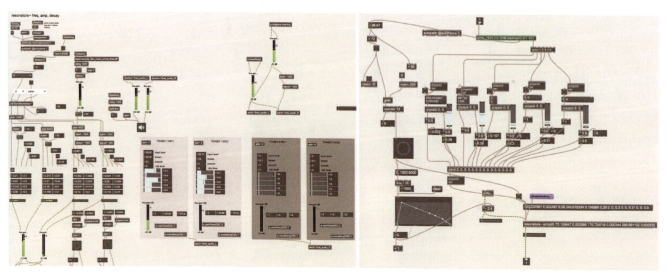

5　MAX/MSP Synch Processor (left) and voice frequency/amplitude analysis core (right) (© 2019 ULR Studio)

Resonant Stacks Huang, Spaw, Marsico

6 Marine grade shrink-wrap application in process
   (Wang © 2016 SHO Architecture)

7 Doubly curved stack halves with shrink wrap applied
   (Huang © 2016 SHO Architecture)

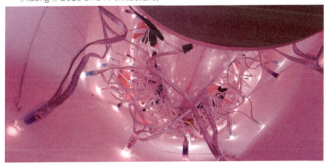

8 Looking down into the inner workings of the stack from above
   (Huang © 2016 SHO Architecture)

9 On site stacks components with RGB LEDs and electronic elements
   exposed (Huang © 2016 SHO Architecture)

ACKNOWLEDGMENTS

This project was supported by the Georgetown Business Improvement District and facilitated by the University of Florida Infinity Fabrication Lab. Project Assistants: Piotr Pasierbiński and Shuyu Wang.

REFERENCES

Auinger, Sam and Bruce Odland. *Harmonic Bridge.* 1998. MASS MoCA, North Adams, MA. Accessed July 15, 2019. https://mass-moca.org/event/bruce-odland-sam-auinger-harmonic-bridge/.

Brooks+Scarpa Architecture Landscape Urban Design. 2013. "Davie-Brown Entertainment." Project Description. Accessed July 15, 2019. https://brooksscarpa.com/davie-brown-entertainment.

Gillis, Matthew. *AIA/LA 2x8 Taut..* A+D Museum Exhibition, June 5, 2012 – June 30, 2012, Los Angeles, CA. Accessed July 15, 2019. https://aplusd.org/exhibition/aia-la-presents-2x8-taut/.

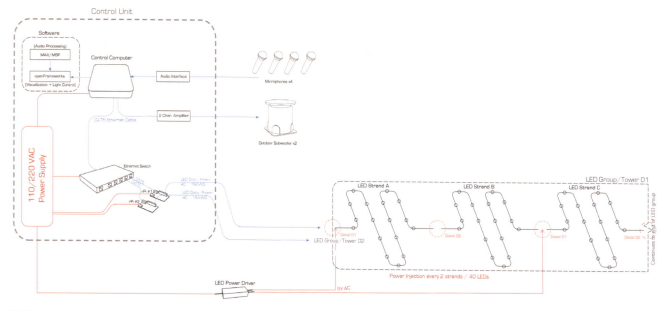

10 Diagram showing component, power, and data connectivity between physical computing system (© 2017 SHO Architecture)

11 The installation encourages visitors to audibly interact and spatially engage with the ever changing atmospheric stacks (Huang © 2016 SHO Architecture)

Resonant Stacks Huang, Spaw, Marsico

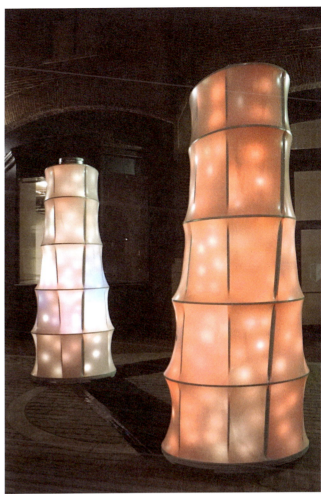

12 Sequence showing animated lighting transitioning across Resonant Stacks (Huang © 2016 SHO Architecture)

Lee-Su Huang received his Bachelor of Architecture from Feng-Chia University in Taiwan and his Master in Architecture degree from Harvard University's Graduate School of Design. He has practiced in Taiwan with various firms and in the United States with Preston Scott Cohen Inc. in Cambridge, and with LA.S.S.A Architects in Seoul, Korea. As co-founder and principal of SHO, his research and practice centers on digital design+ fabrication methodology, parametric design optimization strategies, as well as kinetic/interactive architectural prototypes. Lee-Su is currently a Lecturer at the University of Florida's School of Architecture, teaching graduate and undergraduate level design studios as well as foundation and advanced digital media and parametric modeling courses.

Gregory Thomas Spaw is an Assistant Professor at the American University of Sharjah in the United Arab Emirates. He has previously held the Ann Kalla Assistant Professorship at Carnegie Mellon University and taught undergraduate and graduate studios, seminars and electives at the University of Tennessee. Concurrent with his academic engagement, Spaw is a principal of SHO, a design

collaborative that straddles the territories of teaching, research and practice. His previous professional experience includes work with the award-winning offices of Bohlin Cywinski Jackson, Preston Scott Cohen Inc., and Asymptote. His scholarly pursuits incorporate digital visualization, harnessing parametric workflows, intelligent material fabrication, and responsive environment design.

Jakob Marsico is an interaction designer and media artist. He runs Ultra Low Res Studio, an arts-engineering firm that works with developers and architects to integrate dynamic, experiential installations with the built environment. Jakob currently holds an adjunct instructor position at Carnegie Mellon and is a member of the CoDe Lab in CMU's School of Architecture. He has a BA in Religious Studies from George Washington University and a Masters of Tangible Interaction Design from Carnegie Mellon University.

EXPANDED PERCEPTIONS

Nancy Diniz
Central Saint Martins, UAL

Frank Melendez
City College of New York, CUNY

Blending Physical and Virtual Environments
through Mobile Sensed Data

1   The user experience in Virtual Reality (VR) wearing an Oculus Rift headset and wearable device. The virtual point cloud model is captured with a LIDAR
    scanner and augmented with real-time numerical values and visual attributes that reflect data collected with sensors (© 2018 Augmented Architectures)

OVERVIEW

Our bodies are complex systems that are dynamic and kinetic, allowing us to navigate
through the world, experience our surroundings, and communicate with others through
sensing and data feedback. In order to understand our surrounding environment, we rely
on our human senses: sight, hearing, touch, taste, and smell. However, the limitations of
our human senses do not allow us to perceive all of the invisible, intangible, ephemeral,
multi-layered environmental and biometric phenomena that coalesce and form dense
networks that are important to take into account in multiple fields of design.

Additionally, when individuals are immersed within a Virtual Reality (VR) environment,
typically their sensorial experiences are further dampened, and they are visually cut off
from their surrounding physical environment. There is a distinct separation between the
user's physical surroundings and the immersive virtual space that they are experiencing.
*Expanded Perceptions: Blending Physical and Virtual Environments through Mobile Sensed
Data* is an experimental research project with interactive wearable devices that venture
to embed properties of the physical world seamlessly within the virtual world. The project
capitalizes on VR, ubiquitous computing, sensing, and actuating technologies, to create an
Extended Reality (XR) experience (Figure 1).

In this project, created as part of the Institute for Advanced Architecture of Catalonia
(IaaC) Global Summer School, New York City, 2018, our interdisciplinary team of artists,

2   Scanning the New Lab with a LIDAR scanner (© 2018 MYND Workshop)

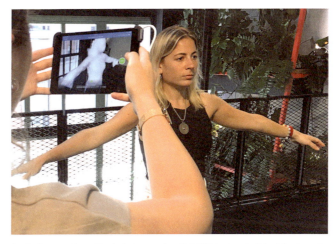

4   Body scanning with photogrammetry (© 2018 Augmented Architectures)

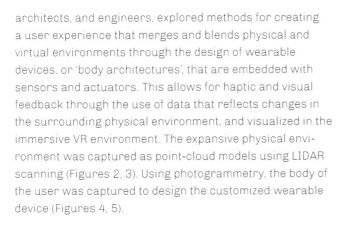

3   Point-cloud mode of the New Lab (© 2018 Augmented Architectures)

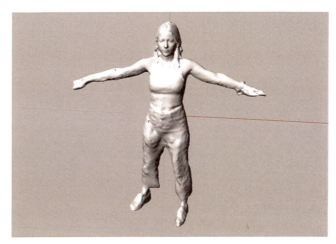

5   Digital model for wearable design © 2018 Augmented Architectures)

architects, and engineers, explored methods for creating a user experience that merges and blends physical and virtual environments through the design of wearable devices, or 'body architectures', that are embedded with sensors and actuators. This allows for haptic and visual feedback through the use of data that reflects changes in the surrounding physical environment, and visualized in the immersive VR environment. The expansive physical environment was captured as point-cloud models using LIDAR scanning (Figures 2, 3). Using photogrammetry, the body of the user was captured to design the customized wearable device (Figures 4, 5).

BODY ARCHITECTURES

Two unique wearable devices were designed and fabricated to capture different kinds of data. This data is sent and mapped in real-time into a digital representation of the physical environment. Through VR, the user of the wearable device can experience visualized representations of the data being collected, which has an effect on the geometries and representation within the digital,

immersive environment. This project sets up a framework that promotes augmenting the human body's interactions with real and virtual worlds. This project supports the 2019 ACADIA theme of 'Ubiquity and Autonomy', as it explores notions of synchronicity of the physical and virtual world as a space, and the virtual as material. The workflow serves to bring a hyper-awareness to our senses, as closed-loop cybernetic systems that utilize 'digitized' biometric and environmental data through the use of 3d scanning and point cloud models, virtual reality visualization, sensing technologies, and actuation (Figure 6). The design of these body architectures relies on hybrid design and transdisciplinary collaborations to explore new possibilities for wearable body architectures that evolve human machine-environment interactions.

The wearable devices focus on two themes. One captures environmental data, in this case CO levels, which is related with issues of health and air quality concerns. The second relates to body proxemics, which is the study of space, how we use it, how it makes us feel more or less comfortable,

WEARABLES DESIGN AND FABRICATION

PATTERNING SCRIPTS   WEARABLE DESIGN   SILICONE CASTING PART 1   ACRYLIC LASERCUT MOULD   SILICONE CASTING PART 2   SENSORS AND ACTUATORS

6   Diagram of the physical computing workflow, sensing and actuation, and wearable design and fabrication process (© 2018 Augmented Architectures)

and how we arrange objects and ourselves in relation to space (Figure 7). The data from the sensors embedded in the wearables is used to actuate different behaviors in the VR environment, through real-time changes in color and streaming numerical values, as well as the physical environment, through haptic sensations (vibration), and ambient effects (lighting) (Figures 8 and 9). The first wearable uses an air quality sensing device that is programmed to relay data levels, which serves as input parameters of the virtual model, resulting in changes of color and scale according to the air quality levels it is sensing. The second wearable integrates a proximity sensor, again, serving as input parameters for the virtual model, and resulting in changes in opacity and transparency. This project aims to experiment with interactive wearable devices that venture to embed the physical world seamlessly with the virtual world by capitalizing on VR, ubiquitous computing, and sensing and actuating technologies.

ACKNOWLEDGMENTS

This project was completed as part of the Institute for Advanced Architecture of Catalonia (IaaC) Global Summer School, New York City, 2018.

Project Team: IaaC GSS NYC Directors: Nancy Diniz, Frank Melendez, Marcella Del Signore, Maria Aiolova. IaaC GSS NYC Tutors: Mint Boonyapanachoti, Sebastian Morales, Dallas Bennett, Michael Robison. IaaC GSS NYC Students: Rabeya Khatoon, Rania Labib, Xinye Lin, Helena Homsi, Yaqub Aisaa, Mohammad Jawad, Sofia Caputo. Model: Renata Venturelli. Host Organization: Terraform ONE, New Lab, Brooklyn Navy Yards, Brooklyn, NY.

IMAGE CREDITS
Figures 1, 3-8: © 2018 Augmented Architectures
Figures 2: © 2018 MYND Workshop

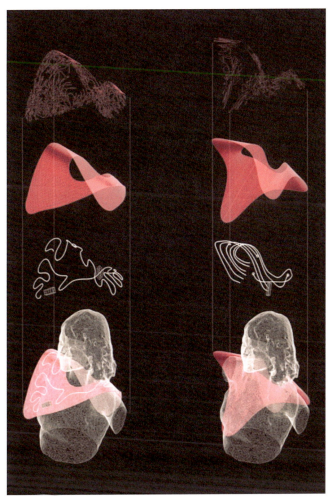

8   Wearable pattern and sensor detail © 2018 Augmented Architectures)

7   Layers of the wearable device (© 2018 Augmented Architecturos)

9   Wearable lighting actuation (© 2018 Augmented Architectures)

Nancy Diniz is a registered architect, entrepreneur, and educator. She is partner of Augmented Architectures and bioMATTERS based in New York City. Nancy has been awarded several fellowships, namely NYSCA/Storefront, MacDowell Colony, EYEBEAM, Seoul Art Space Geumcheon, Arctic Circle, and the Portuguese Foundation of Science and Technology. She is an affiliated researcher at ISTAR Digital Living Spaces Lab, ISCTE, Lisbon Portugal and at WSNL Wireless Sensor Network Lab, XJTLU, Suzhou, China. Nancy is the program Director of the Masters in Biodesign at Central Saint Martins, University of the Arts, London. Previously she held academic positions in the US, China, the UK, Italy and Portugal.

Frank Melendez is an architectural designer, educator, and researcher. He is partner of Augmented Architectures and bioMAT-TERS based in New York City and an Assistant Professor at the City College of New York, CUNY. He is the author of *Drawing from the Model*, Wiley, 2019, and has organized symposia and exhibitions including DATA & MATTER, Venice, Italy, 2018 and Material Interactions, New York, NY, 2017. Frank was awarded a MacDowell Fellowship, 2017, and the George N. Pauly Jr. Fellowship, Carnegie Mellon University, 2013. He holds a BArch from the University of Arizona and an MArch from Yale University.

IRIDESCENCE:
Bio-Inspired Emotive Matter

Behnaz Farahi
University of Southern
California (USC)

1   Iridescence: Bio-inspired emotive collar

What if our clothing could sense the movement and emotions of those around us? How might technology expand our sensory experience and influence our social interactions? And in what ways could our clothing become a form of non-verbal communication, expressed through changes in color and texture?

PRODUCTION NOTES

Client: Museum of Science
             & Industry

Location: Chicago

Date: 2019

The hummingbird is a remarkable creature. The male Anna's hummingbird, for example, has feathers around his throat that appear at one moment completely green. With a twist of his head, however, he can turn them into an iridescent pink. He does this by exploiting the capacity of the microscopic structure of the feather to refract light like a prism, so that the feathers take on different shimmering hues when viewed from different angles. This is how the Anna's hummingbird attracts mates during his spectacular displays of aerial courtship.

2　Hummingbird mesmerizing color change

3　Refraction of light waves makes hummingbird feathers
　appear to change color

4　Close up of color-changing lenticular quills

Inspired by the gorget of the Anna's hummingbird, *Iridescence* is an interactive collar equipped with a facial tracking camera and an array of 200 rotating quills. The custom-made quills flip their colors and start to make patterns in response to the movement of onlookers and their facial expressions.

This project addresses a number of challenging technical issues. First, the design and fabrication of color-changing materials was informed by the logic of lenticular behavior. Not dissimilar to how light is refracted by the feathers of a hummingbird, *Iridescence* uses lenticular lenses laminated onto an array flat colored surfaces to provide color- changing effects. Second, the rotation of the quills is controlled by a series of custom electro-magnetic actuators carefully designed to withstand the natural wear and tear of being part of a 15-month long exhibition. These actuators can be easily removed and replaced by substitute actuators if any of them fail.

Not dissimilar to the way in which the brain, nervous system, muscles, and vision in a hummingbird are synchronized together, this piece is equipped with 200 actuators acting as 'muscles', 40 PCB driver boards acting as a 'nervous system', 4 micro-computers acting as a 'brain' and a facial recognition camera acting as an 'eye', all mounted inside the piece.

Four microcontrollers (Teensy 3.2) work together to orchestrate the collar's behavior. One of these is the master 'brain' in charge of figuring out what the wearable should be doing at any given point in time. The brain communicates with the other three microcontrollers via conductive wires, using messages transmitted as precisely timed electrical pulses. One of the microcontrollers is attached to a camera and two of them are attached to 40 PCB driver boards. These electrical boards act as a 'nervous system'; in which they receive the signals from the brain and transmit them to the 'muscles' actuators.

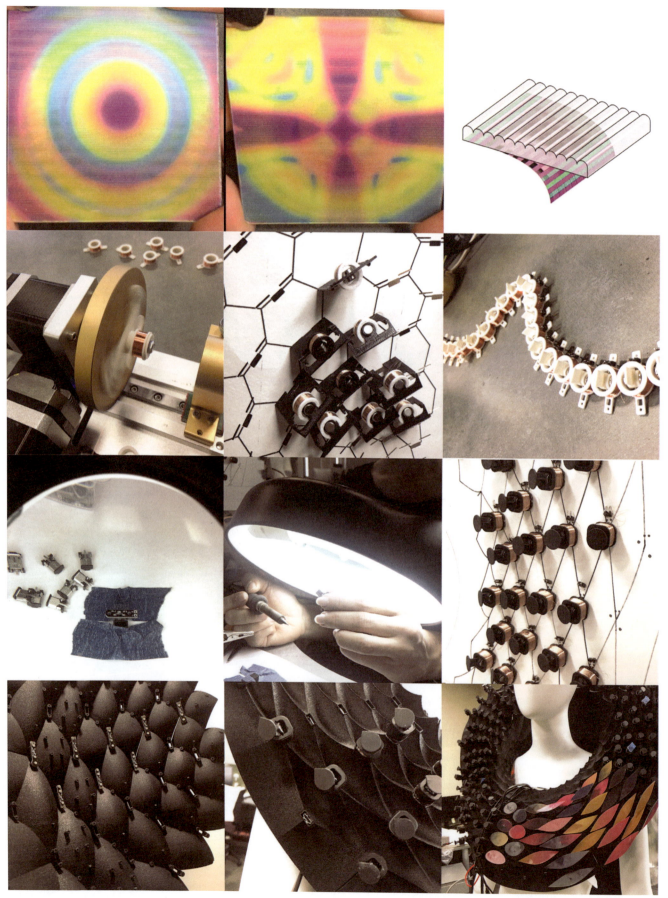

5   Fabrication of lenticular feathers, actuators, and electronics in *Iridescence*

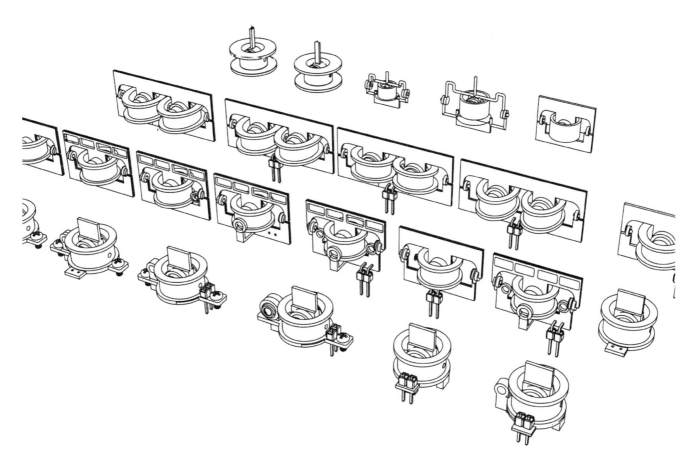

6   Design and fabrication of actuators; more than 20 versions have been prototyped

The design of the actuators evolved over many iterations. It is based on a magnetic field acting upon a permanently installed set of magnets. Each actuator is composed of an assembly of many components. This assembly includes a set of permanent magnets housed on each side of a rotor that is able to flip and change position according to the controlled changes in the magnetic field of a closely coupled magnetic coil. The magnetic field of the coil is switched by reversing the control signal, and thus the rotor flips to the opposite direction. In other words, the permanent magnets located inside the rotor are either attracted or repelled by the field of magnetic coil.

These PCB driver boards were designed to leverage the mature ecosystem built around light emitting diodes (LEDs). By using existing, open source code libraries, we were able to take advantage of code that had been optimized to run on small microcontrollers that then drive thousands of LEDs. Therefore, one of the major engineering challenges in this project was to design and develop electrical boards to control the actuator's behavior using LED driver ICs.

The goal of the project is to explore how wearables can become not only a vehicle for self-expression, but also an extension of our sensory experience of the world. The advantage of using such an innovation can be to gather visual information—such as people's facial expressions— for those individuals with visual impairments or autism who have difficulties receiving or decoding this information. *Iridescence* can also express non-verbally and mimic visual information through its dynamic behavior. To make this work, we borrow from the latest advancements in AI facial expression tracking technology and embed it in bio-inspired material systems.

Overall, this project is an attempt to explore the possibilities afforded by AI facial tracking technology and the dynamic behavior of a smart fashion item, with the intention to address psychosocial issues involving emotions and sensations and to see how these technologies might inform social interaction.

7 *Iridescence* is equipped with a facial tracking camera and an array of 200 flipping quills

Iridescence Farahi

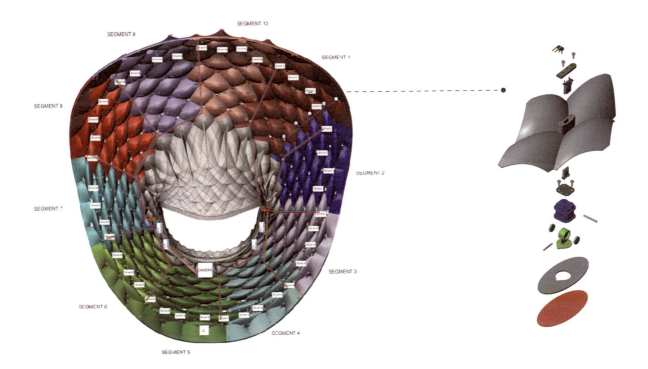

8   Left: Electrical wiring diagram shows location of 40 driver boards, 4 microcontrollers, and a camera
Right: Axonometric diagram shows a quill and its assembly to the collar

ACKNOWLEDGMENTS

This research is part of a broader ongoing collaboration with Paolo Salvagione and Julian Ceipek. I would like to thank them for their advice and helpful contributions to the production of this work. Special thank to Kathleen McCarthy and her team at the Museum of Science and Industry in Chicago for their generous support.

BEHNAZ FARAHI is a designer exploring the potential of interactive environments and their relationship to the human body working in the intersection of architecture, fashion, and interaction design. She also is an Annenberg Fellow and PhD candidate in Interdisciplinary Media Arts and Practice at USC School of Cinematic Arts. She has an Undergraduate and two Masters degrees in Architecture.

IMAGE CREDITS

Figures 1, 4, 7 © 2019 Kristina Varaksina

Figure 2, 3 © Image accessed from video: https://vimeo.com/3331560

Figures 5, 6 © 2019 Behnaz Farahi

Figure 8 © 2019 Behnaz Farahi & Paolo Salvagione

LIGHTWEAVE

Jason Kelly Johnson
California College of the Arts/
FUTUREFORMS

Nataly Gattegno
California College of the Arts/
FUTUREFORMS

1   Lightweave animates an otherwise neglected underpass with cascading patterns of light

A SERPENTINE CHANDELIER THAT BRINGS LIGHT, INTERACTIVITY AND PLAYFULNESS TO A RAILWAY UNDERPASS

Our cities are riddled with left-over and abandoned spaces: slots of land between highways and abandoned lots; spaces that lack jurisdictional clarity and are therefore left neglected. These spaces fragment the city fabric and separate neighborhoods, creating sectioned-off urban spaces and non-defined territories. What if we could take these spaces over and transform them into active, dynamic, and catalytic spaces? What if we could use them to stitch the urban fabric back together again? Could they become catalysts for urban change? *Lightweave* is a permanent installation that attempts to address these issues. It uses light to weave two neighborhoods together again, neighborhoods that had been previously severed by infrastructure.

Lightweave is a large urban chandelier that snakes through a pedestrian underpass, and is bound by the sidewalk, multiple train track lines above, bicycle and vehicular travel lanes, and a large stone wall. The project takes on multiple parameters by occupying the amorphous volume between jurisdictions and uses. It is both a sculptural canopy and a light fixture that emits enough light to safely move pedestrians through; it is artwork that beautifies and activates the underpass, and a way to render an otherwise dark and unwelcoming space safe and well-lit.

PRODUCTION NOTES

Artist:	FUTUREFORMS
Client:	NoMA Parks Foundation
Status:	Built
Dims:	15' x 170' x 30'
Location:	Washington DC
Date:	2019

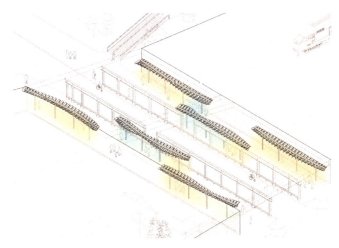

2   Lightweave occupies the full length of the underpass

3   Lightweave extends beyond the underpass

4   Lightweave appears to float above the sidewalk

Lightweave translates ambient sounds from the city into dynamic auroras of patterned LED light. Slowly changing effects are activated by the noise and vibration of passing trains, cars, and other sounds from the neighborhood. The installation animates the underpass and creates a meditative and interactive urban experience.

The artwork consists of six 65-foot long curvaceous sections (390 feet total) of suspended stainless steel and LED lattices. Lightweave is mounted approximately 11 feet above the sidewalk on a steel column and beam structure that does not touch the underpass above in any way to maintain emergency accessibility requirements for the train tracks above.

The lattices were custom built and fabricated in our shop using a CNC tube bender. Once each section was completed, a 'test-fit' was performed in our office hallway to ensure the alignment of the geometries and to catch any fabrication or labeling errors. In parallel, we tested and assembled all the electronics in our studio before integrating them into the

steel lattices. This allowed us to experiment with the LEDs and test the larger affects we aimed to achieve with *Lightweave*.

Each section contains 26 computer-controlled LED modules. Sensors embedded at various locations in each section feed information to a computer that triggers variable and overlapping responses from the LEDS. Individual vibrations send cascading lights through the tunnel, rendering the whole installation as a barometer of activity, a way to read the city and connect to its infrastructural pulse in a more intuitive and visceral way.

Lightweave uses a combination of custom hardware with a professional Pharos lighting controller system communicating with DMX LED drivers, sensors, and the internet. Motion sensing is accomplished with industrial microwave sensors. Sound amplitude input utilizes a LMV324 sound detector board, while programming was completed in a scripting environment called Lua (similar to C or C++).

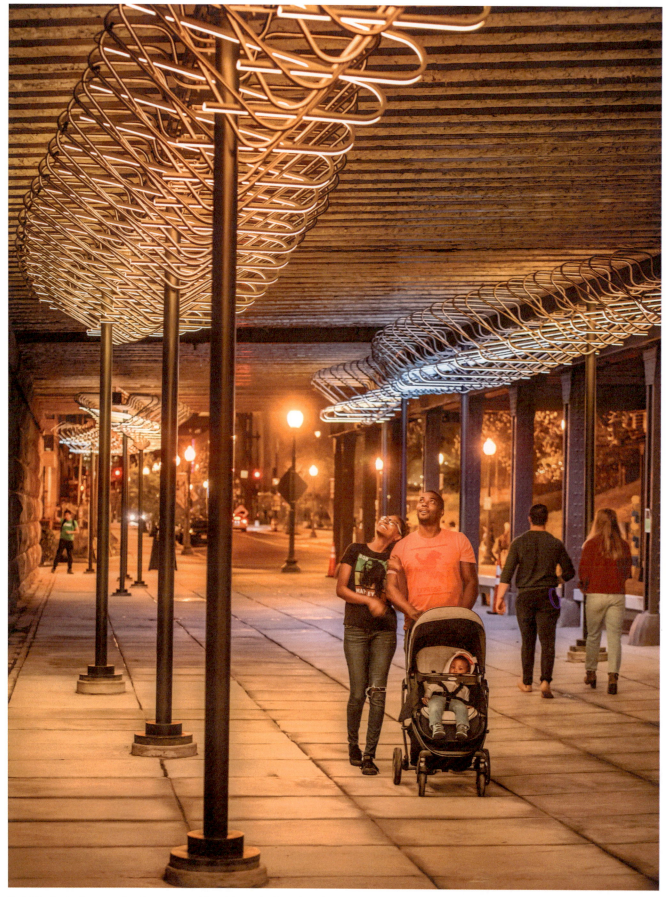

5   Light effects change as vibration sensors pick up information from the trains above and the surrounding environment

6   Fabricating the steel lattices in our shop

7   Producing electronics and testing interactions

8   Confirming the overall geometry in our hallway

9   Testing color, effect and the scale of interactions

ACKNOWLEDGMENTS

Consultants: Endrestudio (Structural Engineering),
Maramoja (Interaction), MC Dean (Electrical Engineering).

IMAGE CREDITS

Figure 3: Photograph by Sam Kittner
Figure 4: Photograph by MCDean
Figure 5: Photograph by Sam Kittner
All other drawings and images by the authors.

Jason Kelly Johnson is co-founder of FUTUREFORMS, a studio
that explores the intersections of art and design with public space,
performance, advanced fabrication technologies, robotics, and
responsive building systems. Jason [b.1973] was born in Canada.
He received his BSc from the University of Virginia and a M.Arch
from Princeton University. He is currently an Associate Professor
of Architecture at the California College of the Arts in San
Francisco, where he co-directs the Digital Craft Lab.

Nataly Gattegno is co-founder of FUTUREFORMS, a studio that
explores the intersections of art and design with public space,
performance, advanced fabrication technologies, robotics, and
responsive building systems. Nataly [b.1977] was born and raised
in Athens, Greece. She received a MA from Cambridge University,
St. John's College, UK, and a M.Arch from Princeton University.
She is currently an Associate Professor of Architecture at the
California College of the Arts in San Francisco.

The Arroyo Bridge: Collaborative Robotics for Large Scale Construction

R. Scott Mitchell
USC School of Architecture

Diana Yan
MADWORKSHOP

Alex Weisfeld
MADWORKSHOP

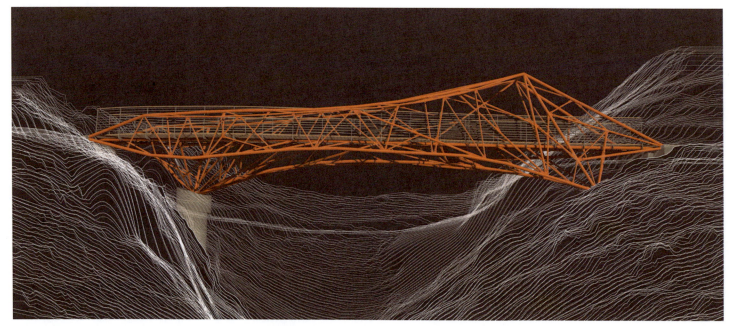

1   The Arroyo Bridge spanning 80 feet (25 meters) over hilly terrain

The Arroyo Bridge is a project in progress. It began initially as a parametric design project at the University of Southern California (USC) School of Architecture, and has developed into a design-build research initiative focusing on the future of collaborative robotics, metrology, and logistics in large-scale, permanent construction. The project is a prefabricated 80 foot (25 meter) asymmetrical pedestrian bridge designed and permitted for permanent installation. The span is comprised of tubular HSS members each connected with either unique part-to-part gusset plates or fishmouth fitted connections. The entire bridge is fully engineered and currently in the final stages of fabrication.

Due to the structure's complex geometry comprised of 299 unique pipes, 234 unique gusset plates, 50 variable-diameter custom connectors, and 4 custom foundation pile-caps, typical methods of weldment fixturing would have been cost prohibitive. This issue pushed our team to develop software for new fabrication techniques. Computational design in Rhino and Grasshopper allowed us to quickly move through iterations with feedback between structural analysis and architectural design.

PRODUCTION NOTES

Architect:	David Martin
Design:	Gigante AG
Engineer:	SGH
Support:	Autodesk Robotics Lab Autodesk Technology Center Boston
Status:	Under Construction
Type:	Pedestrian Bridge
Location:	California
Date:	2019

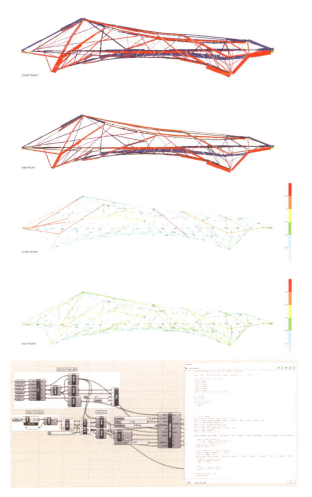

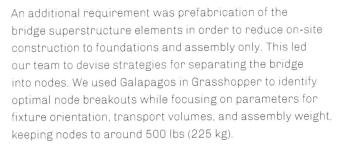

2   Computational tools used to generate from structural analysis

3   Initial prototype with human-robot collaborative process

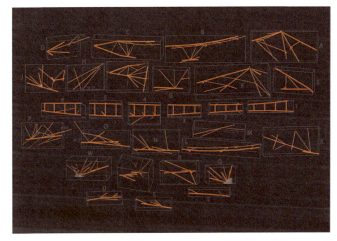

4   Script analysis output for node fixture orientation, transport, and weight

An additional requirement was prefabrication of the bridge superstructure elements in order to reduce on-site construction to foundations and assembly only. This led our team to devise strategies for separating the bridge into nodes. We used Galapagos in Grasshopper to identify optimal node breakouts while focusing on parameters for fixture orientation, transport volumes, and assembly weight, keeping nodes to around 500 lbs (225 kg).

We prototyped fabrication workflows using KUKA robots and KUKAprc. At this point, our team began collaboration with Autodesk Robotics Lab engineers Evan Atherton and Heather Kerrick. Their efforts produced on-site AR visualizations, additional fabrication strategies, and automating robot path planning for multiple robot types. Robot targets were exported from Grasshopper into Autodesk Maya for robot simulation using the Mimic plug-in. Additional Mimic functionality was developed specifically for automating path planning. Mimic can produce KRL or RAPID, which we could take directly to robots.

Among other challenges, finding a suitable space to fabricate the bridge was a priority. In December 2018, our team started a residency at the Autodesk Technology Center, a research facility in Boston focusing on architecture, engineering and construction.

We utilized one of the facility's robotic arms (a linear track-mounted ABB IRB4600) to act as a precision welding positioner and metrology device, thus replacing the majority of standard fixturing elements, and we developed custom tooling for measurement, flat metal pickup, and round metal pickup. Using Mimic, we could move from a production-ready Rhino model to fully simulated and programmed RAPID in 30 minutes on average. Our team tack-welded parts and bracing with robotic precision to assist state-code certified human welders for the final assembly in California.

Owing to the complex geometry and the required joint penetration welds, it was necessary to develop a specialized welding technique using inflatable gas bladders to

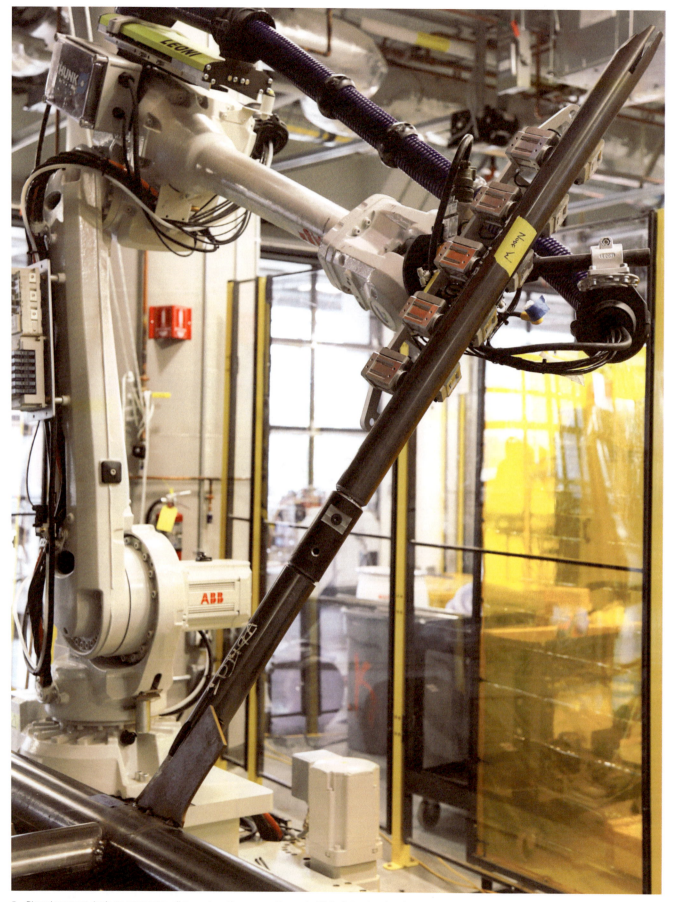

5   Pipe placement during a connector alignment routine, connecting node D5 (in fixture) and node W (assembled later)

6   Organizing pipe inventory in the project area

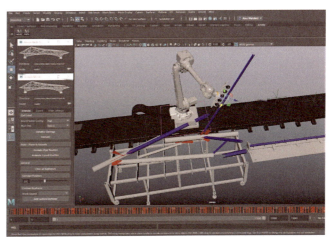

7   Automated path planning in Autodesk Maya using the Mimic plug-in

8   Tooling for robotic gusset placement using a Schunk magnet

9   Tooling for robotic pipe placement using an array of SMC magnets

flood joints with argon. This process removed the need for backer bars on complicated joints. To aid in the final installation, we are now developing new field registration and calibration survey strategies with our partners at Autodesk Research. We are 85% complete at this time and expect to begin installation in early September of 2019 .

ACKNOWLEDGMENTS

Mary and David Martin

MADWORKSHOP Foundation

Autodesk Robotics Lab
Autodesk Technology Center Boston

Adan Macias

REFERENCES

Bechthold, Martin. 2010. "The Return of the Future: A Second Go at Robotic Construction." *Architectural Design* 80(4): 116-21.

Helm, Volker. 2014. "In-Situ Fabrication: Mobile Robotic Units on Construction Sites." *Architectural Design* 84(3): 100-07.

Kerber, Ethan, Tobias Heimig, Sven Stumm, Lukas Oster, Sigrid Brell-Cokcan, and Uwe Reisgen. 2018. "Towards Robotic Fabrication in Joining of Steel." In *Proceedings of the 35th International Symposium on Automation and Robotics in Construction and Mining (ISARC)*.

Kolarevic, Branko, and José Pinto Duarte. 2018. *Mass Customization and Design Democratization*. Abingdon: Routledge.

Stumm, Sven, Johannes Braumann, and Sigrid Brell-Cokcan. 2016. "Human-Machine Interaction for Intuitive Programming of Assembly Tasks in Construction." *Procedia CIRP* 44: 269-74.

Thoma, Andreas, Arash Adel, Matthias Helmreich, Thomas Wehrle, Fabio Gramazio, and Matthias Kohler. 2019. "Robotic Fabrication of Bespoke Timber Frame Modules." In *Robotic Fabrication in Architecture, Art and Design (ROBARCH) 2018*, edited by J. Willmann et al. Springer, Cham.

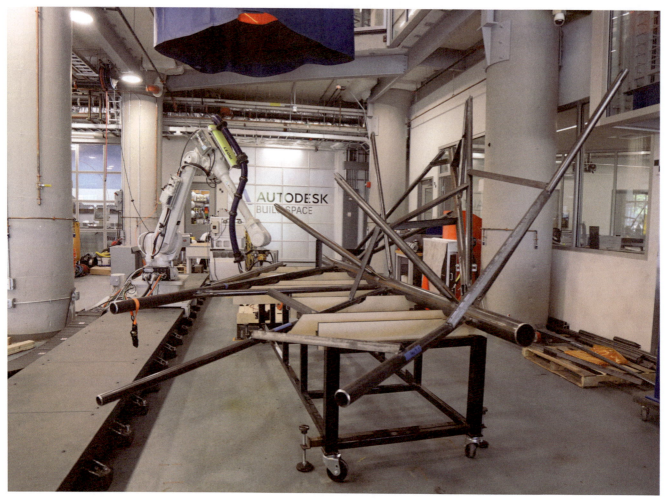

10 A completed assembly on the mobile fixture-cart after adding transport bracing in the Autodesk Technology Center (node P)

R. Scott Mitchell is the owner and principal of Gigante AG, a design-build and fabrication consulting firm based in Los Angeles. He has worked for Gehry Partners, Morphosis, Bestor Architecture and Atelier Van Lieshout (Rotterdam). Earlier in his career, he worked as a laboratory machinist and structural fabricator. He is an Associate Professor of Practice at the USC School of Architecture where he has been teaching digital fabrication and design since 2007. His first book, *Give Me Shelter: Architecture Takes on the Homeless Crisis*, was published by ORO Editions in 2018. He is currently on the non-profit advisory boards of 826LA, a children's educational organization and MADWORKSHOP, a design education foundation

11 Human tack welding parts positioned and measured by an IRB 4600

12 Construction scaffolding for foundation work

13 A shipment of 10 pre-fabricated nodes from Boston to Los Angeles

14 Final structural welds using the argon flooding procedure in California

Diana Yan is a computational designer and Madworkshop Fellow. She received a Bachelor of Architecture from the University of Southern California and a Master in Design Studies from Harvard University.

Alex Weisfeld is a computational designer, robot programmer, and fabricator. He received a Bachelor of Architecture from the University of Southern California.

Component / Assembly: Prototyping Domestic Space

Adam Marcus
California College of the Arts

Matt Hutchinson
California College of the Arts

1   Full-scale stair prototype (L. Maghlakelidze, Y. Liu)

A prototype begins as an experiment which may or may not become a building.
— Barkow Leibinger, *An Atlas of Fabrication* (2009)

This project explores the architectural detail as a locus for reconsidering contemporary domesticity in the context of new technologies of design, fabrication, and assembly. The research, conducted through academic design studios and full-scale prototypes, looks to the Case Study House Program spearheaded by John Entenza of Arts & Architecture magazine in Los Angeles (1945-1966) as a model for how architects can re-conceptualize and re-materialize domestic space through an understanding of digital and robotic fabrication processes. Just as the architects of the Case Study House Program crafted new prototypes for domestic living inspired by the postwar (modernist) logics of mass production, this work speculates how contemporary (postmodernist) logics of mass customization can inform new models of domestic space appropriate for today.

Rather than accepting the architectural detail as a predetermined assemblage of standardized parts or products, this research speculates on the spatial, programmatic, and social possibilities of customizable, parametric, and bespoke details—and how such a paradigm can relate to emerging forms of domesticity.

The pedagogical structure of the studio relies upon focused analysis of precedent as a way to drive both conceptual and material logics. Each project revisits a domestic component

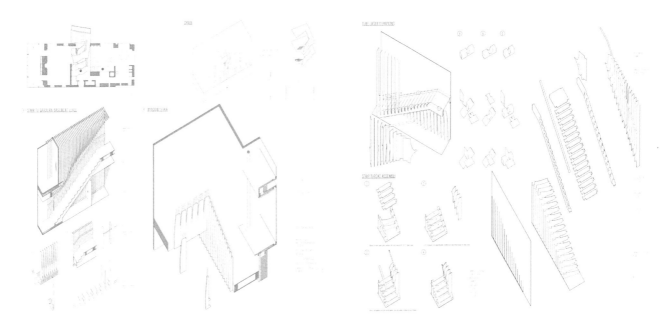

2   Domestic component analysis of NADAAA's Rock Creek House (left) and redesign of component utilizing digital fabrication techniques (S. Moriuchi).

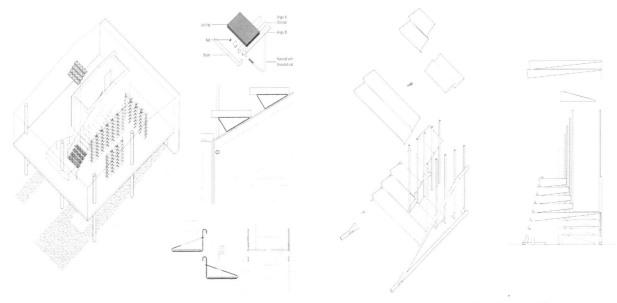

3   Domestic component analysis of Lina Bo Bardi's Glass House (left) and redesign of component utilizing digital fabrication techniques (J. Luo)

from a seminal architectural case study, typically a stair or other aspect of circulation. This component is then reverse engineered in light of contemporary manufacturing techniques that can process standardized, off-the-shelf material components in customized and bespoke ways. Students explore these processes through large-scale study models and physical prototypes that emphasize tectonic fidelity and the effects produced by customized components. Discoveries made at the scale of the joint and detail scale up to a spatial component, a proto-architectural interior condition not yet at the scale of a building, but large enough to understand ideas of public/private relationships within the space. It is only then—after

thoroughly understanding tectonic, space, and effect— that the ideas scale up to a sited architectural proposal. The ambition is to develop new understandings of part/ whole relationships that reflect contemporary modes of living at all scales, from the component to the broader architectural organization.

The research focuses specifically on readily available industrial manufacturing processes as a way to innovate within existing frameworks of architectural production. These include subtractive 2- and 2.5-dimensional cutting and milling, as well as rotary laser cutting, which allows for complex 3-dimensional cuts into standard steel tubing.

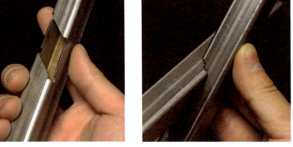

4   The studio partnered with local manufacturers to integrate the production of full-scale laser-cut steel sheet and tube. The workflow required an ability to operate between softwares, scales, and dimensions to translate geometry from a design model to fabrication toolpaths. The rotary laser process, in particular, demanded a comprehensive grasp of solid modeling and the unique constraints of the machine, something to which architecture students at this level typically are not exposed. The iterative process allowed students to refine and optimize tolerance, joinery, and assembly as they worked toward the final proof-of-concept mockup.

5   Full-scale stair prototype with custom laser cut treads/risers and rotary laser cut steel frame (L. Navarro, L. Trinh).

6   Full-scale component prototype with integrated stair and ladder (V. Balunsat, M. Candelaria).

Component / Assembly Marcus, Hutchinson

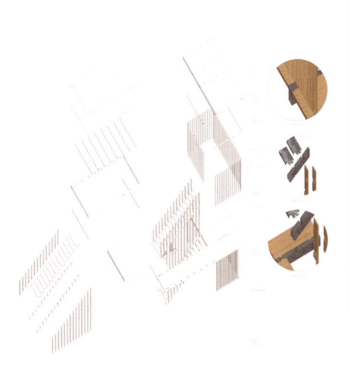

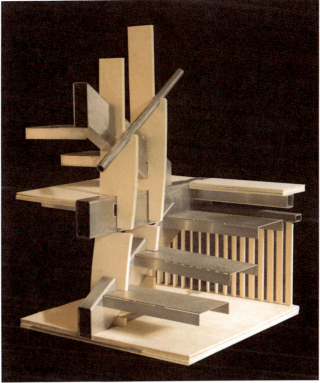

7 Full-scale component prototype integrates rotary laser cut parts for structure, stair stringer, and suspended privacy screen (A. Burlinska, S. Moriuchi)

8   Full-scale stair prototype integrates friction-fit waterjet cut treads and rotary laser cut stringers, without the use of fasteners (J. Guo, H. Jia).

With the support of local industry partners, the students develop full-scale prototypes that constitute proof-of-concept for both tectonic assembly and ideas about customization and variation that inform broader spatial and programmatic strategies.

While 2D laser cutting of sheet goods and even 3D laser cutting of tubes are not new technologies, their application towards holistically bespoke architectural systems is rare. Occasionally such techniques are leveraged in highly custom projects, but it is not common to find the fabrication processes, architectural forms, construction details, and programmatic goals so purposefully and intrinsically linked.

3D tube laser cutting allows for almost complete geometric freedom, yet most of the time it is used for standardized, mass produced industrial parts. In this instance, the studio encourages students to embrace the technology's capacities for mass customization, by emphasizing computational workflows that link variation among parts to carefully calibrated assemblies at the building scale. Detailed understanding of parameters such as tolerance offsets between parts and self-aligning/self-jigging features is incorporated into parametric models that facilitate a feedback loop between digital and physical.

By melding computational workflows and advanced fabrication processes with the pragmatics of building and assembly, this research advocates a subtle but nonetheless radical shift in how we design and make architecture. By recasting the premise of the Case Study House Program in our contemporary context of mass-customization, the work seeks to align programmatic mandates for the flexible, the adaptable, and the bespoke with the manufacturing capabilities that can embed these qualities into architectural components.

ACKNOWLEDGMENTS

Instructors: Matt Hutchinson and Adam Marcus

Students: Vishnu Balunsat, Ania Burlinska, Marlene Cacho, Mia Candelaria, Jiaqi Cao, Jinda Guo, Viviani Isnata, Haonan Jia, Samuel Kilpatrick, Thomas Krulevitch, Tianran Li, Yue Hector Liu, Zixuan Liu, Jingyi Luo, Levan Maghlakelidze, Shunta Moriuchi, Lilliam Navarro, Ronak Patel, Pete Pham, Jae Hyun Seo, Jieh Jia Tan, Leon Trinh, Joshua Van Heidrich, Chuan Zhu

Fabrication Support: Tube Service Co., Seaport Stainless, Autodesk San Francisco Technology Center

Sponsorship: Autodesk San Francisco Technology Center, CCA Faculty Development Grant

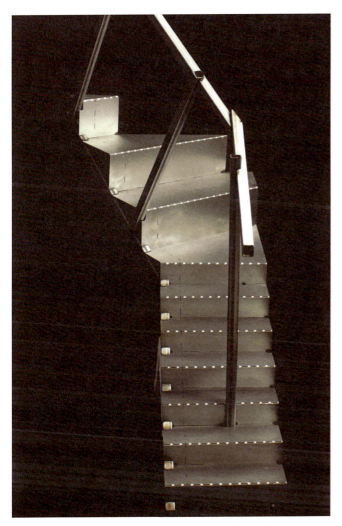

9   Full-scale stair prototype demonstrates intentionally misaligned components that are nonetheless precisely integrated and assembled (S. Kilpatrick, J. Tan).

REFERENCES

Barkow Leibinger Architekten. 2009. *An Atlas of Fabrication*.
Exhibition, 27 Feb 2009 – 27 Mar 2009. London: Architectural
Association.

IMAGE CREDITS

All drawings and images by the students of the
Component/Assembly studio at California College of the Arts.

Adam Marcus is an Associate Professor of Architecture at
California College of the Arts in San Francisco, where he teaches
design studios in design computation and digital fabrication and
co-directs CCA's Architectural Ecologies Lab. He has previously
taught at Columbia University, the University of Minnesota, and the
Architectural Association's Visiting School Los Angeles. He directs
Variable Projects, an award-winning design and research studio
in Oakland, California. Adam is a graduate of Brown University
and Columbia University's Graduate School of Architecture,
Planning and Preservation, and he currently serves on the Board
of Directors for the Association for Computer-Aided Design in
Architecture (ACADIA).

Matt Hutchinson is an architect and educator interested in
exploring the potential convergence of traditional and digital
fabrication processes within architecture. He draws from a diverse
range of professional experiences to inform the multi-disciplinary
and collaborative approach for his own design practice, PATH.
Matt earned his Bachelor of Architecture at Kent State University
and his Master of Architecture at Yale University, currently teaches
as adjunct faculty in the architecture department at the California
College of the Arts in San Francisco, and has recently been a fellow
at Autodesk's Pier 9 Residency program.

Hypersecting Objects

Niccolo Casas
UCL Bartlett

Gabriel Esquivel
Texas A&M University
Garrett Farmer
Texas A&M University
Nicholas Houser
Texas A&M University
Oswaldo Veliz
Texas A&M University

1   In the Hypersecting Objects installation, all the objects participating in the final compositions -the context included- are, at the same time, joined together and preserved distinct; they coexist within the same space in the same time while affirming their own identities. (Garrett Farmer, 2018)

Hypersection is a term, a concept and a procedure debating the processes of transitions that are non mediated. It is intended as a specific way to integrate distinct items, a way that doesn't require adaptation, bending or adjustment, in which it is absolute and not gradual.

The "Hypersecting Objects" installation was constructed to disclose the unexpected and unexpressed qualities of distinct objects that hypersect. Hypersection, in the way it occurs, it connects and separates at the same time; it intentionally preserves and breaks all existing relations, destabilizing what things are and revealing novel emergent and non explicit qualities.

Hypersection displays a unique emerging effect, that of producing continuity within discontinuity. Each hypersection is a non-mediated interaction that concurrently engenders union and separation in an emergent continuous sign that both keeps separate and joins its generators. The non-adherence between superficial patterns or surface components with the architectural body generates a sort of discrepancy, similar to that of slippage, that has the generative quality of creating a series of strangely alluring design moments.

All compositional elements were conceived separately, preserving their formal identities, this by privileging non-mediated interactions and colliding overlays; booleans, overlaps, interruptions, crossings, steps and pauses.

PRODUCTION NOTES

Architects: Niccolo Casas/Gabriel
            Esquivel

Client: Christopher Lawrence
Status: Completed
Site Area: 775 sq. ft.
Location: Bryan, Texas
Date: 12/2018

2   The students worked with simple geometries, primitives and patterns. This was done in order to focus on their non-mediated combination (Aaron Sheffield, 2018)

3   In hypersection, there is no bottom up or top down straight relationship; both scale and hierarchical systematization can be broken with a loss of reference points. (Aaron Sheffield, 2018)

4   Hypersection generates all sorts of strange moments within the overall composition, in which shape, patterns and even structures are interestingly misaligned (Niccolo Casas, 2018)

In the Hypersecting Objects installation, the shift between digital techniques and analog processes became an exploration of material properties, in this case the use of plywood and drywall. What perfectly unrolls as a flat surface in the digital realm might not always result in its material equivalent. In this case both the plywood surface and its trussed skeleton with all of the impurities and kinks gave shape to the formal boolean operations that were first drawn out digitally.

If the exploration of Hypersection delivered researches on figures, patterns, and site as distinct and abstract objects the link between all of them was fabrication. In this, measured accounted steps were used in order to achieve maximal accuracy a flattening technique of the formal digital objects. This transfer of digital object to physical un-rolled prints achieves the first important hypersection. As the flat pieces of paper were cut out to achieve the desired accuracy, with the same criteria the physical material (wood) was cut or machinelly routed considering its properties in order to help us gain an understanding of how hypersection truly works as its own ontology.

The nature of this object/installation was the result of the subtraction and manipulation of primitives producing sharp moments. The process of "smoothing" the unpredicted "kinks" involved a repetitive process of bulking up the seams with drywall compound and sanding techniques. This surface reinterpretation of the object suggests that rather than using digital technology to reverse engineer the construction of the complex form, the digital tools should become a mechanism to better understand material and fabrication potential.

The main ambition of Hypersection was the understating of the objects' hidden qualities via their non- mediated combinations. They students worked by employing cubes, spheres, pipes, cylinders with minimal deformations,

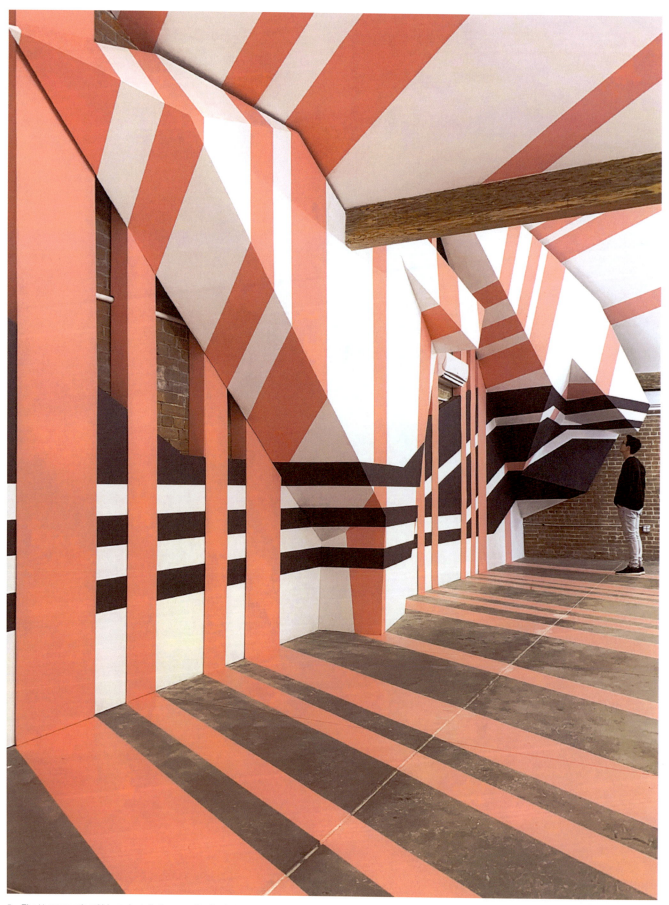

5 The Hypersecting Objects installation was the first attempt to employ hypersection as a founding principle, compositional methodology and construction procedure on a medium-scale architectural project. (Niccolo Casas, 2018)

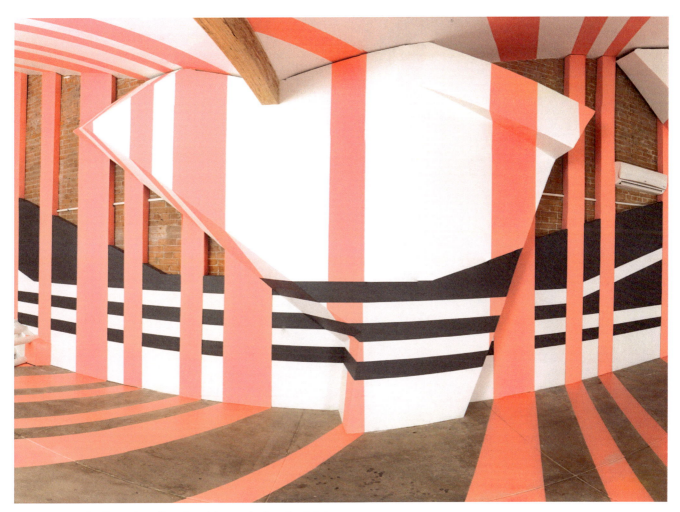

6   The process of rolling and unrolling allowed the transfer from the digital
     to the physical Object (Aaron Sheffield, 2018)

creating patterns both regular and irregular, and investi-
gating super-positions, overlaps and boolean operations.
Eventually, they all developed single proposals, thereby
understanding the potentialities of unrelated and non-mediated combinations. The extreme consequence of such
an operational methodology and philosophical approach
was that, instead of selecting one final proposal to be built,
the students were asked to hypersect their entire projects
as if those were independent objects. This resulted in an
installation design that was a sort of multi-dimensional
hypersection between totally unrelated objects and the site
itself.

ACKNOWLEDGMENTS
Cody Sonnier, Cesar Martinez, Alyssa Thomas, Lauren Lycan,
Hahnur Kim, Hannah Aldridge, Ian Saenz, Mackenzie Dillard, Mindy
Hogan

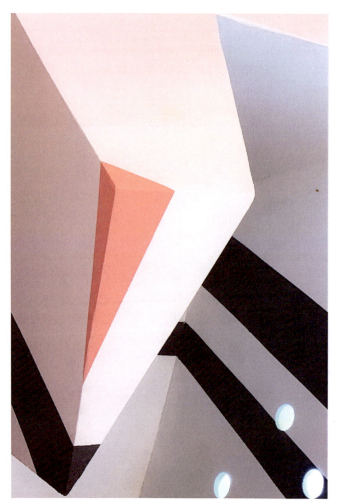

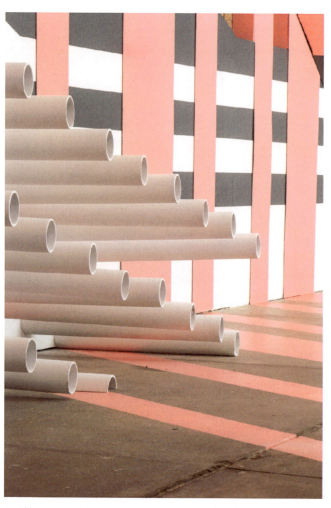

7   All moderated transitions, smooth mediations, bending, attractions and deformations were avoided (Niccolo Casas, 2018)

8   Objects were set to overlap, subtract and intersect freely, without any change or modification required.(Aaron Sheffield, 2018)

IMAGE CREDITS

Figure 1: Garrett Farmer, 2018

Figure 2, 3, 6, 8, 9: Aaron Sheffield, 2018

Figures 4, 5, 7:Niccolo Casas, 2018

Niccolo Casas Italian architect and professor, Niccolo Casas is also the principal and founder of Niccolo Casas Architecture, a visiting faculty member at RISD (Rhode Island School of Design) and a PhD candidate at the Bartlett UCL, London. He runs a multi-disciplinary practice for research and architecture that aims to combine several fields of specializations so as to offer an innovative and unique vision of the academic discipline and profession. His work spans from architecture to couture and fashion-tech, and from design to data visualization and medicine.

Gabriel Esquivel Gabriel Esquivel was born and educated as an architect in Mexico City with a degree from the National University and received his Master's Degree in Architecture from The Ohio State University. Gabriel Esquivel teaches architecture at the College of Architecture at Texas A&M University. He previously taught Architecture and Design at the Knowlton School of Architecture and the Design Department at Ohio State University. Gabriel is the director of the T4T Lab where he examines the integration of digital techniques and analogue conventions to exchange architectural information and its connection to contemporary theory.

Garrett Farmer Garrett Farmer graduated from Texas A&M in 2019 with a bachelor's degree in Environmental Design and a minor in Fabrication & Product Design. He has experience working in various architecture firms, fabrication studios, and non-profit organizations. He currently works in Los Angeles, California at the design firm Ball-Nogues. His interests are in architectural fabrication and aims to get his master's degree in a related field.

Nicholas Houser Nicholas Houser is a 22 y/o designer from Round Rock, Texas, a graduate of Texas A&M, working at xmade Barcelona and starting the M-Arch program at the University of Pennsylvania. His pursuits lay within the strengthening of the connection between the Architectural discourse and profession. Working at firms of

9   In the Hypersecting Object installation, the patterns floating along the surfaces are in reality hypersocting objects that lost their physicality and remained within the spaces as traces of their non-mediated interaction with the visible objects (Aaron Sheffield, 2018)

various degrees and kinds, O'connell Robertson (Austin, Texas), Atelier Sotamaa (Helsinki, Finland), MFGA (New York City, New York), and xmade (Barcelona, Spain), fortify the agenda to reach the goal.

Oswaldo Veliz Ozzy Veliz a graduate of Texas A&M University, has been developing skills within the realm of fabrication. His interests rely heavily on material research, and digital technologies. Throughout the years he has honed skills in places such as at Ball-Nogues Studio where he interned for a year (Los Angeles, California), as a Digital Fabrication Assistant at Texas A&M University where he primarily specialized and explored methods and workflow of 3D Printing. He is currently working at a Boutique Art Studio Voila Creative Studio (Los Angeles, California) as a Designer as well as doing freelance design and fabrication consultancy.

Arctic LiDAR
Logistic Landscapes of the Arctic

Daniele Profeta
Syracuse University

1   3D LiDAR scan visualization image of the Container Harbor in Saint Petersburg (equirectangular still image from the video 'Arctic LiDAR' (© 2019 A/P)

VISUALIZING THE SPACE OF LOGISTICS

ARCTIC LiDAR is an immersive 360° media installation exploring the quickly expanding logistic landscape of the Arctic coast. It was exhibited at the Smithsonian's National Museum of American History during the 2019 ACCelerate Festival to represent Syracuse University. The work was developed in collaboration with Liam Young and STRELKA Institute for Media, Architecture and Design in Moscow.

Logistics can be defined as the detailed coordination of the complex space constituted by infrastructures, information, goods, and people that makes the production and circulation of stuff possible. Stretching across nation-state borders, redefining territoriality through the cartographic space of global supply chains, and constructing an operational state of unencumbered continuous movement of goods, the space of logistics is dramatically transforming the world we inhabit.

Part documentary, part projective narrative, the video presented in this installation articulates projective scenarios for the expanding logistic space of global commerce along the coast of the Arctic. Using 3d LiDAR scanning, this project captures the primary nodes of this far reaching infrastructure—ranging from Dry Ports to Ice Breakers and Rail Terminals—and re-assembles them in a composite, speculative landscape.

PRODUCTION NOTES

Architect: A/P Practice

Client: Syracuse University

Status: Completed

Site Area: 90 sq. ft.

Location: Smithsonian Institute,
             National Museum of American
             History in Washington DC

Date: 2019

2   Arctic LiDAR at the Smithsonian Institution (© 2019 A/P)

3   Installation operating across physical and VR space (2019, © A/P).

4   2.5d relief panels extracted from the 3d LiDAR scans captured on site (© 2019 A/P).

MACHINE VISION AND HUMAN ENGAGEMENT

LiDAR, an acronym for Light Detection and Ranging, is a remote sensing technology that uses light pulses to measure and three-dimensionally map vast territories with ever-increasing precision. A sensor emitting pulses of infrared light, millions of times per second, constructs point-clouds as a representation of the environment being surveyed: a spatial database so detailed that can be used to detect and interact with surrounding objects. Across the territory of the Arctic, it is used to establish politics, proto-cols, and economies of autonomous distribution.

It is through the lens of the apparatus of machinic vision and its network of activations that we can begin to see the traces of this emerging urbanism of logistics across the territory.

Using a Virtual Reality headset, the viewers are transported in the automated landscape of logistics, where driver-less trucks, robotic cranes, and remote-sensing drones operate through the dense point cloud. Immersed in a 360° video moving across this speculative landscape, this operative mode of vision is slowly contaminated by atmospheric elements foreign to the machinic eye, prompting the viewer to develop an intimate engagement with the material. The viewers are caught in an ambiguous territory where a bodily experience of this harsh landscape and its extreme climate reasserts its presence in an otherwise human-less environment. And yet, the observer's point of view is constrained to the rigid linear movement of what appear to be indifferent machines, reinforcing the agency of the automated infrastructure upon the construction of this territory.

ACROSS PHYSICAL AND DIGITAL SPACE

The physical space of the installation engages with the three dimensional database of LiDAR vision by sampling a series of spatial elements surveyed on these sites to construct a space of engagement across multiple mediated realities. The digital trace of the surfaces of cargo containers—one of the artifacts that most dramatically transformed this network of logistics—as well as gantry cranes, ice-breaker

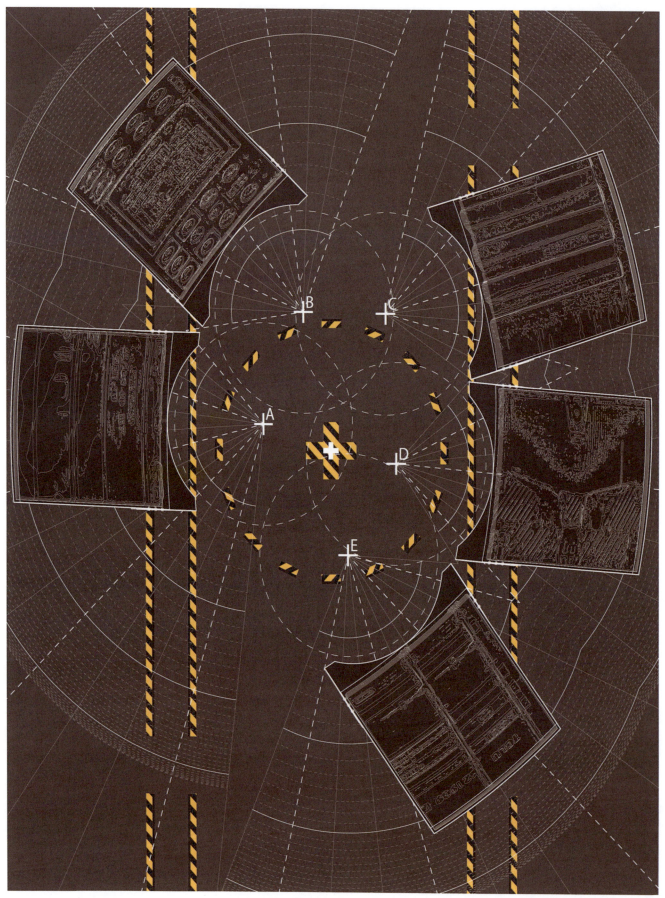

5   Drawing of the unfolded panels showing the overall layout of the installation highlighting the established central viewpoint of the viewer (© 2019 A/P)

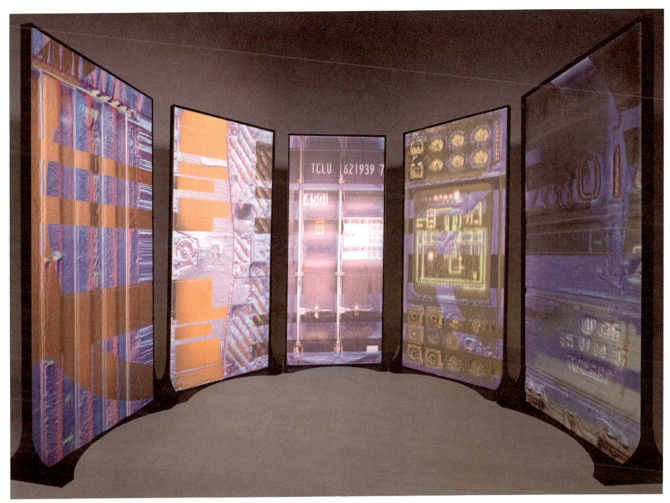

6   Overall view of the five panels each standing in for one of the crucial nodes of the landscape of logistics used in the video installation (© 2019 A/P)

navigation control panels, and train wagons are translated into relief panels to extend and confront the content presented through the VR headset. Rather than focusing on the reproduction of accurate digital copies, these artifacts attempt to highlight the tension between their material surfaces and the machinic vision that surveyed them by juxtaposing their true 'RGB', that is Red, Green and Blue color information, with the 'XYZ' data, a so-called 'normal map' visualizing the directionality of each of the points surveyed. Each panel is CNC milled out of high density foam and is then printed with this edited texture layer.

Ultimately the installation urges the viewers to understand the architecture of logistics beyond a 'technicality', a politically neutral act of management, but rather predicating itself around ideas of anticipation and prediction, acting as a transforming agent of the built environment, of territories as well as of bodies.

ACKNOWLEDGMENTS

This installation was made possible by the generous support of Syracuse University School of Architecture and by the work and contribution of Zexi Tang, Erick Sanchez, Michael Giannattasio, and John Bryant.

The 3d-surveyed material has been collected during an expedition through the Arctic led by Liam Young as part of the 'New Normal' program of STRELKA Institute for Media, Architecture and Design in 2017. Many thanks to Leica Geosystems, who generously donated the use of their equipment for the digital survey of those sites.

Graphic Design by Common Name.

Many thanks to 'The Image Press' in Cicero, NY for their contribution to the prints in this show and to 'Falso Industries' and 'BBD Coaters' in Syracuse, NY for the fabrication of the metal frames.

IMAGE CREDITS
All drawings and images by the author.

7   Close-Up view of one of the relief panels (© 2019 A/P)

8   CNC toolpath following the 3d scanned data (© 2019 A/P)

9   Relief panel and overlayed print highlighting the relationship between machinic vision and human perception of these surfaces (© 2019 A/P)

10 Container Dry Port in Saint Petersburg rendered as an autonomous landscape of motion; equirectangular image from the video 'Arctic LiDAR' (© 2019 A/P)

11 Nickel Harbor in Murmansk as captured by LiDAR scans and edited to embed environmental effects; equirectangular still image from the video 'Arctic LiDAR' (© 2019 A/P)

Daniele Profeta is an Italian architect and designer, and a partner at A/P Practice, a collaborative partnership with Maya Alam. Their projects combine everyday digital habits, contemporary imaging technologies, and traditional craftsmanship to surpass an introverted conversation and open up novel forms of practice. A/P Practice work has received support by institutions including the Smithsonian Institution, the A+D Museum of Architecture and Design in Los Angeles, Syracuse University, and the Festival des Architectures Vives in Montpellier, France.

Daniele holds a Master of Architecture from Princeton University and completed his undergraduate studies between La Sapienza University in Rome and KTH School of Architecture in Stockholm, where he graduated with Honors.

LightTank
a cross-reality sculpture

Uwe Rieger
arc/sec Lab
University of Auckland

Yinan Liu
arc/sec Lab
University of Auckland

1   LightTank at the Ars Electronica Festival 2018 (Photo: Tom Mesic)

LightTank is an interactive cross-reality installation that augments a lightweight space-frame structure with digital constructions in the form of holographic line drawings.

The project was developed for the Ars Electronica Festival and presented in the Cathedral of Linz in 2018. It aims to expand principles of augmented reality (AR) headsets from a single person viewing experience to a communal multi-viewer event. To achieve this goal, LightTank uses an anaglyph stereoscopic projection method that, combined with simple red/cyan cardboard glasses, allows the creation of 3D imagery. Four LiDAR laser scanners (LiDAR-UK 2019) monitor four large transparent projection walls. These are assembled to an X-shape to form an inhabitable, tower-like construction.

The project was conceived by the arc/sec Research Lab at the University of Auckland. Giving equal attention to both design aspects, the physical and the digital, the Lab develops user responsive architecture, where dynamic properties of the virtual world are an integral part of the built environment. Embedded in the School of Architecture, the Lab aims to re-connect the intangible computer world with the multisensory qualities of architecture and urban spaces. With a focus on intuitive forms of user interaction, the arc/sec Lab uses large-scale prototypes and installations as the driving research method to test and to demonstrate new design principles of hybrid constructions. These investigations stretch widely across the disciplines. LightTank`s sensor solution was developed in collaboration with the Augmented Human Lab at the Bio-Engineering Institute at the University

PRODUCTION NOTES

Architect: Uwe Rieger & Yinan Liu

            arc/sec Lab in collaboration with the Augmented Human Lab

Client: Ars Electronica

Status: Completed

Location: Mariedom, Linz, Austria

Date: 2018

2   LightTank at the Cathedral of Linz

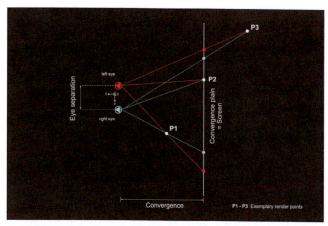

3   Anaglyph stereoscopic rendering principle

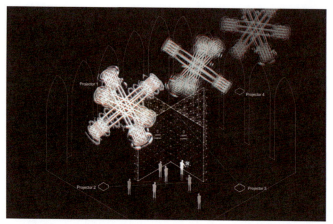

4   Physical screen intersecting with digital object

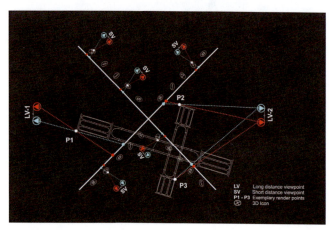

5   Multi-perspective anaglyph rendering principle

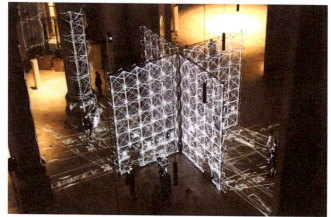

6   Transparent screen in X shape setup.

of Auckland, which focuses on enabling human-computer interfaces as natural extensions of body, mind, and behaviour.

Next to building upon the principles and technologies of previous installations (arc/sec Lab 2019), LightTank takes advantage of two stage techniques to generate free-floating imagery. One is the use of a gauze fabric as a projection carrier and the second is the application of stereoscopic imagery on transparent surfaces.

Examples showing the effective use of gauze projection screens to create inhabitable environments are the performances Hakanaï (Adrien M & Clair B 2013) and Shiro (Nonotak Studio 2016). These setups use projections to generate the dynamic appearance and disappearance of two-dimensional light-walls. While the projection material and the projection logic are similar, LightTank follows a different approach, whereby screens are not used as ephemeral dividers, but as invisible surfaces to display stereoscopic information that translates into a three dimensional AR environment.

A comparable immersive effect is created with the 4D Box system (Culture Yard 2018). Through wearing active shutter glasses (PhysOrg 2009), the audience is able to see stage actors operating in an augmented environment. The setup combines stereoscopic projections with a theatre effect called "Pepper's Ghost" that uses a transparent film to reflect images onto the stage (Nickell 2005, 291). However, the presented AR environment remains rendered from a single view perspective, solely visible for the seated audience on one side of the film.

LightTank offers a 360° solution by rendering stereoscopic images with multiple perspectives on a four-sided transparent gauze structure. This allows for viewing and interaction from multiple positions. The projected scenery consists of two components: small 3D icons and large spatial digital constructions. The small holographic icons are rendered with a short distance viewpoint and allow a 'touch' at arm's length. Aligned in a shelf-like arrangement, they are monitored by 2D LiDAR laser sensors. Comparable to a holographic touch screen, the icons allow the visitor to trigger and control the large constructive animations. These expand over the whole screen and are rendered

LightTank Rieger, Liu

7   3D glasses with anaglyph filters (Photo: Tom Mesic)

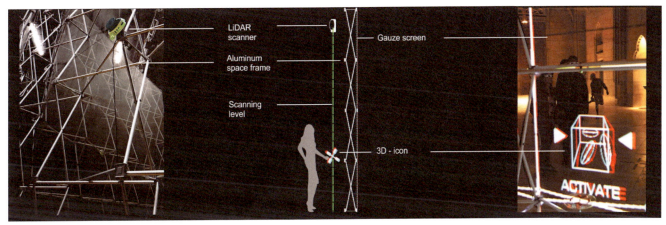

8   LiDAR sensors monitoring visitor interaction with holographic icons

for two opposing, long distance viewpoints. The virtual constructions are calibrated 1:1 to superimpose both the aluminium space-frame structure and the architecture of the cathedral. The combination of physical structure, sensors and digital construction creates a user interactive inhabitable hybrid sculpture, blurring the boundaries between the tactile and the virtual.

ACKNOWLEDGMENTS

The project was designed and developed by the arc/sec Lab, Uwe Rieger and Yinan Liu, at the School of Architecture and Planning at the University of Auckland, www.arc-sec.com

The sensing solution by was developed by the Augmented Human Lab, Roger Boldu, Heetesh Alwani, Haimo Zhang, Suranga Nanayakkara at the Auckland Bioengineering Institute at the University of Auckland, www.ahlab.org

REFERENCES

Adrien M & Claire B. 2013. "Hakanaï." Accessed May 20, 2019. https://www.am-cb.net/projets/http-www-am-cb-net-projets-hkn.

arc/sec Lab. 2019. "Projects." Accessed May 20, 2019. https://www.arc-sec.com.

Culture Yard et al. 2018 "4D Box." Accessed May 20, 2018, https://ars.electronica.art/error/en/4dbox/.

LiDAR-UK. 2019. "What is a Lidar." Accessed May 20, 2019, http://www.lidar-uk.com/what-is-lidar/.

Nickell, Joe. 2005. *Secrets of the Sideshows*. 4th ed. Lexington, Kentucky: University Press of Kentucky.

Nonotak Studio. 2016. "Shiro". Project page. Accessed May 20, 2019. https://www.nonotak.com/_SHIRO.

PhysOrg. 2009 "Active Shutter 3D Technology for HDTV." Accessed May 20, 2019. https://phys.org/news/2009-09-shutter-3d-technology-hdtv.html.

IMAGE CREDITS

Figures 1, 7, 9, 11: Photos by Tom Mesic, Ars Electronica, August 9, 2018; licensed under creative commons (attribution: non commercial), https://www.flickr.com/search/?text=ars%20electronica%20LightTank

All other drawings and images by the authors

9   LightTank displaying the Swarm Scene (Photo: Tom Mesic)

Uwe Rieger is a co-founder of the Berlin-based interdisciplinary group [kunst + technik] e.V. and the architecture office XTH-berlin. Since 2006, he has served as Associate Professor for Design and Design Technology at the University of Auckland, where he established the arc/sec Lab for Cross-Reality Architecture and Interactive Systems. As an architect and researcher, Uwe's work focusses on responsive architectural systems using mixed reality concepts. His large-scale installations have been exhibited at renowned institutions such as the Museum of Modern Art Barcelona, the Venice Architecture Biennale, Ars Electronica, the International Building Exhibition IBA, the National Museum of Indonesia, and the National Museum of New Zealand Te Papa Tongarewa.

Yinan Liu received a MArch(Prof)(Hons) degree from the University of Auckland. She is the lead technologist at the arc/sec Lab and coordinator of the Digital Research Hub at the School of Architecture and Planning at the University of Auckland. Yinan is the founding partner of arc/sec Solutions ltd., which develops customised applications for cross-reality environments.

10 LightTank video 3:10

11 LightTank with the view through the main nave of the Cathedral of Linz

Wilding Agents

Nicolas Azel
Carnegie Mellon University

Marantha Dawkins
Carnegie Mellon University

1   Aggregated field of simulated rover behavior on a vacant lot

Wilding Agents merges machinic behavior and plant community interactions to create living, dynamic intelligences and resilient landscapes. The central proposition of this project is a behavioral rather than compositional model for design, in which the material and logical relationship between agent and environment is codetermined: a rover catalyzes synthetic urban environments by automating ecological participation in undervalued urban space. The rover builds an intimate relationship with its environment as not its ward but its memory, as it reads and writes information onto the landscape.

Ecosystems "grope from one temporal equilibrium to the next," with each assemblage creating a context that generates and conditions subsequent states. The critical structural difference between ecosystems and contemporary urban infrastructure is that an ecosystem's aim is resiliency, not stability (Mostafavi 2003, 5). While urban infrastructure is built on a foundation of positivist frameworks of control (DeLanda 1997, 144), an adaptive design methodology can un-bind urban design approaches from deterministic urban fabric. *Wilding Agents* seeks to achieve this decoupling by intersecting computation and urban ecology using a multi-leveled behavioral model that accepts a range of hyperlocal inputs including field conditions, infrastructural capacity, and community preference. The model is comprised of a custom seed and plant behavior database; a community interface; and the rover, which uses sensors to inform planting behaviors. Simulating rover and plant dynamics reveals the model's expansion into urban and ecological networks and connects it to larger-scale issues like stormwater management, habitat connectivity, and soil health.

PRODUCTION NOTES

Location: Pittsburgh, PA

Date: 2018

2   Vacancy and green network in the Larimer neighborhood of Pittsburgh

In *Vehicles: Experiments in Synthetic Psychology*, neuro-scientist and cyberneticist Valentino Braitenberg describes a series of vehicles that make use of simple interactions between motors and sensors to produce behaviors like fear, aggression, love, and exploration. Adding threshold devices enables the emergence of value systems, deci-sion-making, and phenomena that look very much like logic and knowledge. But if, for example, a vehicle must perform a calculation too large for its limited parts, it may use the landscape as a tool, i.e. marking the ground to represent large numbers, then crawling back to read the numbers for calculation. The vehicle is "never able to comprehend these large numbers at any one moment. But using itself as an instrument in a larger scheme involving the environment... it ends up with the correct result" (Braitenberg 1984, 24). The implications of an agent-based behavioral system, which simultaneously learns from and changes mutable field conditions, are profoundly ecological. The *Wilding Agents* behavioral model is designed to test plant and robotic interaction through landscape transformation.

Rather than producing, controlling, and navigating data-rich digital environments towards specific performative goals, the intention behind this work is for the machine to be data poor and the environment to be materially, intelligently, and ecologically rich. This project probes the potential for a hybrid intelligence that entangles accessible hardware and simple behavioral coding with plant behavior and urban ecology. Choreographing behavioral reinvigoration of vacant land reshapes the way value can be conceived and distributed in the city; sites are engaged as ecological tissue, urban infrastructure, and cultural medium. Simulations of the project model reveal patterned urban networks that have the potential to challenge normative procedures of land acquisition, aggregation, development, and displacement; and to relieve pressures on overburdened city infrastructures using a non-linear design methodology. *Wilding Agents'* open-ended epistemological framework recasts the relationship between the biological and mechanical to untether itself from anthropocentric biases and build toward resilient urban ecologies.

3   The rover's site behavior combines a data-driven wandering algorithm and sensor-based responses
    to encourage the Braitenbergian emergence of resilient ecologies

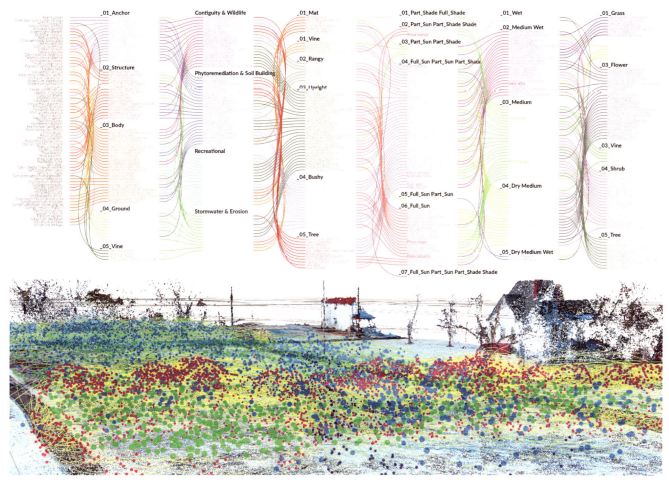

_01_Anchor
_02_Structure
_03_Body
_04_Ground
_05_Vine

Contiguity & Wildlife
Phytoremediation & Soil Building
Recreational
Stormwater & Erosion

_01_Mat
_01_Vine
_02_Rangy
_03_Upright
_04_Bushy
_05_Tree

_01_Part_Shade Full_Shade
_02_Part_Sun Part_Shade Shade
_03_Part_Sun Part_Shade
_04_Full_Sun Part_Sun Part_Shade
_05_Full_Sun Part_Sun
_06_Full_Sun
_07_Full_Sun Part_Sun Part_Shade Shade

_01_Wet
_02_Medium Wet
_03_Medium
_04_Dry Medium
_05_Dry Medium Wet

_01_Grass
_03_Flower
_03_Vine
_04_Shrub
_05_Tree

4   The database organizes plants into communities using functional, morphological, aesthetic, logistical, and environmental classifications, conceptualizing planting in terms of interdependent communities that allow for diverse, robust, low maintenance, functional, adaptive, and richly layered landscapes

REFERENCES

Braitenberg, Valentino. 1984. Vehicles: Experiments in Synthetic Psychology. Cambridge, Mass.: MIT Press.

DeLanda, Manuel. 1997. A Thousand Years of Nonlinear History. New York: Zone Books.

Mostafavi, Mohsen. 2003. "Landscapes of Urbanism". Landscape Urbanism: A Manual for the Machinic Landscape. London: Architectural Association.

IMAGE CREDITS

All drawings and images by the authors.

Nicolas Azel is an urban designer and educator whose works seek to engage landscape systems for the promotion of egalitarian communities and increased ecological health. He specializes in design computation, with a focus on complex urban systems and landscape ecology. Some of Nico's past work includes community planning, infrastructural systems planning, and public parks design, as well as coding custom 3D modeling plugins, visualizing complex datasets, and developing interactive simulations of storm water runoff. He is currently based out of Pittsburgh where he works as an Urban Designer at Evolve::Environment Architecture, and teaches at Carnegie Mellon University School of Architecture.

Marantha Dawkins is an urban designer whose work focuses on the convergence of urbanization, landscapes of climate change, and the formation of ecological niches. Marantha's recent research has probed expressivity, subjectivity, and symbiosis as they relate to ecological relationships and performance. She currently teaches in the School of Architecture at Carnegie Mellon University.

ACADIA 2019 CREDITS

CONFERENCE CHAIRS

Kory Bieg is an Associate Professor of Architecture at the University of Texas at Austin. He received his Master of Architecture from Columbia University and is a registered architect in the states of California and Texas. Since 2013, he has served as Chair of the TxA Emerging Design + Technology conference, and co-Director of TEX-FAB Digital Fabrication Alliance. He has served on the Board of SXSW Eco Place by Design and the Association for Computer Aided Design in Architecture.

In 2005, Kory Bieg founded OTA+, an architecture, design, and research office that specializes in the development and use of current, new, and emerging digital technologies for the design and fabrication of buildings, building components, and experimental installations. OTA+ uses current design software and CNC machine tools to both generate and construct conceptually rigorous and formally unique design proposals

Danelle Briscoe received her Master of Architecture degree from Yale University where she was awarded the Eero Saarinen Design Excellence Award. Her Bachelor of Architecture degree is from the University of Texas at Austin with Honors. Her ten years of work experience includes being a designer at Frank Gehry Partners, LLP, designer at Marmol+Radziner LLP (both in Los Angeles)and UT residency at Centerbrook Architects (in Connecticut).

In 2016, Danelle completed her book titled Architecture Information Modelling. Danelle has served on the Board of Directors for ACADIA and also on the Editorial Board for the International Journal of Architectural Computation (IJAC)

Clay Odom founded the design practice of StudioMODO in 2009 to develop design, branding, conceptual art, and furniture projects and research.

Clay is an Associate Professor at The University of Texas School of Architecture. His research involves inquiry into the generation and manipulation of a range of subjective spatial, contextual, experiential, and para-cinematic outcomes - such as atmosphere, sublimity, and delight, which emerge through objective, effective processes of design, fabrication, and installation.

CLOSING PANEL

Michelle Addington is dean of The University of Texas at Austin School of Architecture, where she holds the Henry M. Rockwell Chair in Architecture. Formerly, she served as Gerald Hines Chair in Sustainable Architectural Design at the Yale University School of Architecture and was jointly appointed as a Professor at the Yale University School of Forestry and Environmental Studies. Prior to teaching at Yale, she taught at the Harvard University Graduate School of Design, the Technical University of Munich, Temple University and Philadelphia University.

Ian Bogost is the Ivan Allen College Distinguished Chair in Media Studies and Professor of Interactive Computing at the Georgia Institute of Technology, where he also holds appointments in the Scheller College of Business and the School of Architecture. He is a Founding Partner at Persuasive Games LLC, an independent game studio, and a Contributing Editor at The Atlantic. The author or co-author of ten books, Bogost's latest is Play Anything.

Neil Leach teaches at Tongji University, FIU and the EGS, and has also taught at the AA, Harvard GSD, Columbia GSAPP, Cornell, SCI-Arc and USC. He is an academician in the Academy of Europe, and is the recipient of two NASA Innovative Advanced Concepts fellowships to fund research into developing 3D print technologies for the Moon and Mars. He has published 40 books including: Designing for a Digital World (Wiley, 2002), Digital Tectonics (Wiley, 2004), Digital Cities (Wiley, 2009), Machinic Processes (CABP, 2010), Robotic Futures (Tongji UP, 2015), Swarm Intelligence (Tongji UP, 2017), Computational Design (Tongji UP, 2017), Digital Fabrication (Tongji UP, 2017) and 3D Printed Body Architecture (Wiley, 2017).

Marcelyn Gow is principal of servo los angeles, a design collaborative invested in the development of architectural environments integrating synthetic ecologies with shifting material states. servo's work has been exhibited at the Venice Architecture Biennale, the Centre Pompidou, Archilab, Artists Space, the SCI-Arc Gallery, the MAK Center for Art and Architecture, the Storefront for Art and Architecture and the San Francisco Museum of Modern Art (SFMoMA) and is in the permanent collections of SFMoMA and the FRAC Centre. Gow received her Architecture degrees from the Architectural Association and Columbia University, as well as a Dr.Sc. from the ETH Zurich. Her doctoral dissertation Invisible Environment: Art, Architecture and a Systems Aesthetic explores the relationship between aesthetic research and technological innovation. Gow is currently the Coordinator of SCI-Arc's M.S. Design Theory & Pedagogy postgraduate program and she teaches design studios and history and theory seminars at SCI-Arc.

Kathy Velikov is an Architect, Associate Professor at University of Michigan's Taubman College, and current President of ACADIA. She is founding partner of the research-based practice rvtr, which serves as a platform for exploration and experimentation in the intertwinements between architecture, the environment, technology, and sociopolitics. She is a recipient of the Architectural League's Young Architects Award and the Canadian Professional Prix de Rome in Architecture. Her work has received numerous awards and has been published and exhibited internationally. Kathy is co-author of Infra Eco Logi Urbanism (Park Books, 2015) and is currently working on a new book, Ambiguous Territory: Architecture, Landscape and the Postnatural (Actar, 2020).

SESSION CHAIRS

Daniel Koehler is a city-architect, and co-founder of lab-eds. He is an assistant professor for architecture computation in the School of Architecture at The University of Texas at Austin. Before, Daniel taught in the BPro-program at the Bartlett School of Architecture in London, and was a postdoctoral research fellow at Innsbruck University. Daniel has studied Architecture at the University of Applied Arts in Vienna, and he completed his PhD at Innsbruck University. His work has been exhibited in Prague, Milan, Graz, Montreal, London, and is part of the permanent collection of the Centre Pompidou. He is the author of "The Mereological City", a study on the part-relationships between architecture and its city in the modern period. His current research focuses on the urban implications of distributive technologies.

Aleksandra Jaeschke is an Assistant Professor of Architecture and Sustainable Design at the University of Texas at Austin. A graduate of the Architectural Association in London (AA Diploma 2005), she holds a doctorate from Harvard GSD (Doctor of Design, 2018), and is a licensed architect in Italy where she practiced at AION, an architectural firm she co-founded and co-directed until her move to the U.S. In 2013, AION held a solo exhibition Eco-Machines in the Wroclaw Museum of Architecture in Poland. In recognition of the work developed by the studio, she received the Europe 40 Under 40 Award for 2011. Jaeschke's current interests range from mainstream discourses on sustainability and broader notions of ecology, to cross-scalar integrative design strategies and the role of architects in transdisciplinary projects. She is the 2019 Wheelwright Prize winner.

Alvin Huang, AIA, NOMA is a Los Angeles based architect with a global profile. He is an award-winning architect, designer, and educator specializing in the integrated application of material performance, emergent design technologies and digital fabrication in contemporary architectural practice. His work spans all scales ranging from hi-rise towers and mixed-use developments to temporary pavilions and bespoke furnishings.

His design work has been published and exhibited widely and has gained international recognition with over 40 distinctions at local, national, and international levels including being selected as one of 50 global innovators under the age of 50 by Images Publishing in 2015, being featured as a "Next Progressive" by Architect Magazine in 2014, and being named one of Time Magazine's 25 Best Inventors of 2013.

Adam Marcus is an Associate Professor of Architecture at California College of the Arts in San Francisco, where he teaches design studios in design computation and digital fabrication and co-directs CCA's Architectural Ecologies Lab. He has previously taught at Columbia University, the University of Minnesota, and the Architectural Association's Visiting School Los Angeles. He directs Variable Projects, an award-winning design and research studio in Oakland, California, and he is a partner in Futures North, a public art collaborative dedicated to exploring the aesthetics of data. Adam is a graduate of Brown University and Columbia University's Graduate School of Architecture, Planning and Preservation, and he currently serves on the Board of Directors for the Association for Computer-Aided Design in Architecture (ACADIA).

Tsz Yan Ng is an Assistant Professor at Taubman College, University of Michigan. Her material-based research and design primarily focus on experimental concrete forming (hard) and textile manipulation (soft), often times in direct exchange and incorporating contemporary technologies to develop novel designs for building and manufacturing. A common thread to her work investigates questions of labor in various facets and forms – underscoring broader issues of industrial manufacturing innovation, of human labor, crafting, and aesthetics. She's the principal of an independent architecture and art practice with built works in the US and China. Her practice, collaborative in nature and interdisciplinary in scope, ranges in scale from textile manufacturing facilities to commercial retail interiors and installations. Ng joined Taubman College as the Walter B. Sanders Fellow (2007-08) and was also the Reyner Banham Fellow at the University of Buffalo from 2001-2002.

Behnaz Farahi is a designer and creative technologist based in Los Angeles working at the intersection of fashion, architecture and interactive design. Trained as an architect and specializing in physical computing and 3D printing, her ultimate goal is to enhance the relationship between human beings and their environment by following morphological and behavioral principles inspired by natural systems.

Behnaz is a recipient of a number of prestigious awards including the 2016 World Technology Design Award and the 2016 Innovation By Design Fast Company Design Award. She is currently an Annenberg Fellow and is completing her PhD in Interdisciplinary Media Arts and Practice at the USC School of Cinematic Arts.

Gabriel Esquivel was born and educated as an architect in Mexico City with a degree from the National University and received his Master's Degree in Architecture from The Ohio State University. He previously taught Architecture and Design at the Knowlton School of Architecture and the Design Department Ohio State University.

After joining the architecture faculty at Texas A&M University, he has investigated the benefits and vehicles of a heterogeneous model that integrates both technology and architecture's proprietary devices. Gabriel began to explore different possibilities of research through fabrication in partnership with the Department of Aerospace Engineering, specifically on the relationship of composite and SMA materials with architectural automated surfaces. Gabriel is the director of the T4T Lab at Texas A&M University where he examines the integration of digital technology to exchange architectural information and its connection to contemporary theory.

Jason Kelly Johnson is lead artist and founding design partner of FUTUREFORMS. He brings to the team an expertise in computational design and advanced digital fabrication, through the lens of critical art production and interactive technologies. Jason [b.1973] was born and raised in Canada. He received a Bachelor of Science from the University of Virginia, and a Masters of Architecture from Princeton University. Johnson is currently an Associate Professor at the CCA in San Francisco, CA.

Güvenç Özel is an architect, artist and technologist. He is a Suprastudio Lead at UCLA A.UD IDEAS Program, and the principal of Ozel Office. His work is at the intersection of architecture, technology and media. His projects and experimental installations were exhibited in museums and galleries in the USA and Europe, including Istanbul Museum of Modern Art and The Saatchi Gallery in London. His recent design and research on 3D printing was awarded one of the top prizes at NASA's 3D Printed Habitats Competition. His latest installation Cypher was sponsored by Google's Artists and Machine Intelligence Program and debuted at SXSW. At UCLA IDEAS, his masters design studio research focuses on virtual reality, machine learning/ AI, robotics and sensing interfaces with support from leading companies such as Autodesk, Microsoft, Oculus and others.

Ersela Kripa is an Assistant Professor at Texas Tech College of Architecture, a registered architect, and founding partner of AGENCY, an architectural research, design, and advocacy practice established in New York City in 2010 with Stephen Mueller. Born and raised under communist dictatorship in Albania, Ersela's work is particularly focused on uncovering the machinations of the securocratic regimes that surveil and control public lives. She uses data as agency in marginalized urban environments by operating where hacker culture meets the city, cataloguing, analyzing, and co-opting ways in which citizens intersect with urban systems.

Ersela is recipient of the 2010-2011 Rome Prize in Architecture, the 2018 Emerging Voices Award from the Architectural League of New York, two MacDowell Colony fellowships, and the New York Foundation for the Arts fellowship. Ersela's work has been exhibited at the 12th Architectural Venice Biennale, the Hong-Kong Shenzhen Urbanism Biennale, Storefront for Art and Architecture, among others.

Ian Bogost is the Ivan Allen College Distinguished Chair in Media Studies and Professor of Interactive Computing at the Georgia Institute of Technology, where he also holds appointments in the Scheller College of Business and the School of Architecture. He is a Founding Partner at Persuasive Games LLC, an independent game studio, and a Contributing Editor at The Atlantic. The author or co-author of ten books, Bogost's latest is Play Anything.

Matias del Campo is a registered architect, designer and educator. Founded together with Sandra Manninger in Vienna 2003, SPAN is a globally acting practice best known for their application of contemporary technologies in architectural production. Their award-winning architectural designs are informed by advanced geometry, computational methodologies, and philosophical inquiry. This frame of considerations is described by SPAN as a design ecology. Most recently Matias del Campo was awarded the Accelerate@CERN fellowship, the AIA Studio Prize and was elected into the boards of directors of ACADIA. He guest edited an edition of AD, Architectural Design. SPAN's work is in the permanent collection of the FRAC, the MAK in Vienna, the Benetton Collection, and the Albertina. He is Associate Professor at Taubman College for Architecture and Urban Planning, University of Michigan

Virginia San Fratello draws, builds, 3D prints, teaches, and writes about architecture as a cultural endeavor deeply influenced by craft traditions and contemporary technologies. She is a founding partner in the Oakland based make-tank Emerging Objects. Wired magazine writes of her innovations, "while others busy themselves trying to prove that it's possible to 3-D print a house, Rael and San Fratello are occupied with trying to design one people would actually want to live in". She also speculates about the social agency of architecture, particularly along the borderlands between the USA and Mexico, in her studio RAEL SAN FRATELLO. You can see her drawings, models, and objects in the permanent collections of the Museum of Modern Art, the Cooper Hewitt Smithsonian Design Museum, and the San Francisco Museum of Modern Art.

Uli Dangel is an Associate Professor and Program Director for Architecture at The University of Texas at Austin where he teaches courses in design, construction, architectural detailing, and structural design. He received a Diploma in Architecture from Universität Stuttgart and a Master of Architecture from the University of Oregon. His professional career led him to London where he worked for internationally renowned architecture firms Foster and Partners as well as Grimshaw. He is a registered architect in Germany, the United Kingdom, and Texas.

Uli Dangel's research and teaching focus on the use of wood in construction, its influence on building culture and craft, and how it contributes to the advancement of sustainable practices at the scale of local and global economies. Birkhäuser Basel published his books Sustainable Architecture in Vorarlberg: Energy Concepts and Construction Systems and Turning Point in Timber Construction: A New Economy in 2010 and 2017 respectively.

Dana Cupkova is a Co-founder and a Design Director of EPIPHYTE Lab, an interdisciplinary architectural design and research collaborative. She holds an Associate Professorship at Carnegie Mellon University's School of Architecture and serves as the Track Chair for the Master of Science in Sustainable Design program. She was a member of the ACADIA Board of Directors from 2014 to 2018, and currently serves on the Editorial Board of The International Journal of Architectural Computing (IJAC). Dana's work positions the built environment at the intersection of ecology, computational processes, and systems analysis. In her teaching and research, she interrogates the relationship between design-space and ecology as it engages computational methods, thermodynamic processes, and experimentation with geometrically-driven performance logics. In May 2018 Epiphyte Lab received the Next Progressives design practice award by ARCHITECT Magazine, The Journal of The American Institute of Architects.

ACADIA
ORGANIZATION

The Association for Computer Aided Design in Architecture (ACADIA) is an international network of digital design researchers and professionals that facilitates critical investigations into the role of computation in architecture, planning, and building science, encouraging innovation in design creativity, sustainability and education.

ACADIA was founded in 1981 by some of the pioneers in the field of design computation including Bill Mitchell, Chuck Eastman, and Chris Yessios. Since then, ACADIA has hosted over 30 conferences across North America and has grown into a strong network of academics and professionals in the design computation field.

Incorporated in the state of Delaware as a not-for-profit corporation, ACADIA is an all-volunteer organization governed by elected officers, an elected Board of Directors, and appointed ex-officio officers.

CONFERENCE
MANAGEMENT

PEER REVIEW
COMMITTEE

CONFERENCE CHAIRS

Kory Bieg, *Associate Professor, The University of Texas at Austin School of Architecture*

Danelle Briscoe, *Associate Professor, The University of Texas at Austin School of Architecture*

Clay Odom, *Associate Professor, The University of Texas at Austin School of Architecture*

WORKSHOPS CHAIRS

Ben Rice, *Lecturer, The University of Texas at Austin School of Architecture*

EVENTS COORDINATOR

Riley Moore, *Chief of Staff, The University of Texas at Austin School of Architecture*

CONFERENCE ADMINISTRATIVE SUPPORT

Jasmin Blas-Mendieta, *Student Program Coorindator, The University of Texas at Austin School of Architecture*

Justin Taylor, *Administrative Associate, The University of Texas at Austin School of Architecture*

Kelsey Stine, *Communications Coordinator, The University of Texas at Austin School of Architecture*

Maria Carlsen, *Assistant to the Dean, The University of Texas at Austin School of Architecture*

TECHNICAL SUPPORT

Robert Stepnoski, *Senior Lecturer, The University of Texas at Austin School of Architecture*

WEBSITE

Kory Bieg, *Associate Professor, The University of Texas at Austin School of Architecture*

COPY EDITING FOR PUBLICATION

Gabi Sarhos

GRAPHIC IDENTITY

Bruno Canales, Kory Bieg, Danelle Briscoe, Clay Odom

LAYOUT + DESIGN

Crystal Torres, Kory Bieg, Danelle Briscoe, Clay Odom

PUBLICATION EDITORS

Kory Bieg, Danelle Briscoe, Clay Odom

THE UNIVERSITY OF TEXAS AT AUSTIN SCHOOL OF ARCHITECTURE (CONFERENCE ACADEMIC HOST)

Michelle Addington, *Dean, The University of Texas at Austin School of Architecture*

Francisco Gomes, *Associate Dean for Academic Affairs, The University of Texas at Austin School of Architecture*

Allan Shearer, *Associate Dean for Research and Technology, The University of Texas at Austin School of Architecture*

Charlton Lewis, *Associate Dean for Student Affairs, The University of Texas at Austin School of Architecture*

Ulrich Dangel, *Program Director for Architecture, The University of Texas at Austin School of Architecture*

Igor Siddiqui, *Program Director for Interior Design, The University of Texas at Austin School of Architecture*

Hope Hasbrouck, *Program Director for Landscape Architecture, The University of Texas at Austin School of Architecture*

CONFERENCE
MANAGEMENT

The Association for Computer Aided Design in Architecture (ACADIA) is an international network of digital design researchers and professionals that facilitates critical investigations into the role of computation in architecture, planning, and building science, encouraging innovation in design creativity, sustainability and education.

ACADIA was founded in 1981 by some of the pioneers in the field of design computation including Bill Mitchell, Chuck Eastman, and Chris Yessios. Since then, ACADIA has hosted over 30 conferences across North America and has grown into a strong network of academics and professionals in the design computation field.

Incorporated in the state of Delaware as a not-for-profit corporation, ACADIA is an all-volunteer organization governed by elected officers, an elected Board of Directors, and appointed ex-officio officers.

PRESIDENT
Kathy Velikov, *University of Michigan*
president@acadia.org

VICE-PRESIDENT
Jason Kelly Johnson, *California College of the Arts*
vp@acadia.org

SECRETARY
Brian Slocum, *Universidad Iberoamericana*
secretary@acadia.org

VICE-SECRETARY
Mara Marcu, *University of Cincinnati*

TREASURER
Mike Christenson, *North Dakota State University*
treasurer@acadia.org

VICE-TREASURER
Jason Kelly Johnson, *California College of the Arts*

MEMBERSHIP OFFICER
Phillip Anzalone, *New York City College of Technology*
membership@acadia.org

TECHNOLOGY OFFICER
Andrew Kudless, *California College of the Arts*
webmaster@acadia.org

DEVELOPMENT OFFICER
Alvin Huang, *University of Southern California*
development@acadia.org

COMMUNICATION OFFICER
Adam Marcus, *California College of the Arts*
communications@acadia.org

BOARD OF DIRECTORS
2018 (Term: Jan 2019 - Dec 2019)

Brandon Clifford
Mara Marcu
Tsz Yan Ng
Lauren Vasey
Andrew John Wit
Behnaz Farahi
Adam Marcus
Gilles Retsin
Jane Scott
Skylar Tibbits
Melissa Goldman *(alternate)*
Phillip Anzalone *(alternate)*
Matias del Campo *(alternate)*
Manuel Jimenez Garcia *(alternate)*
Christoph Klemmt *(alternate)*
Gernot Riether *(alternate)*

ACADIA
ORGANIZATION

Virginia San Fratello draws, builds, 3D prints, teaches, and writes about architecture as a cultural endeavor deeply influenced by craft traditions and contemporary technologies. She is a founding partner in the Oakland based make-tank Emerging Objects. Wired magazine writes of her innovations, "while others busy themselves trying to prove that it's possible to 3-D print a house, Rael and San Fratello are occupied with trying to design one people would actually want to live in". She also speculates about the social agency of architecture, particularly along the borderlands between the USA and Mexico, in her studio RAEL SAN FRATELLO. You can see her drawings, models, and objects in the permanent collections of the Museum of Modern Art, the Cooper Hewitt Smithsonian Design Museum, and the San Francisco Museum of Modern Art.

Uli Dangel is an Associate Professor and Program Director for Architecture at The University of Texas at Austin where he teaches courses in design, construction, architectural detailing, and structural design. He received a Diploma in Architecture from Universität Stuttgart and a Master of Architecture from the University of Oregon. His professional career led him to London where he worked for internationally renowned architecture firms Foster and Partners as well as Grimshaw. He is a registered architect in Germany, the United Kingdom, and Texas.

Uli Dangel's research and teaching focus on the use of wood in construction, its influence on building culture and craft, and how it contributes to the advancement of sustainable practices at the scale of local and global economies. Birkhäuser Basel published his books Sustainable Architecture in Vorarlberg: Energy Concepts and Construction Systems and Turning Point in Timber Construction: A New Economy in 2010 and 2017 respectively.

Dana Cupkova is a Co-founder and a Design Director of EPIPHYTE Lab, an interdisciplinary architectural design and research collaborative. She holds an Associate Professorship at Carnegie Mellon University's School of Architecture and serves as the Track Chair for the Master of Science in Sustainable Design program. She was a member of the ACADIA Board of Directors from 2014 to 2018, and currently serves on the Editorial Board of The International Journal of Architectural Computing (IJAC). Dana's work positions the built environment at the intersection of ecology, computational processes, and systems analysis. In her teaching and research, she interrogates the relationship between design-space and ecology as it engages computational methods, thermodynamic processes, and experimentation with geometrically-driven performance logics. In May 2018 Epiphyte Lab received the Next Progressives design practice award by ARCHITECT Magazine, The Journal of The American Institute of Architects.

Henri Achten, *Czech Technical University in Prague*

Viola Ago, *Rice University*

Sean Ahlquist, *Taubman College, University of Michigan*

Chandler Ahrens, *Washington University in Saint Louis*

Masoud Akbarzadeh, *University of Pennsylvania*

Suleiman Alhadidi, *University of New South Wales*

Ana Anton, *Institute of Technology in Architecture, ETH Zürich*

Phillip Anzalone, *New York City College of Technology*

German Aparicio, *California Polytechnic State University - Pomona*

Imdat As, *University of Hartford*

Joshua Bard, *Carnegie Mellon University*

Amber Bartosh, *Syracuse University*

Martin Bechthold, *Harvard Graduate School of Design*

Chris Beorkrem, *University of North Carolina, Charlotte*

Kory Bieg, *The University of Texas at Austin*

Johannes Braumann, *Institute for Advanced Architecture of Catalonia*

Danelle Briscoe, *The University of Texas at Austin*

Nicholas Bruscia, *University at Buffalo*

Jason Carlow, *American University of Sharjah*

Paolo Cascone, *COdesignLab*

Joseph Choma, *Clemson University*

Mike Christenson, *University of Minnesota*

Angelos Chronis, *Austrian Institute of Technology*

Brandon Clifford, *Massachusetts Institute of Technology*

Greg Corso, *Syracuse University*

Kristof Crolla, *Chinese University of Hong Kong*

Dana Cupkova, *Carnegie Mellon University*

Pierre Cutellic, *Institute of Technology in Architecture, ETH Zürich*

Mahesh Daas, *University of Kansas*

Martyn Dade-Robertson, *Newcastle University*

Daniel Davis, *WeWork*

Matias del Campo, *Taubman College, University of Michigan*

Marcella Del Signore, *Tulane University*

Antonino Di Raimo, *University of Portsmouth*

Rachel Dickey, *University of North Carolina, Charlotte*

Nancy Diniz, *Central Saint Martins, University of the Arts London*

Mark Donohue, *California College of the Arts*

Gabriel Esquivel, *Texas A&M University*

Alberto T. Estévez, *Universitat Internacional de Catalunya*

Behnaz Farahi, *University of Southern California*

Thom Faulders, *California College of the Arts*

Michael Fox, *California Polytechnic State University - Pomona*

Pia Fricker, *University of Helsinki*

Madeline Gannon, *Carnegie Mellon University*

Richard Garber, *New Jersey Institute of Technology*

Manuel Jimenez Garcia, *Bartlett School of Architecture UCL*

Guy Gardner, *University of Calgary*

Jordan Geiger, *University at Buffalo*

David Gerber, *University of Southern California*

Melissa Goldman, *University of Virginia*

Marcelyn Gow, *Southern California Institute of Architecture*

Yasha J. Grobman, *Technion Israel Institute of Technology*

Onur Yuce Gun, *Massachusetts Institute of Technology*

Soomeen Hahm, *Bartlett School of Architecture UCL*

Erik Herrmann, *Ohio State University*

Alvin Huang, *University of Southern California*

Weixin Huang, *University of Florida*

Molly Hunker, *Syracuse University*

Matt Hutchinson, *California College of the Arts*

Nathaniel Jones, *Arup, London*

Jyoti Kapur, *University of Borås*

Neil Katz, *Skidmore, Owings & Merrill LLP*

Aysegul Akcay Kavakoglu, *Altınbaş University*

James Kerestes, *Ball State University*

Sumbul Khan, *Singapore University of Technology and Design*

Axel Killian, *Massachusetts Institute of Technology*

Christoph Klemmt, *University of Cincinnati*

Tobias Klein, *Tilburg University*

Daniel Koehler, *The University of Texas at Austin*

Axel Körner, *University of Stuttgart*

Sotirios Kotsopoulos, *Massachusetts Institute of Technology*

Ersela Kripa, *Texas Tech University, El Paso*

Christian Lange, *The University of Hong Kong*

Julie Larsen, *Syracuse University*

Carla Leitao, *Rensselaer Polytechnic Institute*

Russell Loveridge, *Institute of Technology in Architecture, ETH Zürich*

Gregory Luhan, *University of Kentucky*

Ryan Vincent Manning, *quirkd33*

Sandra Manninger, *Taubman College, University of Michigan*

Mara Marcu, *University of Cincinnati*

Adam Marcus, *California College of the Arts*

Bob Martens, *TU Wien*

Iain Maxwell, *University of Technology Sydney*

Matan Mayer, *IE University*

Malcolm McCullough, *Taubman College, University of Michigan*

Wes McGee, *Taubman College, University of Michigan*

Duane McLemore, *Mississippi State University*

Frank Melendez, *City College of New York*

AnnaLisa Meyboom, *University of British Columbia*

R Scott Mitchell, *University of Southern California*

Stephen Mueller, *Texas Tech University, El Paso*

Rasa Navasaityte, *The University of Texas at Austin*

Taro Narahara, *New Jersey Institute of Technology*

Andrei Nejur, *University of Pennsylvania*

Catie Newell, *Taubman College, University of Michigan*

Tsz Yan Ng, *Taubman College, University of Michigan*

Marta Nowak, *University of California Los Angeles*

Clay Odom, *The University of Texas at Austin*

Betul Orbey, *Dogus Universitesi, Istanbul*

Guvenc Ozel, *University of California Los Angeles*

Derya Gulec Ozer, *Istanbul Kemerburgaz University*

Dimitris Papanikolaou, *University of North Carolina, Charlotte*

Ju Hong Park, *Massachusetts Institute of Technology*

Kat Park, *Skidmore, Owings and Merrill, LLP*

Santiago Perez, *University of Western Australia*

Nicholas Pisca, *Gehry Technologies*

Ebrahim Poustinchi, *Kent State University*

Maya Przybylski, *University of Waterloo*

Seung Ra, *Oklahoma State University*

Gilles Retsin, *Bartlett School of Architecture UCL*

Gernot Riether, *New Jersey Institute of Technology*

Christopher Romano, *University of Buffalo*

Jenny Sabin, *Cornell University*

Virginia San Fratello, *San Jose State University*

Jose Sanchez, *University of Southern California*

Axel Schmitzberger, *California Polytechnic State University - Pomona*

Mathew Schwartz, *New Jersey Institute of Technology*

Tobias Schwinn, *University of Stuttgart*

Jane Scott, *University of Leeds*

Jason Scroggin, *University of Kentucky*

Nick Senske, *Iowa State University*

Bob Sheil, *Bartlett School of Architecture UCL*

Igor Siddiqui, *The University of Texas at Austin*

Brian Slocum, *Lehigh University*

Aldo Sollazzo, *Institute for Advanced Architecture of Catalonia*

Kyle Steinfeld, *University of California, Berkeley*

Robert Stuart-Smith, *University of Pennsylvania*

Satoru Sugihara, *ATLV*

Martin Summers, *University of Kentucky*

Joshua Taron, *University of Calgary*

Peter Testa, *Southern California Institute of Architecture*

Geoffrey Thun, *Taubman College, University of Michigan*

Therese F. Tierney, *University of Illinois Urbana- Champaign*

Zenovia Toloudi, *Dartmouth College*

Kenneth Tracy, *Singapore University of Technology and Design*

Carmen Trudell, *California Polytechnic State University - San Luis Obispo*

Richard Tursky, *Ball State University*

Lauren Vasey, *University of Stuttgart*

Kathy Velikov, *Taubman College, University of Michigan*

Tom Verebes, *New York Institute of Technology*

Joshua Vermillion, *University of Nevada, Las Vegas*

Maria Voyatzaki, *Aristotle University of Thessaloniki*

Emily White, *California Polytechnic State University - San Luis Obispo*

Aaron Wilette, *WeWork*

Andrew John Wit, *Temple University*

Christine Yogiaman, *Singapore University of Technology and Design*

Lei Yu, *Tsinghua University*

Machi Zawidzki, *Singapore University of Technology and Design*

SPONSORS
2019

PLATINUM SPONSOR

GOLD SPONSOR

Zaha Hadid Architects

SILVER SPONSORS

GRIMSHAW

Page/

HKS LINE

form•Z

Altair

BRONZE SPONSOR

SMITHGROUP

SOM

SPONSOR

EDUCATION SPONSOR

CHAOSGROUP

MEDIA PARTNERS

The Architect's Newspaper

ADVERTISING SPONSOR